First Published in the UK in 2003 by;
COLUMBIA PUBLISHING WALES LIMITED
Glen More,
6, Cwrt y Camden,
BRECON LD3 7RR
Powys, Wales. UK
Tel/Fax 01874 625270
dng@columbiawales.fsnet.co.uk

A CIP catalogue record for this book is available from the British Library and the National Library of Wales.

ISBN 0-9538945-4-1.

Cover Design and Typesetting by R C C Evans
rcce@picorama.com

Printed in Wales by: Creative Print and Design Wales,
Ebbw Vale NP23 5SD.

To Greg and Pauline.

THE RISE AND FALL OF TENBY RACES

1846-1936

BY RICHARD LAWRENCE

Best Wishes

Richard Lawrence

CPW BOOKS.
Columbia Publishing Wales Limited

"FOR MY SONS

MY LIFE"

CONTENTS

PREFACE

My interest in Tenby Races began in the mid 1970's when I first heard the tale of the "Oyster Maid Affair". I enquired further of my father. He told me all he knew of those involved at the time, but warned that I should be careful not to stir up a hornet's nest. Tenby was the scene of a huge betting coup involving some of the 1920's biggest racing and gambling figures. The scandal went unproven and made fortunes for the gamblers involved, but it also heralded the beginning of the end for the Tenby Races, one of Britain's biggest racing fixtures in its time. This tale of riches and treachery, coupled with a 1960's National newspaper story by the former jockey Dick Francis and some old race cards, gave me the impetus to search for the truth behind the "Oyster Maid Affair" and its effect on Tenby races. As Dick Francis said himself in his piece headlined 'Welsh Special', the scandal was "probably the biggest and most bitterly resented betting coup in the history of National Hunt racing". Unfortunately, my intrigue was not matched by forthcoming information, with many newspaper reports and personal accounts being sketchy or having disappeared mysteriously. So the project was shelved until the early 1980's when a stroke of luck sent me a new avenue for investigation.

I was in the antique trade when an old box tied up with baler-twine came into my possession after a Tenby house clearance. Upon opening this, I could not believe what I had found. There were masses of photographs, receipts, letters and all sorts of material relating to Tenby Stables. I now had names of people whom I could contact, one of whom was Mr Ben Hooper, who lived near Kilgetty; he was responsible for building the fences and the hurdles at the racecourse when the meeting re-opened after the First World War and remained in this capacity until the meeting closed in 1936. He was an absolute minefield of information and he led me to other contacts; but there were still those who refused to talk about it. One vital contributor I was able to visit was Violet Pritchard, nee Smith, Robert Weaver Smith's daughter, then in her late 80's. An afternoon with Violet was priceless; at the cost of a bottle of Gordon's and twenty Players there was little that she did not know. It was she who directed me to the Evergreen Inn to see Ray Wilding, as he had been given a lot of photographs some years before. When I enquired, Ray took a picture frame off the wall which had rugby rosettes set in it, but when he turned the frame over, there were hidden pictures of horses and jockeys from the Tenby Stables fitted into it. There were six pictures altogether, which I kept in exchange for the re-framing of his prized rugby rosettes. Things were now moving along very briskly and I approached Fulmar Television Company of Cardiff as to the making of a documentary film about the gambling coup, for which I supplied the story and the photographs: 'The Tenby Sting' December 2000. After this documentary was televised I received numerous telephone calls and letters, most of which were of great importance and it was then that I decided to write a book covering the complete history of Tenby Races from 1846-7 to its end in 1936-7.

The main force behind the book is to try and recount how important Tenby Races were in the racing calendar, with the top jockeys, horses and trainers in the UK and Ireland visiting every January to compete at the highest level of National Hunt Racing. One question that the book outlines is whether the infamous "Oyster Maid Affair" of 13th January 1927 led to the downfall of races. In my mind, the Tenby Races would certainly have grown into the biggest National Hunt Meeting of its kind in Wales had it not been for the scandal that lost the trust, and later the presence of the bookies on the Welsh course. Today though, Tenby Races is a part of the country's history that few know about.

But as we shall see, it is quite worth remembering....

AUTHOR'S THANKS

Many thanks to Mr Arthur Ormond, editor of the Tenby Observor, for his invitation to his offices and access to the huge leather bound volumes in their archive that provided invaluable information about the social climate of the era under research, as well as the racing scene. This really opened the door and gave a much wider aspect, especially on the Mr Deer/Harrison saga. I would also like to thank Mr Neil Dickinson, the present editor of the Tenby Observor, without whom this book would not have been possible. At this stage I must mention Mr Charles Birt, whose knowledge of certain criteria has been an absolute goldmine. I would also like to thank Julie Sutcliffe at the Tenby Library, who has been as enthusiastic as myself over the last twenty years or so, and has always found time to help me. Also Tenby Museum from the days of John Tipton to the present, when Mr Mark Lewis has been more than helpful, especially with my pestering telephone calls, and the earlier research help from (the late) Elizabeth King. Also, Messrs Weatherbys have been more than helpful. I hope that the book proves as enjoyable to read as it has been to research and write.

RICHARD LAWRENCE

INTRODUCTION

This is the story of a racecourse, which from humble beginnings in early Victorian Wales, grew into what was to become the hub of Welsh racing and the centre of the Welsh National Hunt's social racing calendar. It is also the story of a Welshman who lived with a passion for horses, for women, and the good life; who as a boy, had a vision, that one day he would become a ruler of men and of horses, and the possessor of all that his heart could desire. It is also the story of lust and greed, of cunning and trickery, of riches and fortune, and the final loss of them all, and the loss of a soul. The setting is the Welsh coastal town of Tenby; known to poet Dylan Thomas; birthplace of Robert Recorde, the Elizabethan mathematician; home of Augustus and Gwen John, 20th Century artists; and of Dick Francis, jockey and best-selling author of novels. Tenby has been and always will be known to hosts of the great and famous, as well as to the ordinary men and women, without whom, there would be no life in this magical little town at all. But, there was soon to be another notch carved into the mediaeval walls of this historical little town, perhaps a notch carved so deep that the memory of the name Oyster Maid would last longer than the mediaeval stone walls of Tenby itself.

RICHARD LAWRENCE

CHAPTER ONE
"THE EARLY DAYS"

Tenby races were formed by a small group of local owners and breeders in 1846, but the first records of any racing in Tenby were recorded in 1847, and the results were published in the Racing Calendar. The meeting took place over two days: August 25th and 27th. Three races were run each day; on the first day all three winners were owned by Mr. Henderson and on the second day, Mr Bullin won two of the races with his horse, four-year-old Faith.

"Taken from the Racing Calendar"

Wednesday, August the 25th THE CORPORATION PLATE of 25 sov. Added to a Sweepstake of 5 sov. each, h.ft. the second horse saved his stake; heats, two miles.

Mr Henderson's br. m. Lady Charlotte, 5 yrs, 10st 11lb, 2, 1, 1Mr F Jacob's br. h. Pharaoh, aged, 11st 7lb, 1, 2, dr
Mr D Griffiths's b.f. Jenny Lind (h.-b.), 3 yrs, 8st 7lb, 3, dr
Mr Lort Phillips's ch.g. Greedy Sam (h.-b.), aged, 11st, 4, dr

The Ladies' Cup of 15 sov. added to a Sweepstake of 2 sov. each, h.ft. for horses that never started in any race previous to the time of entry, heats, a mile and a half, was won by Mr Henderson's br.f. Susan, 3 yrs, 8st, beating four others.

The Tradesmen's Stakes of 3 sov. each, h.ft. with 20 added, heats, two miles, was won by Mr Henderson's br. m. Lady Charlotte, 5 yrs, 9st 7lb, beating four others.

FRIDAY.— A Handicap Hurdle Stakes of 5 sov.each, h. ft. with 25 added. The second saved his stake, heats, two miles, over four hurdles (4 subscribers) was won by Mr Protheroe's Chance by Confederate, aged, 9 st 7lb, beating two others.

The Stewards' Plate of 25 sov. added to a Sweepstake of 5 sov. each. h.ft. the owner of the second horse recd. back his stake, 2 mile heats (4 subscribers) was won, at two heats, by Mr Bullin's Faith, by Elis, 4 yrs, 10st, beating Jenny Lind, 3 yrs, 8st 4lb, and one other.

The Selling Stakes of 2 sov. each, with 15 added, the second saved his stake, heats, one mile and a half (4 subscribers) was won by Mr Bullin's Faith, 4 yrs, 9st 1lb, beating Greedy Sam, aged, 10st 8lb, and two others.

Hunts Directory of 1850, reports racing for two days in August, with Evening Balls. The races are run on a flat piece of land, west of the town but casual matches or trials of speed are sometimes held on the south sands. From 1854 onwards the Tenby Observor contained notices and reports of the race meetings. The first such notice was of races to be held on Tuesday and Thursday 12 and 14 September 1854, usually with 4 races to be held upon each day.

The programme for the opening day read as follows:

"Corporation Plate of 20 guineas", over a mile and a half "Stewards Cup value 20 sovereigns", over two miles, and to include six flights of hurdles, "The Hack Handicap" for farmers and tradesmen, "A Handicap Hurdle Race"

Second Day

"Tenby Stakes Handicap, three sovereigns each entrance fee"

"Selling Stakes, two sovereigns each entrance fee"

"A Handicap Hurdle Race, two sovereigns each entrance fee"

"The Forced Handicap, of three sovereigns each entrance fee"

Conditions and Rules:

1 Three horses to start for each race or the public money will not be added.
2 The second horse in each race to save his stakes if four start.
3 Each horse to pay FIVE SHILLINGS for scales and weights.
4 Stakes to be made good at the time of entry.
5 Disputes to be referred to the stewards, and their decision to be final.
6 Horses to be entered for the Corporation Plate and Handicap Hurdle Race, at the Cobourg Hotel, on Saturday, 9th September.
7 Horses for the second day, to be entered on Tuesday 12th, before eight p.m.
8 The winner of the Selling Stakes to be sold by auction immediately after the race, and the surplus, if any, to go to the race fund.
9 Colours to be declared in writing at the time of entry.

Stewards Ordinary at the Cobourg Hotel on the 12th, and at the White Lion Hotel on the 14th. Stewards Balls on Tuesday and Thursday evenings. Cricket match and Regatta, to be held as usual.

RACE BALLS

On Tuesday 12th and Thursday 14th September. Dancing from 9 p.m.

Ladies tickets……………………………..6s..0d

Gentlemen…………………………………7s 6d

Tickets to be procured at the Lion and Cobourg Hotels, the Library, and at Mr. Thomas Thomas, Grocer, High Street, Tenby.

Mrs Fanny Price Gwynne in 'Allen's Guide to Tenby' gives the following account of the races: the races are held annually, on the flat land over the Marsh, the property of L Mathias Esq, of Lamphey Court. They are held about September and are of two days duration. The horses are chiefly bred in the principality, but celebrated racers from England, also run here. Carriages are charged 2s 6d as entrance fee to the race ground. Horses are charged about 1s. There is also a rude little booth, dignified with the title of The Stand…Parties preferring this stand to their carriages, may purchase a ticket for one or both days.

In 1856 the races were again held on a Tuesday and a Thursday in September. The weather on Tuesday was very fine, but the attendance was not by any means large. About 2p.m., the course was cleared for the first race:

The Tradesmen's Plate, of twenty sovereigns, added to a sweepstakes of five sovereigns each, two forfeit.

Phantom……………………...	Weaver	1
Confederate…………………...	J Rees	2
Deception………………….	J Mathias	0
Faro………………………..	F Morgan	0

A Handicap Hurdle Race of five sovereigns each, £2 forfeit, with £20 added

Phantom…………………….	Weaver	1	1
Eighty-seven……………...	J R James	2	2
Deception………………….	J Mathias	3	4
Haidee……………………...	J Rees	4	3

The Hack Selling Race. Two sovereigns entrance, half forfeit, with £15 added

Madam Landau……………….	Rogers	1	1
Colt by Foxberry……………...	J Rees	2	3
Flirt………………………….	T Davies	0	dr*

| Welsh Girl..................... | J R James | 0 | dr* |
| Fugleman........... | Thomas and Harries | 3 | 2 |

On Thursday the weather was favourable, but the concourse of spectators very small.

About 2p.m. the bell was rung for The Tenby Stakes:

A handicap of five sovereigns each, two forfeits, with £25 added.

Confederate......................................	1
Madam Landau..................................	2
Florence..	distance

A handicap hurdle race of five sovereigns each, £2 forfeit, with £20 added.

Haidee..	1	1
Beeswing..	2	dr
Flirt..	3	dr

The forced handicap of three sovereigns each, with £15 added. Forced for winners, free for losers.

Confederate......................................	1	1
Colt by Foxberry................................	2	dr
Madam Landau..................................	3	2

* dr. – Withdrawn or dropped out.

On Tuesday and Thursday evenings the stewards race-balls took place, under the able stewardship of Arthur Lort Phillips Esq, and H I Puxley Esq, and were well attended.

Visitors to the Tenby Races of 1856 and staying at The Cobourg Hotel were as follows:

William Bateman, London; Miss Mary Anna Buckby, Begelly Rectory; R H Buckby Esq, Worcester College, Oxon; S Beynon Esq, Trewern; R Beynon Esq, Jesus College, Oxon; T J Beynon and the Misses Beynon Trewern; Mr, Mrs & Miss Coney Esq, Braywick Grove, Maidenhead; Miss Cooke, Carew Rectory; Baroness De Rutzen, Slebech Hall; Miss De Rutzen, Mr De Rutzen, Slebech Hall; William Davies Esq, Merthyr; Mr Hassard Hume Dodgson Esq and family, Putney, Surrey;

Miss Evans, Gloucester; Mr, Mrs & Miss Franks, Knock Long, Limerick; The Misses Gabb, Abergavenny; Miss Gascoyne, Haroldston House, Haverfordwest; Mr & Mrs E J Gibb, Glasgow; Charles Hansom Esq, Clifton; Mr, Mrs & Miss Hockley, Huscombe, Surrey; Richard Jenkins Esq, Marchogllwyn; Rev Leach, St Petrox Rectory; The Misses Lucas, Westbury, Glos; Montague R Leverson Esq, 18 Queen Square, London; Mrs G Maycock, Clifton; Hon William Noel, Clanna Falls, Lydney, Glos; Mr, Mrs & Miss Partridge, Beaufort; Mrs Perry, Clifton; Mrs Prosser, Marchogllwyn; Mr &

Mrs Powell, Birmingham; Miss Richardson, Gloucester; Thomas Skone Esq, Bethany Cottage, Haverfordwest; Mrs Wartnaby, Leicestershire; William Webster Esq and family, Upton Hall, Birkenhead; Mr Cavendish Walll, Dudmeston, Bridgenorth; Mrs John Berry Walford, Abergavenny, Miss Williams, York Place, Clifton; Colonel Yerbury and family, Bradford; Capt Bissette, 56th Regiment; P Callen Esq, 71st Highland Light Infantry; Capt Carpenter, 7th Fusiliers; Lieutenant Follett, 7th Fusiliers; Lieutenant Hobson 7th Fusiliers; Lieutenant Kempson, 7th Fusiliers; Thomas Mirehouse Esq, Brownslade; Mr W Peel Esq, Haverfordwest; Mr X Peel Esq, Parc Glas.

On Tuesday 138 persons were at the ball.

At the conclusion of the races on Thursday, some rustic sports were got up, consisting of a donkey-derby, a sack race and also "pig-racing". A copy of the original race card is shown opposite, luckily by someone who marked the placings and weights. The reason for the two columns are for qualifying heats. Hence two jockeys named in the "Hack Selling Race". However, it could also mean that the first named jockey fell off. If so, the horse could be caught by another jockey and ridden to claim any prize money. This was allowed and happened on many occasions.

The two-day meetings held in September, continued until the early 1870's, when they moved to November and December. The following article was written in a national racing paper by Mr Garry Moore who was a jockey in the race concerned:

In the Castlemartin Stakes at Tenby in 1870 the course was then on the marsh, below the railway station. There were nine runners, the start being under the limekilns, a point exactly opposite the grandstand on the other side of the course.

All the horses were at the starting post under starters orders, with the exception of Zion Hill by Mount Zion, owned by Mr F D Saunders of Glanrhydw, and ridden by Mr Tom Ince Bowen. After a preliminary canter in front of the grand-stand, he galloped around to the starting point, Mr Bowen shouting to all the riders there to clear the way, as he could not stop his mount, which was now going round the course for a second time, out of control.

Mr Bowen could not retain him within bounds, as he made for the stone walls, which intersected the marsh; he jumped a stone wall well over six feet high, with Mr Bowen still in the saddle. However at the second wall Mr Bowen came to grief, unfortunately breaking a few bones.

The race was then run without Zion Hill, and I won it on Jerry, Milkmaid being second, ridden by Mr W H P Jenkins. A mare by Claret and ridden by Mr Trewent was third.

Mr Frank Gulston, a winner of the Diamond Sculls, had a safe mount on Harkaway, but was probably more at ease in his skiff with the sculls, than

BY AUTHORITY OF THE STEWARDS.

TENBY RACES, 1856.

SECOND DAY.

THURSDAY, 18th SEPTEMBER.

THE TENBY STAKES, of *Five Sovereigns* each, *Two* forfeit, with £25 added. Three times round and a distance. The Winner to pay £5 to the Fund.

st	lbs		
12	4	Mr. E. Chard's b m *Madam Landau*, 6 years; white body, red sleeves, blue cap	2
11	7	Mr. Heywood's b h *Confederate*, 4 years; green jacket, purple cap	1
10	0	Mr. Thomas b c by *Fatherly*, out of *Ambassadress*, 3 years; purple cap	
11	7	Mr. Viner's *Beeswing*, 4 years; white body, pink sleeves, black cap	
10	0	Mr. Jones' b m *Flirt*, 6 years; pink jacket and blue cap	
9	7	Mr. C. Morgan's b m *Haidee*, by *Pegasus*, out of *Jane*, 4 years; blue jacket, green cap	3
10	4	Mr. —— *Florence*; puce body, amber sleeves, puce cap	

A HANDICAP HURDLE RACE, of *Five Sovereigns* each, £2 forfeit, with £20 added. Heats—twice round and a distance, over Hurdles. Winner to pay £2 to the Fund.

st	lbs		
10	0	Mr. C. Morgan's b m *Haidee*, by *Pegasus* out of *Jane*, 4 years; blue jacket, green cap	1	1
10	7	Mr. Jones' b m *Flirt*, 6 years; pink jacket and blue cap	2	2
10	7	Mr. Viner's *Beeswing*, 4 years; white body, pink sleeves, black cap	3

THE FORCED HANDICAP, Of *Three Sovereigns* each, with £15 added. Forced for Winners. Free for Losers. Heats—once round and a distance. The Winner to pay £1 to the Fund.

1	Mr. G. Lort Phillips' br g *Deception*, aged; crimson jacket, black cap		
2	Mr. X. Peel's b g *Eighty-Seven*, by *Pharaoh* out of *Buttercup*, by *Uncle Toby* out of *Dairy Maid* by *Candidate*, 5 years; green jacket, purple cap		
3	Mr. Waits' br g *Phantom*; crimson and white jacket, and white cap	6
4	Mr. Richards' c g *Eagleman*, by *Mango*, Dam by *Ascot*, Grand-dam *Gift*, by *Tamworth*; red jacket, amber sleeves	3
5	Mr. E. Chard's b m *Madam Landau*, white body, red sleeves, and blue cap	4
6	Captain Rhys' .... green jacket, and purple cap	2
7	Mr. C. Morgan's g *Paris*, blue jacket, green cap	
8	Mr. Thomas b c by *Fatherly*, out of *Ambassadress*, black body, crimson sleeves, and black cap	2
9	Mr. Jones' b m *Flirt*, pink jacket and blue cap	
10	Mr. Viner's *Beeswing*, 4 years; white body, pink sleeves, black cap	1
11	Mr. Heywood's *Confederate*, 4 years; green jacket, purple cap	
12	Mr. C. Morgan's *Haidee*, 4 years; blue jacket, green cap	3
13	Mr. —— *Florence*, puce body, amber sleeves, puce cap	1

CONDITIONS.

Three horses to start for each race, or the whole of the stake money will not be added. The second horse in each race to save his stake if four start. Each horse to pay Five Shillings entrance to be made good at the time of entry. Disputes to be referred to the Stewards, and their decision to be final. Newmarket rules will be strictly adhered to.

Stewards' Ordinary at the Cobourg Hotel. Ball in the Evening.

JOHN LEACH, Esq. .... } Stewards.
ARTHUR LORT PHILLIPS, Esq. }

T. THOMAS, Secretary.
G. BOWEN, Clerk of the Course.

when seated in the saddle with the reins.

Mr Saunders was so disgusted with the pranks of Zion Hill, that at the Gate House Hotel that evening, he asked me to take him away, as he did not want to see him anymore. I took Zion Hill home the next day, and intended to run him at Llanstephan races. This I did, but when I mounted him, he took the bit, and ran away with me for four miles on the turnpike road, and when he stopped, it was of his own sweet will. He was then put in a double-harness, where he worked well, as he could not run away on his own. He was then sold to Mr T M Offin, of Down Hall, Rayleigh, Essex, whose brother was Master of the Essex Foxhounds. Mr Offin was a fine horseman, standing well over six feet tall, and who ridiculed the idea of any horse running away with him. "I was to hear no more from Mr Offin or Zion Hill", said Mr Moore.

Garret Moore was the eldest son of John Moore of Jockey Hall, the Curragh; both he and his brother, Willie, spent their lives in horse racing, later training on the flat and NH. Better known as Garry, he was a natural horse-man, who combined skill, strength, and elegance, to an unequalled degree and he raced many times at Tenby with great success.

Bristol races had been going through a very lean time, and a Mr Frail attempted a revival by inviting the Prince of Wales to the 1874 meeting: special trains were laid on and thousands upon thousands turned up to spectate and entries were excellent, as the prize money had been catapulted into ridiculous sums; The Bristol Royal Chase was run for the first time with a prize of £1805, only £80 less than the Grand National prize. There were twenty runners, and the race was won by Mr Garry Moore on Scots Grey. Mr Moore at the time was leading Irish Amateur Champion Jockey. He also won the 1875 Great Metropolitan Chase at Croydon, on Fawley. In 1879, he won the Grand National on The Liberator, trained by his father at Jockey Hall, the Curragh, later in 1880 he was second with the same horse to Empress in the Grand National. Being well over six feet and a natural twelve stone he retired in 1885, due to a weight problem, and took up training at Seven Barrows where almost a century later Peter Walwyn was to have great success. As a trainer his biggest success was The Eclipse Stakes with Surefoot.

However, he was a poor businessman, and the despair of his gambling owners. His riding instructions to first time amateurs were "Wish you luck, really sorry I cannot be there, but you will not come unstuck; wear a low rein, a stiff chin, keep your elbows in, and go like the merry winds of Hades".

Mr G Lort Phillips, The Squire of Lawrenny.
A major horse breeder, and owner.
Lawrenny Castle in the background.
circa.1860

(Left to Right) Mr Henry Dennis, Mr Henry Dyke Dennis and Mr Henry Dyke Dennis Jnr

Three generations of the Dennis family at Park House Racing Stud, Tenby (circa.1860)
The Dennis family were the owners of the Ruabon coalmines and brickworks and were
all great sporting men. Park house was sold by the Dennis family to Mr Prettyjohn
during World War II, after a Queen Bee aircraft crashed into the front drive of
Park House, seriously frightening one of Mr Dyke Dennis's prize mares
whilst heavily in foal.Mr Henry Dyke Dennis sucessfully sued the
War Ministry, sold up and left.

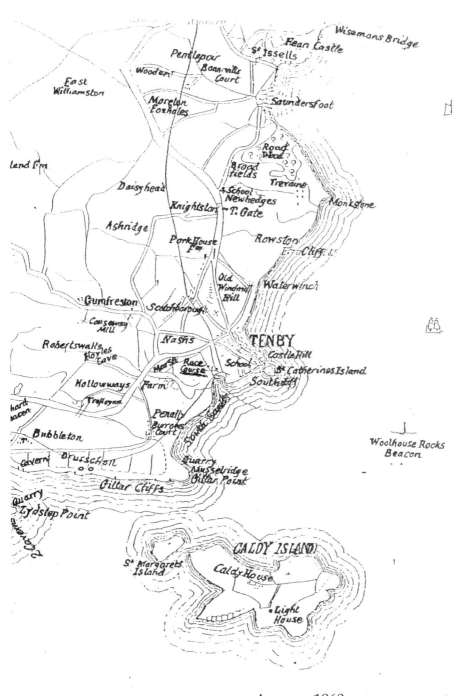

Approx 1860

19

Tenby races continued to be a great success for the next few years, but it was felt that they now needed a more adventurous course, over a more challenging area of the countryside. It was not advisable to move too far from Tenby, and to continue to attract the same support, from both the public and the equine society, as one would not work without the other, and prove to be a financial success. After making several enquiries, they were offered the use of the "Lodge Farm", by the owner, Mr Vickerman of "Hean Castle".

The first meeting at Lodge Farm was on December 7th and 9th 1875 and was to be an excitable yet moderate affair. The course was described in the Tenby Observor as being well fitted for steeple chasing, with the banks being good, and an all-round view being obtained from the new grandstand and other coigns of vantage. And on both days the ground was capital going.

The Tenby Observor on Thursday, 2nd December carried this notice:

TENBY
STEEPLE-CHASES
(Under Grand National Rules,) will take place on
Tuesday and Thursday, Dec 7th & 9th 1875
At Lodge Farm, New Hedges

E J REED, Esq. CB MP	}
J F LORT PHILLIPS, Esq	}
O GEORGE Esq 1st Life Guards	} *Stewards*
J N MOORE Esq	}
Captain WARBURTON RE	}

FRED BOWERS, *Hon Sec & Clerk of Course*

FIRST DAY
THE LAWRENNY PLATE

Of 40 sovs, added to a sweepstakes of 3 sovs, each, for *bona fide* hunters; four years old 11st; five years 11st 12lbs; six and aged 12st 3lbs; winners once 7lbs; twice 14lbs; three times 2lbs extra; entrance one sov. each to the fund, the only liability for non-starters; three miles over a banking course. To close and name on or before Tuesday, November 23rd to Messrs Weatherby, or the Hon Sec, *Royal White Lion Hotel,* Tenby.

THE LADIES PLATE

Of 25 sovereigns, added to a sweepstakes of 2 sovs each, for *bona fide* Hunters; four years old 12st 7lbs; five years 12st 10lbs; six and aged 13st; the winner to be sold for £200; if for £150 allowed 3lbs; £100, 7lbs; £80, 10lbs; £60, 14lbs; £40, 21lbs; entrance 1 sov each to the fund, the only liability for non-starters; two miles over the flying course. The winner to be sold in the usual manner. To close and name as for the Lawrenny Plate.

THE INNKEEPERS' PLATE

Of 19 sovereigns, for bona fide Hunters, for Galloways not exceeding 14 hands 3 inches high; 11st each; 7lbs allowed for every inch under that height; entrance 1 sov to the fund; two miles over the Flying Course. To close and name to the Hon Sec, at the *Royal*

20

White Lion Hotel, Tenby, by 9 pm Monday December 6th.
THE STEWARDS' PLATE
Of 19 sovereigns, for *bona fide* hunters; four years old 11st; five years 11st 12lbs; Six and aged 12st 3lbs; winners, of 19 sovs or otherwise, once 7lbs; twice 10lbs; three times 14lbs extra; entrance one sov to the fund; two miles over the flying course. To close and name as for the Innkeepers' Plate.

SECOND DAY
THE TENBY PLATE
Of 30 sov, added to a sweepstakes of 3 sovs each, for *bona fide* hunters; four years old 11st; five years 11st 12lbs; six and aged 12st 3lbs; winners once 7lbs; twice 14lbs; three times 21lbs extra; the winner of the Lawrenny Plate to carry 7lbs extra; entrance 1 sov to the fund, the only liability for non-starters; two miles over banks. To close and name as for the Innkeepers' Plate.

THE BOROUGH MEMBER'S PLATE
Of 25 sovs, given by E J Reed Esq, CB, MP added to a sweepstakes of 3 sovs each. For bona fide hunters, the property of farmers and tradesmen residing in
South Wales; four years old 11st; five years 11st 12lbs; six and aged 12st 3lbs; entrance 1 sov to the fund, the only liability for non-starters; two miles over banks. To close and name as for the Innkeepers' Plate.

THE VISITORS' STAKES
Of 20 sovs, added to a sweepstakes of 2 sovs each; 1 sov entrance to the fund, the only liability for non-starters; conditions the same as for the Innkeepers' Plate; the winner of that race to carry 7lbs extra; two miles over the flying course. To close and name as for the Innkeepers' Plate.

THE GARRISON PLATE
Of 19 sovs, for *bona fide* hunters; four years old 11st; five years 11st 12lbs; six and aged 12st 3lbs; winners once 7lbs; twice 14lbs; three times 21lbs extra; entrance 1 sov to the fund; two miles over the flying course. To close and name as for the Innkeepers' Plate.

SELLING PLATE
With 20 sovs added; the conditions the same as the Ladies Plate; Winners of the Ladies' Plate 7lbs extra.

Any objection must be made in writing, accompanied with five sovereigns, and should it be considered frivolous the money must be forfeited to the fund.

Three horses, bona fide the property of different owners, to start, or the added money will be withheld.

Proper colours to be declared to the Hon Sec at the time of entry, or 1 sov fine will be inflicted, to be paid before weighing.

All Galloways to be measured at the Royal White Lion Stables by ten o'clock on the morning of the first day.

Certificates, signed by masters of fox or stag hounds, must be registered at Messrs Weatherby's Office a clear week before the day of the race, accompanied by a fee of 2s-6d.

Each jockey to pay 5s for weighing in each race.

NO GAMBLING BOOTHS, OR PLAY OF ANY DESCRIPTION, ALLOWED
ON THE COURSE.
THE DECISION OF THE STEWARDS WILL BE FINAL.

A GRAND PIGEON MATCH
will be held on Wednesday Dec 8th
The Stewards' Ordinary at the *Royal White Lion Hotel*,
Tuesday, December 7th.
Race Ordinary at the *Cobourg Hotel*, Thursday, December 9th.

The Fly by Night Colt

Over he went like a bird
Victorian Steeplechasing by Finch Mason

The Tenby Observor also printed this report on the races:

Being the first meeting at the new venue, it was not as successful as first anticipated, due mainly to simple teething problems, which were rectified by the Committee, in readiness for the following year. However, the meeting of December 1876, whether as to the number of horses that competed for the several stakes, the company on the ground, the attendance at the ball on Tuesday at the Royal Assembly Rooms, or the large number of gentlemen that sat down to the ordinaries at the Royal Lion and Cobourg Hotels, must be considered as the most successful that we have had for many, many years. The entries were far above average and good fields were presented.

The weather too was all that could be desired, especially on the first day, when the sun shone out at times with a warmth and brilliancy that resembled more of a day in the Spring than in the middle of December. The result was a large attendance of ladies and gentlemen, who occupied seats in their carriages, amongst them being Mr Crawshay-Bailey of Belfield, Tenby, with a large party, and whose splendid drag, was the admiration of all.

The second day was not so warm, with a cold southeast wind blowing in from the sea, but there was still a very good attendance, and any little drawback resulting from the weather was made up by the pertinacity with which the races were contested. Through the kindness of Mr C R Vickerman of Hean Castle, the course was the same, as that run over last year, situated on the Lodge Farm, about one and a half miles from the town.

The stewards present were Mr J F Lort Phillips of Lawrenny, Mr O George, Mr Crawshay-Bailey, Mr Curre, Mr W F Roch, Mr M Owen and Mr M Lloyd. Mr Reed MP would also have been present, but an important engagement rendered it necessary for him to return to London on Monday. The presence of these gentlemen on the course, and the large contributions to the meeting given by the Squire of Lawrenny, Mr Crawshay-Bailey and Mr Reed MP, show that they take more than a passing interest in providing sport in this part of Wales. The genial proprietor of the Royal Lion Hotel, Mr F Bowers, was as usual, Hon. Secretary and clerk of the course, and most ably did he perform his duties. We congratulated him upon the success attending his exertions in the matter.

Mr C Ackland-Allen made an efficient starter, Mr R J Olive of Carmarthen, presided over the scales, while Mr J Gregory of the Royal Gate House Hotel fulfilled the somewhat difficult task of judge, most satisfactorily.

"OPEN STEEPLE-CHASE"

A plate of 50 sovereigns, for bona fide Hunters; 4 yr old, 11st, 5yr old , 11st 12lbs, 6 yr old and aged, 12st 3lb, winners 7lb extra. Entrance £2 to the fund; three miles over a banking course.

12-3, Mr T Roch's, Sammy, Mr Roch, 1
12-10, Mr F Bower's, Snuff, T Gwyther, 2
12-3, Mr Summer's, The Buck, Hitchings, 3

Cymrw, Lady and Phoebe also came to the post. Lady, whilst running for the first bank, riding right into it, fell and threw Rudd heavily. In the second mile, at the first bank from the stand, Phoebe went the wrong side of the flag, but Mr Tom Phillips gallantly took the fence a second time. A capital race ensued with Snuff leading the van until coming into the turn by the farmhouse, when he came to grief at the last bank, and so spoiled his chance of winning. Sammy won by 20 lengths, with as much between second and third.
Betting: 6-4…Lady, 2-1…Sammy, 4-1…The Buck

"THE MAINDIFF COURT SELLING PLATE"

A plate of 25 sovereigns, given by Mr Crawshay-Bailey Esq for *bona-fide* hunters; 4 y.o. 11st.....5 y.o.11st 12lb,…6 y.o. and aged….12st 3lb; winners once 7lbs; twice 10lbs extra; the winner to be sold for £150; if for £100, allowed 5lbs; if for £80,10lbs, if for £50 ,14lbs - two miles over flies; entrance £1-10s, to the fund. The winner to be sold by auction, immediately after the race, and the surplus, if any, to be divided between the owner of the second horse and the fund.

11-2, Mr Cotton's, Lancaster, Owner, 1
11-13, Mr Olive's, Rainbow, Tom Phillips, 2
11-12, Mr Lloyd's, Astolpho, T Gwyther, 3
Six came to the post, but in taking the second bank Ruby fell.

Betting: 6-4 against Longstop…3-1 against any other. Lancaster won easily, with 6 lengths between second and third. The winner was sold to Mr Morris Owen for 88 guineas.

THE LAWRENNY RED-COAT PLATE

Of 30 sovereigns for bona fide Hunters - entrance £2 to the fund; three miles over the flying course; gentlemen riders in hunting costume, that have never ridden for hire.

12-10, Mr Cotton's, Gambler, Mr A Jones, 1
10-00, Mr Bower's, Ruby, Mr Newman, 2
12-12, Mr Wallace's, Bedford, Owner, 3

Boxer and Pembroke also came to post, and a capital race was the result. Ruby refused, and Pembroke bolted in the second mile. A splendid run was made for the finish, Mr Jones landing the winner by half a length. An objection was lodged against the winner, on the grounds that Mr Jones was not in the "Hunting Costume". The objection was allowed, and the stakes were awarded to the second horse.
Betting: 2-1 on, Bedford, 3-1 Pembroke.

THE INNKEEPER'S PLATE

Of 20 sovereigns for Galloways not exceeding 14 hands 3ins 11st each with 7lbs allowed for every inch under that height; entrance £1-10 shillings to the fund. Two miles over the flying course, winners 7lb extra.

11-7, The Duke of Montrose's, Just in Time, Millar, 1
11-7, Mr Bower's, Admiral, Mr Newman, 2
11-7, Mr M. Owen's, Lady, Mr Roch, 3

Five showed to the front, and a very good race ensued. Just in Time made the running, with Admiral lying close up for the whole distance. Just in Time, however, was landed the winner by half a length.

Betting: evens, Just in Time, 2-1, Admiral.

Race-ball and Supper will take place at

the Royal Assembly rooms on Tuesday. Ladies ticket 8s 6d; Gentlemen 15s.

A later report of this dance is as follows:
About 130 ladies and gentlemen were present. The room was of a charming appearance, and the supper was as usual served in the style so well-known to the frequenters of Balls at the Royal Assembly Rooms, and for which the proprietor is so justly celebrated. Dancing commenced to the strains of "Ashman's Band", and was kept up till the small hours of the morning, which were far advanced.

****

Many more race meetings were to be held very successfully at Lodge Farm, annually in November or December, until the races moved to Knightston Farm in 1887, where the Hunt Steeplechase and Hurdle Races were to be held annually every January, with one summer meeting also.

During this era of Victorian Fencing, there are three jockeys whose names stand head and shoulders above all others, and it would be an injustice to the readers if I were not to mention them.

Firstly, Tom Olliver (D.o.B not known, Died 1874). Swarthy faced and black haired, of Spanish gypsy blood, he was born in Sussex as one of 16 children. There was no money, no schooling and very often no shoes for the Oliver family. Tom added the extra "l" to his name to give himself his own particular identity. He was able to do anything with horses and soon worked his way into the world of hunting and steeplechasing. His phenomenal success brought him fame but little in the way of fortune, as he was hopeless with money. Against a background of stable boys earning £10 per year, top-flight jockeys expected £5 per ride and £10 a winner, while for an important victory in which a gamble had been landed, £50 was the recognised fee. But Olliver, who would put his hand into his pocket for every chance-met beggar, was permanently on the verge of bankruptcy and was frequently imprisoned for debt. Usually the officers of the locally stationed regiments, many of whom he had coached in the art of cross-country riding, came to his aid during these confinements.

Tom won the Grand National three times, in 1842 on Gay Lad, 1843 on Vanguard and in 1853 on Peter Simple, the oldest horse ever to win the Grand National at 15 years of age, which he also trained. He was also second three times and third once. He also won the Liverpool Steeplechase at Maghull in 1838 on Sir Henry.

For a time he was the landlord of "The Star Inn" at Leamington, but later moved to Prestbury, near Cheltenham, where he became an important figure. He coached a bevy of Cheltenham based jockeys including Tommy Pickernell, George Stevens, William Holman, William Archer and Josie Little, who repaid him by beating him by 1 ½ lengths on Chandler for the 1848 Grand National. He also coached a rebellious Cheltenham schoolboy who hero-worshipped him. Adam Lindsay-Gordon later immortalised him in his racy ballads of hunting and chasing:

"He cares not for the bubbles of fortune's fickle tide
Who like Bendigo can battle and like Olliver can ride."

Later in life he became a trainer at Wroughton and proved himself just as skilful in that branch of his profession. He handled the 1874 Derby winner, George Frederick, but he died without seeing the fruits of the victory, leaving the honour and his priceless store of knowledge to his head lad, Tom Leader.

His wit never deserted him, when later in life he replied to the lengthy query of a fussy owner over the staying capacity of an extremely slow horse, with this glorious riposte: "Honoured Sir, your horse can stay four miles, but it takes a hell of a long time to do it."

The second jockey, George Stevens (1833–1871), holds the record of riding five Grand National winners. He won in 1856 on Freetrader, 1863 on Emblem, 1864 on Emblematic and in 1869 and 1870 on The Colonel.

He was born near Cheltenham and, like every boy of promise in the area, was coached by Tom Olliver. From a letter written by Olliver to a friend of Steven's just before the 1869 Grand National, we learn something of the old maestro's approach to the big race. "If Stevens lays away from his horses and be not interfered with, it will be like a lot of terriers leading a staghound a gallop – tell him it is a long way from home to the last half mile. I have no doubt he will say that I am an old fool, but recollect old Tom Olliver's words. Be cautious and go not too soon, the post is the place to win at." Stevens obeyed these instructions to the letter and won by three lengths. In fact he customarily rode a waiting race. Stevens also won the Cheltenham Steeplechase three times, in 1863 and 1865 on Emblem and in 1870 on Daisy. He was a frail looking man of delicate health and weighed less than nine stone and rode only occasionally. He won only 76 chases in 22 seasons, but his win percentage was extraordinarily high. He was killed in June 1871 when his hat was blown off riding down Cleeve Hill, causing his staid cob to shy and whip around violently throwing the best cross-country jockey in England head first against a stone. He was 38 years old.

Last but not least was Arthur Nightingall (1868–1944). A member of the famous Epsom racing family, Arthur was the son of John Nightingall. The finest professional jockey of his day, he was noted for his coolness, judgment and his exceptional strength in a finish. After the close finish to the 1894 Grand National, which he won on Why Not, correspondents claimed that he could have won the race on any of the first three past the post. He was a noted exponent of the 'lean-back' seat and his tall spare frame could be seen swinging gracefully back, almost touching the horse's quarters, as he landed over Aintree's drop fences. He won the Grand National three times, 1894 on Why Not, 1890 on Ilex and 1901 on Grudon. He also won the Lancashire Chase, 1890 on Ilex and 1898 on Keelson, The Scottish Grand National in 1894 on Leyburn, The Grand Sefton in 1893 on Why Not, The Liverpool Hurdle in 1890 on Toscano, The Grand International Chase in 1890 on M.P. and The Great Sandown Hurdle in 1900 on Spook and 1901 on Goldfinder. He also rode many winners in France, Austria and Germany, including the big chase in Baden-Baden on Pampero.

He subsequently became a fine trainer, taking over Priam Lodge from Jack Jones. His patrons included H.R.H. the Prince of Wales and Lord Marcus Beresford. He paid meticulous attention to horse management and to schooling and his horses rarely fell. A gentle man, with an aesthetic face and excellent manners, he was widely loved and respected in Epsom and when he died aged 76, his ashes were sprinkled over the Derby course.

What makes the mention of these jockeys all the more exciting is that they all rode at Tenby Races during their illustrious careers.

********** **

At Tenby in January 1893 a newspaper carried a special note which read "This meeting which was arranged to take place at the course on Knightston Farm, has been looked forward to with a great deal of interest….it being that the race committee had erected a new and commodious stand, to be known as The Grandstand, the new stand being on a more advantageous site, than that occupied by the old stand, and which also possesses other advantages, all tending to the comfort and enjoyment of the spectators".

Notice

The Tenby Hunt Steeple-Chases and Hurdle Races will take place under National Hunt Rules on Wednesday and Thursday, 23rd and 24th of January. All entries close on Tuesday January 15th, to Mr George Chiles, at the Cobourg Hotel, Tenby; or Messrs Weatherby, London; except for the Knightston Selling Hurdle Race Plate, which will close by 7pm the night before the race, at the Cobourg Hotel. Arrangements have been made, whereby, the owners of horses staying at The Cobourg, Royal Lion, or Royal Gate House Hotels, will have their horses stabled free of charge. The course is of all grass and within two miles of Tenby.

C W R STOKES Hon Sec

There were eight jumps at Knightston race-course, with the water-jump bigger than that at Liverpool, Tenby's being 15 feet, as against 12 feet 6 inches of water at Liverpool. Yet, it was the banks on this course that made the racing so exciting, for both rider and spectator.

The course was one and a half miles round, over natural countryside, with some banks on its outline, running right handed down into a valley, hidden from the view of the spectators, until coming up the hill and back into view again.

"FIRST DAY'S RACING"

January 23rd 1893

The weather in early morning was very gloomy with a cold north wind. As the day grew it somewhat brightened, but there were several showers. A large number of visitors came into the town by the morning trains, and the streets wore a very animated appearance. Just before the commencement of the races quite a gale of wind sprang up from the WNW, and made it very cold and uncomfortable on the course. It seemed to search out nearly every corner of the Grandstand, and was of icy chilliness. The atmosphere was clear, and a burst of sunshine added materially to the enjoyment of the large number of people who came to the course in carriages and on foot. The course was in capital going order, and was not at all heavy except at the gateways, where the mud was churned up a great deal by the carriage traffic. A plentiful supply of gorse and ashes, however, soon remedied this. The Grandstand was exceedingly well patronised, and there was a very large crowd at the rails. It is impossible to give a complete list of those in the Grandstand, but among those present were Colonel Saurin, Colonel and Miss Lewes, Mr A P Saunders, Mr W H Richards (Mayor of Tenby); Colonel and Miss Goodeve, Mr H H Goodeve, General Bowen, Captain Westby, Captain Crossman, Mr C E Burrell, Mr A T Harrison, Mr C W R Stokes, Colonel Denne, Mr A Powell, Mr T A Rees, Mr J F Lort Phillips, Lawrenny, Miss Philipps, Mrs and Miss Hawksley, the Misses Reid, Mr Brookman, Mr J Rogers, jun., Mr W G Lewis, Mr B Rees, Captain Moreton Thomas, Captain Cochrane, R N., Mrs Cochrane, Mr G H Smyth, *Mr W Francis, Mr W Lewis, Miss Vickerman, Mr Davies, Mrs Maxwell, Miss Lewes, Miss Howells, Miss Newland, Miss Lewes, Llanlear; Mrs Maunsell, Mr and Mrs Saurin, Miss James, the Misses Broughton, Mr Garnon, Mr Coombes, Mr G Prothero, Mr J Gifford, jun., Dr J G Lock, Mr S G Rogers, Mr Grabbam, Mr W A Jenkins, Mr Fishwick, Mr T Chiles and Mr H Mortimer Allen, the Tenby photographer.

* Mr William Francis – Dick Francis's grandfather. He lived at Wedlock Farm, Tenby and was a farmer and horse dealer and trainer.

The sport provided was exceedingly good, the fields being large; and it will be seen that in the last race, every horse entered, started; an almost unprecedented event.

Larger fields it would be almost impossible to get. This was especially the case in the Penally Banking Race, the Tenby Maiden Hurdle, and the Licensed Victuallers' Optional Plate. The former, a new race, we were glad to see attracted so many competitors. Though two of the horses in the Town Steeplechase coming to grief early in the struggle, it proved quite a walk-over for Mr A P Saunders Davies's Fairy Queen. Cunning Boy was fairly demoralised after falling down at the dry ditch, and bolted for Tenby, having apparently had enough of it. Tom Phillips pluckily, notwithstanding his recent accident, remounted Congress II, and made him go the course, but he was not in it, the spill having given Fairy Queen a lead of nearly once round the course. Dean Swift went well for the Maiden Hurdle, and won easily; and the Squire of Lawrenny's Macheath proved one of the gamest horses at the meeting. The merits of Columba in the Licensed Victuallers' Optional Plate were unrecognised by the knowing ones, and it proved a godsend for the pencillers - although, if it had not been for the crowding at the first hurdle, which caused a few collisions, and Bangaway to come to grief, there is no doubt that Mr Shirley's representative would have caused a still greater surprise. The merits of St Columba were appreciated by that astute owner and he has made a bargain, although he had to give 160 guineas for him. By-the-bye, the race fund will considerably benefit by this transfer, as St Columba fetched 90 guineas more than his selling price, and half will go to the fund. We are glad this is so, as the committee are in want of money, the summer meetings causing a deficiency.

Supt. Evans and a strong force of the County Constabulary were on the ground, but their services were not in great requisition, the crowd being most orderly.

THE STEWARD'S ORDINARY

This was held at the *Cobourg Hotel* last night when Mrs J B Hughes placed a capital spread on the table, the menu being as follows:-
Hors D'Oeuvres, Oysters, Caviar. *Potages* – Mock Turtle, Palestine. *Poissons* – Salmon, Fillets of Sole. *Entrees* – Oyster Patties, Quenelles of Chicken. *Releves* – Boiled Turkey, Roast Turkey, Tongues, Sirloin Beef, Saddle of Mutton. Game – Pheasants, Partridges, Golden Plover. *Entremets* – Christmas Pudding, Mince Pies, Rhubarb Tart, Jellies, Vanilla Ice Cream. Cheese Straws, Devilled Biscuits. Iced Nessebrode Pudding. (The oysters no doubt, coming from the renowned Caldey Island oyster beds.)

Among those who sat down were Colonel Denne (Chairman), Mr John Evans (Lavallin House), Vice-Chairman; Major Glascott, Messrs Edwards (*Sporting Chronicle*), Mr Page (*Sporting Life*), G Chiles, G Richards, T. Morgan (*Western Mail*), E Muncaster, Davey, Mackenzie, Parsley, Heywood and G Daw (*Tenby Observor*), A Davies, H Goodeve, S G Rogers, Captain Crossman, Messrs C E Burrell, W Lewis (Milford House), Mr Shiel (Owner of St Columba), W Lewis (Tenby), W Morgan (Cardiff), H Turner (Worcester), E Morgan (Cardiff), Mr Jepson.

After the removal of the cloth, the Chairman, in a few prefatory remarks, proposed the health of the Queen, the Prince and Princess of Wales, and the rest of the Royal family (Drank with applause). Major Glascott said he rose to propose success to Tenby Races – (applause) – and he thought a vote of thanks was due to some of those members of the Race Committee who worked hard for their success. He knew that meetings like these were difficult to keep up, and it reflected the greatest credit upon those men who managed to keep up such a meeting as this every season. He was sorry he did not see more representative men present, who ought to be there looking after the interests of this town. (Applause.) He, however, did see their capital friend, Mr Chiles, whom they all knew had done so much to promote the interests of sport in Tenby. (Applause.) Then there was his friend, Mr George Richards, whose judging today, except with regard to one race – (laughter) – could not be excelled. He was sorry to see one person absent for reasons which they all deplored, he alluded to Mr C W R Stokes*. (Applause.) No man had done more for Tenby Races than he has done. (Hear, hear.) The toast was drank with enthusiasm.

Mr G Chiles returned thanks, and said it always afforded him pleasure to promote any kind of sport, as he thought it brought a great many people, who they would not otherwise have, to the town. (Applause.) He was very much pleased with the races to-day, and he trusted they would have as good a day on Thursday. He should like to propose the health of the poor backers (laughter). Mr George Richards also returned thanks, and made a few humorous remarks with respect to the trouble of judging.

The Chairman then rose to propose the Visitors present. (Applause.) His own experience of Tenby only extended over about four years at that table, but he was very pleased to meet the same faces there year after year – (applause) – and he hoped that they would continue to come there – firstly, as a matter of business; and secondly, because it is a pleasure for them to come. If it was a pleasure for them to come, he could assure them it was a pleasure for Tenby people to see them.

Others present during the race days were as follows:
Mr W H Montague Leeds, Tenby; Captain N Collins, Gravesend; Mr Eric Cattley, Winchester, Mr Sackville Owen, Mr Hill; Mr E H Lewis Bowen, Glynfrew; Mr Richard Lloyd, Pentypark; Captain E Travers, R A, Tenby; Captain Pollick R A, Pembroke Dock; Captain A S Mathias, Llangwarren; Captain Lindsay Brabazon, 2nd Welsh Regiment; Mr C Buckhill, Eastbourne; Sir David Hughes Morgan, Bart, Penally; Mr Hughes Morgan, Penally; Mr Jim Hughes Morgan, Penally; Mr Haddon Howard, Shepperton; Mr H Oakshott, Cheshire; Mr D G Estridge, Ferryside; Major R C E Barclay, Manorbier; Mr John D Newton, Llandaff; Mr Stuart Chester, Cardiff; Mr J L H Williams, Narberth; Dr E W Price, Narberth; Mr G R Vickerman, Saundersfoot; Mr J G Protheroe Beynon, Whitland; Mr L Pugh; Captain Turner, Hean Castle; Mr W L Tregoning, Ferryside; Mr G E Tregoning; Mr D Carbon Swan; Mr G L Tregoning; Mr G Parry, St David's; Dr Lionel Owen, Mayfield, Narberth; Captain Hugh Allen, Cresselly; Mr W F Protheroe Beynon, Welsh Regiment; Mr Spencer Miles, Treforest; Lord Suffienld, Amroth Castle; the Hon George Coventry, Amroth Castle; Major E A Forbes, Begelly; Mr Porter, Plaish Hall, Salop; Major Tyrrell Beck, M C, D S O, London; Sir Frank Newnes, Bart, London; Captain F W Martin, 2nd East Lancs Regiment, Pem-
*I can find no reason for his absence.

31

broke Dock; Lieutenant Colonel Delme Davies-Evans, Dr Tristram Samuel, Pembroke; Mr David Evans, Mr Hoskyns, Baron de Rutzen, Mr B Cousins, Harrow on the Hill; Mr R E A Jones, King's Own Royal Regiment, Tenby; Mr C H Bromfield, Tenby; Mr Roy Eccles, Broadway, Laugharne; Mr A G O Mathias, Pembroke; Mr O F Lowless, Pembroke; Mr A H Eccles, Broadway; Lieutenant-Commander Pender Pender, DSO, RN, Astridge, Tenby; Mr Buckley, Mr Lewis, Hean Castle; Captain J Howell, MFH, Amroth Castle; Colonel Spence, Colby, CMG, DSO, Ffynone; Sir David Spence, Colby, Ffynone; Mr H G Hoxson, Pembroke Dock; Captain Burden, 2nd East Lancs Regiment; Mr H W Neville, General Sir Frederick Meyrick, Bart; and party, Bush, Pembroke; Mr Gerald Baker, Nythaderyn, Tenby; Captain Thresh, 2nd East Lancs, Pembroke Dock; Mr H Seymour Allen, Cresselly; Major W Stewart, Llanfairarybryn, Llandovery; Mr M F P Lloyd, Glanseven, Llangadock; Mrs Roy Eccles, Broadway, Laugharne; Miss Newell, Oxford; Mrs Gerald Baker, Nythaderyn, Tenby; Mrs Lort Stokes, Tenby; Mrs Thresh, Pembroke Dock; Mrs W Stewart, Llandovery, Miss M E Stewart, Llandovery; Miss Betty Lloyd.

The ladies at the Race-Ball were described as follows:

THE DRESSES

Miss Stephens, of Broomhill, Kidwelly, wore a gold lace frock; Miss Stella Moore, Woofferton Grange, was attired in pale pink georgette and lace; Mrs Bickerton Edwards, black georgette with diamante trimmings; Miss Sianden Paine, mauve georgette with floral appliqués; Miss Iris Jennings, iridescent sequin dress; Miss Lloyd, black satin and jet; Mrs David Percival, gold brocade; Miss Joyce Williams, peacock taffetas; Lady Price, in black; Mrs Spence, Colby, black and white georgette, trimmed with diamante; Mrs Gwyn Mathwin, Bofs de Rose brocaded velvet; Mrs John Newton, gold lace and polinsky; Miss A Vaughan, yellow georgette, trimmed with mauve and silver beads; Miss Nesta Price, period frock in white taffetas; Mrs Lionel Owen, silver lame, trimmed with white fox fur; Miss Joyce Prentis, apricot and silver; Miss Phyllis Howell, pink georgette, trimmed with diamante; Mrs R G Bailey, cyclamen georgette, over silver tissue; Miss M Roderick, red chiffon, trimmed with palest pink ninon, with silver broderie Anglaise on the rounded skirt panels. Mrs Hope, wife of Admiral Hope, wore multi-coloured and gold tissue, trimmed with silver lame, and in her hair was a pearl and ruby tiara. Chatting to her was Mrs Hugh Nicholson in black taffetas, with hems of emerald taffetas and gold thread embroideries on skirt, finished with a big bustle bow with emeralds on side. She chaperoned Miss Rosemary Nicholson, who was in a charmingly girlish gown of white georgette, embroidered with pearls in a diamond design and underlined with palest pink georgette; Miss Dorothy Davies-Evans' gown of crimson charmeuse was embroidered with gold and crimson silk in a half-moon design; Miss Miles wore a white georgette gown with black hems and a bold design of gold and silver sequins; Mrs Stokes, eau de nil georgette in bead, embroidered petals; Miss Gwyneth Taylor's gown of silver tissue fell at the hem in deep points of silver lace; Mrs Gray's pretty gown of silver tissue was trimmed with tiny apple green flowers on the skirt panels; Miss Stephens' gold lame gown was trimmed with gold and shaded blue sequin bands; with a side drapery similarly bordered. Miss Betty Lloyd wore a dainty dress of pink georgette; Mrs FitzStephen Lloyd wore silver tissue, with pearl bead fringes hanging from the waist; Colonel W J Evans, DSO, secretary of the Hunt Week, brought Mrs Evans, who was wearing a becoming black gown with black lace edging the skirt; Miss Reid was in black, and Mrs Vickerman wore white lace with circle of ruched taffetas on the skirt; Miss Curzon wore black, with diamante skirt embroideries.

* * * * * * * * * * *

In 1894, it was decided to move the annual meeting of January forward to March, in order to obtain weather more acceptable to all concerned, but especially for the supporters, as there was a hope of better weather during this month, because a great majority of the people were now travelling from very distant parts of the UK. But this did not prove to be of any advantage, and so in 1895, the meeting was once more to revert to the month of January, and the Tenby Observor carried this report:

JANUARY 1895
TENBY HUNT STEEPLE CHASES AND HURDLE RACES
Wednesday and Thursday, January 23rd and 24th

STEWARDS
W H Richards Esq, Mayor of Tenby; Clement J Williams Esq; J F Lort Phillips Esq, M F H; H Gwyn Saunders Davies Esq; C E Burrell Esq; Colonel Goodeve A A G; Lieut-Colonel Denne, late 4th D G; Captain Cochrane, R N, HMS Rupert; Colonel Quirk, D S O, Welsh Regiment; Colonel Suarin; Colonel Macpherson, R E; Colonel Knox R A; John Evans Esq, M O H; J V Colby Esq; W J Buckley Esq, M F H; Henry Lawrence Esq; Morris Owen Esq; T D S Cunningham Esq, Isle of Caldy; Captain Moreton Thomas; Bowen P Woosnam Esq; W T Summers Esq; W M Singer Esq; A Mortimer Singer Esq;

General Laurie; H Seymour Allen Esq, M F H; C W R Stokes Esq; A Powell Esq; Captain Crossman; Captain L Jenkins.

> Clerk of Scales – Lieut-Colonel Denne
> Judge – Mr George Richards
> Clerk of the Course – Mr H J Gregory
> Stakeholder – Mr George Chiles
> Starter – Mr George W Ormond
> Hon Sec – C W R Stokes Esq, 6 Croft Terrace, Tenby.

Last year the date of this fixture was changed to the first week in March in the hope that the weather would be more favourable for outdoor sport. This, unfortunately, was not the case, and consequently at the preliminary meeting of subscribers it was decided, certainly only by a small majority, that the Races should again be held during the week immediately succeeding that of the Hunt Week. The principal reason for this, stated at the time, was that many who came to Tenby for the Hunt Week festivities would be induced to prolong their stay in Tenby, in order to enjoy the sport provided at one of the few good old-fashioned country meetings, which has survived many vicissitudes, and which for a long series of years has been looked forward to with interest by most of the county families. One disadvantage of its taking place in January is that the weather is more than ordinarily treacherous, and except for the fact that it is a very rare thing indeed to have a long spell of wintry weather in Tenby and its vicinity, and it would in nine cases out of ten render racing almost an impossibility. There is an inherent faith, however, in Tenby, founded on long experience, that hard frosts and deep snow are most transient in their visitations in this part of the country, and that whilst others are either ironbound in icy fetters or buried under a mantle of snow several inches in depth, that the country hereabouts is not only visible, but sufficiently soft to make good running a possibility. For some few seasons past the only fault to be found with the course has been that, thanks to Jupiter Pluvius, it has been too soft and that the breezes have wafted inland a little too much sea fog* to enable those present to fully enjoy the spectacle.

*The sea fog was a common occurrence in the winter months, but never was it so bad as that of the January Meeting, in 1927, of which we read later.

This year considerable anxiety was felt as to whether we were not going to experience a repetition of our previous bad luck, and up to Tuesday morning the outlook was most unpromising. Certainly we had no snow, and the thermometer only fell sufficiently below freezing point to give a skimming of frost in the most exposed situations. This soon went and the keen air had had a beneficial effect in drying the surface of the land and the roads without at all interfering with good going on the course proper. Other parts of the country did not seem so fortunate, as owners of horses at a distance wired to say they would not bring their horses, owing to frost and snow. Reassuring telegrams were sent them and on Tuesday afternoon there were undeniable prospects of a good sport taking place under most enjoyable climatic conditions for January.

"A MENTION OF A FEW OF THE RACES"
THE LAWRENNY PLATE of 40 Sovs
35 sovs to the winner; 5 sovs to the second.

An optional selling Steeplechase; four years old, 10st 10lbs; five, 11st 10lbs; six and aged, 12st 5lbs; if entered to be sold by auction for 70 sovs, allowed 7lbs; if for 50 sovs, allowed 10lbs. Entrance 2 sovs. About three miles over banks.

Mr Lort Phillip's Macheath, aged (£70), 12st 5lb, W Warlow, 1
Mr W Thomas's br m Alice, aged (£70), 11st 12lbs, S T Jones, 2
Mr J V Colby's (late Major Moore's) b g King Cole,
By Rhidorrock, aged (£70), 11st 12lb, C Galvin, 3
Mr A H Hall's Natas, aged, 12st 5lb, S Dean, 0
*Mr W Francis's Annie Laurie, aged, 12st 5lb, Brychan Rees, 0
(thrown off early)
Mr R H Harries's (late Mr L Rees's) Forester, by Jaffa, aged (£70), 11st 12lb,
Tom Phillips 0
Captain White's b g Free and Easy, aged, 12st 5lb, Owner, 0

* William Francis – Dick Francis's grandfather.
   Betting: 3 to 1 agst Macheath and Annie Laurie, 7 to 2 Forester, 4 to 1 Alice, 8 to 1 King Cole and Natas, 10 to 1 others.
   Macheath led at the start, closely followed by Free and Easy and King Cole. Annie Laurie's rider was thrown early in the race. Macheath came away at the finish and won by nine lengths; a good finish between second and third. This victory was very popular, with loud cheers greeting the horse on returning to the Paddock, and at 3-1 the local public won plenty of money.

THE LICENSED VICTUALLERS' OPTIONAL SELLING HURDLE RACE

Of 40 Sovs 35 sovs to the winner, and 5 sovs to second. Four years old, 11st; five, 11st 10lbs; six and aged, 12st 3lbs; if entered to be sold for 70 sovs, allowed 10lbs; if for 50 sovs, allowed 14lb, Entrance 2 sovs, Two miles over eight flights of hurdles.

Mr L Shiel's ch h St Columba, by Baliot, out ofAmelia, by Vestminster, aged (£70), 11st 7lb, Owner, 1

Captain M Lindsay's ch m Avona, aged, 12st 3lb, W Lindsay, 2
* Mr Herbert Sidney's Golden Oriole, 6 yrs (£70), 11st 7lb, Owner 3
* Champion Jockey 1900
Mr R Moynan's Measure for Measure, 5 yrs, 11st 10lb, Mr J Lewis 0
Mr W R Shirley's Bangaway, 6 yrs (£50), 11st 3lb, W Eardwicker 0
Mr M A Shipway's br h Annandale, by Galliard-Argua, aged (£70), 11st 7lb, J P Evans 0
Mr T Sheehan's (IRE) b g Victor II, by Old Victor, dam byWild Oats, aged (£70), 11st 7lb Owner 0
Mr W G Lewis's br g Congress II, aged, 12st 3lb, J Griffiths, 0
Mr A P Saunders Davies's Grape Vine, aged, 12st 3lb, Mr G S Davies , 0
Sir Cuthbert Slade's (late Mr D Crane's) Briarwood, 5 yrs, 11st 10lb, Owner, 0

Betting: 3 to 1 each agst Briarwood and Grape Vine, 4 to 1 agst Measure for Measure, 5 to 1 agst Avona, 7 to 1 each agst St Columba and Golden Oriole, and 10 to 1 agst others.

The whole lot got off close together. Some mistakes were made at the first hurdle, and Bangaway fell giving his rider a nasty shaking. The rest kept well together, but eventually Columba came away and won by half a length. A good race for second place. The winner was put up by Mr E Grabham, the Auctioneer, and was knocked down to Mr Shirley for 160 guineas.

* * * * * * * * * * *

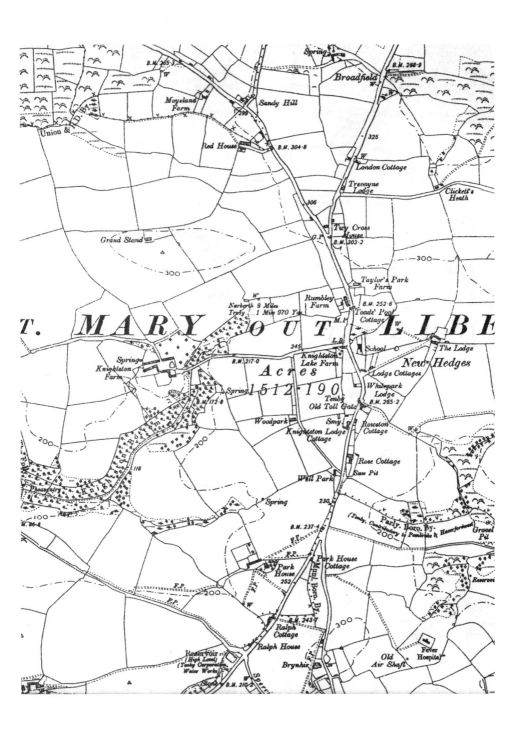

OS Map circa. 1895, showing Race Course and new Grand Stand

1895 was a year of great significance for Tenby Races. Brychan Rees, the veterinary surgeon was now joint Licensee of the Lion Hotel, along with his wife, Hilda Erederica Elizabeth Rees, and carried on the business of hoteliers, the owner being Mrs Rees's mother, wife of the late Fred Bowers. The Lion Hotel owned the two stables in Upper Frog Street, known as Brychan's Yard, and what is known today as the Mews, which was a few yards away. Frederick Brychan Rees was born on Tuesday January 22nd 1895, the day before the Race Meeting at Tenby, on Wednesday 23rd and Thursday 24th. Can you imagine the pandemonium that ensued?! The Hotel bursting at the seams, his wife in bed with a newly born son, and the busiest week of the year for a veterinary surgeon. Also, he had taken a nasty bump when thrown from Annie Laurie in the Lawrenny Plate on the first day.

So, a future champion jockey was born, and what better an introduction into the world than to choose to be born during Tenby Race Week. The next three decades were to introduce a new breed of horseman, one that was eager and quick to learn; to seize opportunities for themselves, which had not been available to the previous generation. On the 25th May 1896, a daughter was born into the Rees family, Sarah Letitia Norah Rees, and on the 25th January 1898 another son, Lewis Bilbee Rees, once more, born during Race-Week like his elder brother Fred, and also destined to become a champion.

It was during these next few years that David Harrison started to show a great deal of interest in the Tenby Racing Scene. He was born in 1876 at Deer Park, Tenby. His father, Thomas Ashton Harrison, whose profession was described as that of a Gentleman, was a keen follower of racing. David was now almost twenty and had become a very good friend of George Stokes, who was born on September 25th 1875, and was baptised privately, as he was not expected to live for more than a few days or so, but, he did live, and Tenby Races would not have become the success that it was without him. There was no doubt that he played a key part in its future and indeed in it's inevitable downfall, and his own untimely death. He was in fact a witness at David Harrison's marriage to Grace Morris on April 18th 1906. She was the daughter of Henry Morris, a clergyman, of The Norton, Tenby, and after their marriage in 1906, moved into The Grove in Heywood Lane, Tenby.

In the following year 1896, there were very few entries for the January Meeting, and on the first day there were only twenty-eight entries for the five races and out of this number, five had failed to attend. In the matter of bookmakers and betting men, there was perhaps a larger number present than last year, but the amount of business done was not up to expectation. In the Lawrenny Plate, there was a very unfortunate accident. Macheath, which had recently been purchased from Mr Lort Phillips by Mr L F Craven, fell very awkwardly whilst taking one of the banks and throwing his jockey clear, broke its back. In order to put it out of its misery, its throat was cut, but this was to no avail. Eventually a shotgun was obtained from Knightston Farm and the animal was put down. This brought an air of shock and surprise to all those who attended, as to why the committee had no shotgun or revolver of their own in the committee room throughout the whole meeting. It was obviously something that had been somehow overlooked and it was ensured that in the future, this would not happen again. However, it left a very sour taste in the mouth for all of those in attendance, especially the ladies, and the following day was very poorly attended.

In 1897, Brychan Rees had become joint secretary with Mr C W R Stokes and the date of the meeting was again brought forward to March 4th and advertised as a Spring Meeting. The weather was absolutely unbearable and the attendance was very small, although the entries for the races were excellent. However, on the second day, the rider of Pen Hilda, Mr H Griffiths, sustained a nasty head injury whilst being thrown at the water jump; his injuries were attended to by Dr Beamish Hamilton, the official surgeon, who had been appointed by the committee. Dr Beamish Hamilton complained that there was no stretcher available to move the injured man to a hospital room, and one had to be made up very quickly, and two policemen conveyed the injured man to the committee room under the stand. The surgeon did the best that he could and saved the life of Mr Griffiths. Dr Hamilton again complained to the committee that there should be a hospital room with access to clean linen and hot water, and a proper hospital bed, not the committee meeting table, which he had to use. Mr C W R Stokes noted that this would be seen to. "Also," commented Mr C W R Stokes, "due to the lack of support it is understood that there will be a considerable financial loss, which added to the loss of last year, will create a heavy debt, which will have to be faced by the committee. Judging from past meetings it is apparent that the Tenby Races were losing their popularity and success, and something will have to be done to rectify this deficiency," he said.

In the Cresselly Steeple Chase Mr George Stokes saw his first horse run, as an owner. It was Bubble, a six year old ridden by T Crank, but was not placed. The race was won by Mr Lort Phillips's Memphis, aged 12st 10lb ridden by C Galvin. The race was three miles over banks and was won by 2 lengths at 2-1. Mr Lort Phillips 'declaring to win'*, it proved a popular winner amongst the local betting public. Mr Brychan Rees also had a runner in the race, Greenlight ridden by Mr T Sheehan, but was unplaced.

*If an owner has two runners or more in the same race, he must give his preference to the horse which he thinks has the best chance, by 'declaring to win!" with that horse.

In the Lawrenny Selling Steeple Chase of two and a half miles over banks, Mr J F Lort Phillips's Memphis was again an entry, and Mr Lort Phillips fancying his chances for a second time with the same horse, he again 'declared him to win', there was tremendous applause, and it was backed down to 2-1 on, and with Mr C Galvin again in the seat, carrying 12st 11lb, won by a neck, with a deafening noise of cheering and chanting at the finish post. Mr Brychan Rees also ran Greenlight again, in the Tenby Hurdle over 2 miles gaining a second place, with Mr P Sheehan riding.

*If an owner has two runners or more in the same race, he must give his preference to the horse which he thinks has the best chance, by 'declaring to win!" with that horse.

****

1898 saw the official arrival of Mr David Harrison, as an owner. He had bought an aged steeplechaser, by the name of Countess, under the guidance of Brychan Rees, with whom it was stabled. He had also struck up a very strong friendship with Brychan Rees, as we shall later read about.

The committee had now decided to move the meeting to February 2nd and 3rd for 1898, and had commissioned Hereford Agents, Smith and Page, to organise their future race meetings.

February 2nd & 3rd 1898

The first day included:

Penally Steeplechase, 25 sovereigns
Town Steeplechase, 40 sovereigns
Visitors Hurdle, 40 sovereigns
Cresselly Steeplechase, 30 sovereigns
Licensed Victuallers Selling Hurdle, 30 sovereigns

Second day:

Deer Park Open Hunt Steeplechase, 30 sovereigns
Stewards Steeplechase, 30 sovereigns
Lawrenny Selling Chase, 30 sovereigns
Knightston Selling Hurdle, 30 sovereigns

The Deer Park Open Hunt Steeple Chase was sponsored by David Harrison.

New entry fees were introduced by Smith & Page.

Admission to ground, 1s
Carriage and one horse, 3s

Carriage and Pair, 5s
All other carriages 10s and in each case, 1s for each occupant.

In addition, admission to the Grandstand 3s 6d per person. Saddle horses not allowed on the ground. A private carriage enclosure will be reserved for subscribers of two guineas and upwards.

Tickets for standings and outside bookmakers 3s 6d each, to be obtained from the Hon Secs before taking to the ground, and any person refusing to pay on demand, will be treated as a trespasser, with the course being Private Property.

NO LISTS, CLOGS, STOOLS, or any Ready Money Betting Allowed (This meant that no person to hinder or prevent others from moving around by forming an area of their own for betting with filthy shekels and wads of the crown, and using a side-pack saddle in doing so... work that one out if you can!). Cheap Rail Tickets will be issued by the GWR. All horses to be entered by January 26th.

It seemed that Smith and Page meant business; but it did not go down too well, as on both days there were no more than three runners in each of the ten races. The admission was poor due to the fact of the entrance fees and charges, although there was a fair crowd, but the going was very heavy and the weather was miserable and unsettled.

On the first day, David Harrison ran his horse Countess in the Cresselly Steeple Chase, riding himself and coming third of three runners. He ran Countess again the second day in the Knightston Selling Hurdle, again riding himself with the same result. Brychan Rees also ran Lady Fitzraven on both days, ridden by P Sheehan, with the same result, third on both days.

David Harrison was now enjoying the first taste of being involved in the racing scene, and had bought a few more horses, under the watchful eye of Brychan Rees. In 1899, the races were again held in February, on the 9th and 10th. On the first day the weather was terrible, with storms and heavy gales. Many people stayed at home, but those that had committed themselves to travel did attend. It was found impossible to open the whole front of the Grandstand, due to the severe gales. Many people sheltered in the paddock when the races were not in progress, and it was almost impossible to walk anywhere because of the mud. During the afternoon, there were two serious accidents. Firstly in the Cresselly Steeple Chase, St Teilo, owned by Mr Frank Bibby, fell and broke a leg and had to be shot, then in the next race Jacobus II, owned by Mr J F Barrett, fell at the notorious water jump and broke its back, again it was shot. On this occasion, both horses were put out of their misery within a very short space of time. Among the stewards in attendance were: J F Lort Phillips, Lawrenny, Colonel Denne, Major Glascott, Mr C W R Stokes,

41

W G Parcell, Mr T Ashton Harrison**, W J Buckley, Dr Lawrence, Capt Cass and Col Goodeve. The suspicious running of Salius in the Visitors Hurdle Race attracted the attention of the stewards, who held a meeting after the race. The owner and jockey were summoned to the stewards' room. After hearing the explanation of the owner Mr John Widger (IRE) and his jockey Mr T Hair, it was resolved that the case be reported to the National Hunt Committee.

**David Harrison's Father

On the first day in the Penally Steeple Chase of two and a half miles over banks, Brychan Rees's Little Norah, ridden by Mr P Sheehan, made all the running for two miles, but came second to Mr Gregory's Alnwick.

Tenby Races 1898
Penally Steeplechase Cup

(Left to Right) Brychan Rees, Secretary, Sir David Hughes Morgan Bart, Chairman of the Western Mail, George Stokes, Solicitor, Henry Lawrence, Steward.

The other races were as follows:

VISITORS HURDLE
40 sovereigns, two miles
Mr T J Widger's (IRE), Rupee, Owner 1
Mr J Widger's (IRE), Salius, T Hair 2
Mr F Bibby's, Rickardstown, Mr A Wood 3

LICENSED VICTUALLERS SELLING HURDLE
30 sovereigns, 2 miles
Mr J Widger's (IRE), Keymer, Mr T J Widger 1
Mr R Inman's, Hawick, D Davies 2
Mr J V Colby's, Rose Garland, L Oxenham 3

CRESSELLY STEEPLE CHASE
40 sovereigns, 3 miles over banks
Mr C Smith's, Mary Stuart, Mr P Sheehan 1
Mr J V Colby's, Electric, L Oxenham 2

Electric and Mary Stuart made the running for the first two miles, Mary Stuart fell but was remounted and won. St Teilo fell badly and was shot.

TOWN STEEPLE CHASE
40 sovereigns, Two miles over flying course
Mr F Bibby's, Terpsichore II, Edward Thomas 1*
Finished alone.

* Edward Thomas was Mr J F Lort Phillips's stud groom and later trainer of Kirkland. NB. Mr Frank Bibby had bought Kirkland the previous year as a two year old in Ireland.

Mr J Barrett's Jacobus II ridden by Mr P Sheehan, fell at the water and broke its back and was shot.

On the second day, although it rained in the morning, there was an improvement in the weather. The going was very heavy and there were no accidents. All the races went off on time.

STEWARD'S STEEPLE CHASE
40 sovereigns, 3 miles
Mr F Bibby's, Terpsichore II, Edward Thomas 1
Mr J Harty's, Natasha, Mr P Sheehan 2
Betting 5-4 on Natasha

A very pretty race was run and was well fought out. Natasha led at the water, first time round; thereafter the two could be covered by a sheet. Turning into the straight, Terpsichore II came away and won a magnificent race by two lengths. Because there were only two runners the prize was reduced to 25 sovereigns, with entry reduced to 1 sovereign.

THE LAWRENNY PLATE
of 30 sovereigns. Entry 1 sovereign
15 sovereigns given by Mr F Bibby and matched by Mr J F Lort Phillips for half bred
horses, bred in South Wales, and maidens at the time of entry to the race.
Two miles over the flying course
Mr F Bibby's, Lady Lovelace, Edward Thomas 1
Mr L F Craven's, Solva, Mr Benchley 2
Capt M Lindsay's, Lois, F Parker 3
Lady Lovelace won by 20 lengths Betting 3-1 on

TENBY HURDLE RACE
30 sovereigns, two miles
For horses which have never won, except for banking races up to time of closing.
Mr F Bibby's, Rickardstown C Glavin 1
Mr W Grove's, Port Phyilis, Mr Grove 2
Mr D Harrison's, Rascal, R W Smith 3 *
Rickardstown made all the running and won easily.

DEER PARK OPEN STEEPLE CHASE
3 miles over banks
Mr C Smith's, Mary Stuart, Mr P Sheehan 1
Capt Bell's, Connaught Ranger II, Mr Benchley 2
Mr J V Colby's, Electric, Tom Phillips 3
Betting 5-4 on Connaught Ranger - 5-4 Mary Stuart, won by neck.
*Robert Weaver Smith, who was to become the holder of the license for the Tenby stable
of David Harrison.

The Cresswell Quay Open Handicap Chase

CHAPTER TWO
THE SOCIAL SCENE AND AS A RESORT

At the turn of the century, Tenby was very, very popular, and the Great Western Railway was running to perfection. In the past, the only horseflesh was either travelling to Tenby Races or to Ireland via Pembroke Dock, and of course travelling back again. But with the opening of Tenby Racing Stables, David Harrison would have access by rail to virtually any of the racecourses in the UK and Ireland. There were two blacksmith-farriers in Tenby itself; one being John Griffiths in Upper Frog Street and the other was George Sinnett in the South Parade. There was also Henry Nash at Knightston Gate, New Hedges, whose grandson David still runs the family business Well Park, as a Caravan Park. Henry Nash was used by David Harrison mostly on the duration of the Annual Races in January, and also the summer meetings, when they were held. The apprentice to Henry Nash was one Herbert Mason, and when Henry Nash retired Herbert converted his outbuildings at Rose Cottage on the opposite side of the village road to open his own smithy, where he

Knightston Smithy (left to right) Herbert Mason and Henry Nash.

carried on the business until he retired in the 1960's. As a young lad of about ten I used to earn 6d every Saturday for pumping the bellows in the old forge; it was hard work for a little lad, because almost every Saturday during the hunting season there would be a meet nearby, and there were a lot of horses in the New Hedges area in those days. As soon as Mr Mason had finished work, he would give me the 6d and pat me on the head, and say, "Don't be late next week son, there's a big meet in the town". I would run straight to Mrs Weigh's little cottage near Lodge Gate, and spend 2d on a bottle of her home-made ginger beer, which was renowned throughout the county.

There were two saddlemakers; Mr John Evans, in Tudor Square, who also ran a retail saddlery business from the same premises. Then there was John James, at No 4 Crackwell Street, who sold to the trade only, and was basically full time keeping David Harrison's stable supplied. He was one of the businessmen known as a part of the Tenby Triangle. Because opposite was Oliver Thomas the Bookmaker, and a few doors away was The Sun Inn, where all the jockeys and the lads spent their leisure time. It was in fact in John James

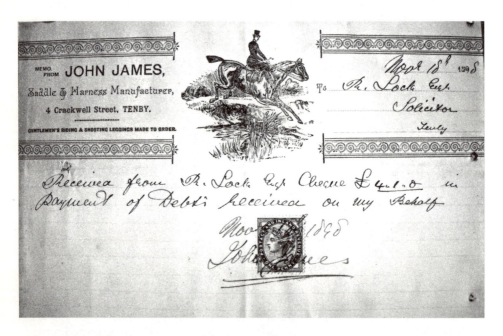

the Saddler's that Dick Francis's grandfather would sit on a chair in the corner, as he visited most days to keep up with the news of the town, and where the next winner was coming from.

There was plenty of work in the town, especially for apprentices, as many tradesmen were emigrating to Australia.

"FREE EMIGRATION TO AUSTRALIA"
Free passages are granted by the Government of Queensland:-
To General Servants, Cooks, Housemaids, Nurses, Dairy Maids, etc,

wages, £25 to £50 a year all found. To Married and Single Farm Labourers. wages £30 to £50 a year with board and lodging. Assisted Passages on payment of £4 to:

Artizans (all kinds), Bricklayers, Quarrymen, Blacksmiths,
Cabinet Makers, Rope Makers, Carpenters & Joiners,
Gardeners, Shoemakers, Butchers,
Grooms, Shipwrights, Bookbinders, Saddlers,
Shepherds, Bakers, Plasterers, Tailors & others
Plumbers and Painters

At Wages about double English Rates. Each Ship carries an experienced Surgeon and Matron. Families have separate sleeping compartments. Work can be carried on in the open air all the year round. Beef and Mutton 3d a lb; Tea 2s 6d a lb; Flour 15s a cwt; Sugar 3d a lb. Apply personally or by letter to:

AGENT-GENERAL FOR
QUEENSLAND, 32, Charing Cross, London, SW; or to
G STONE, THE RAILWAY, TENBY.

Other attractions to the town, apart from the glorious beaches, and the theatrecals, were the De Valence Gardens, the Tenby Baths, and of course Sea Fishing.

"TENBY BATHS"
SEA AND FRESH WATER

These Baths, fitted with all the latest improvements for the
Comfort and convenience of Bathers
ARE NOW OPEN!
Hot Sea Water Bath, 1/6
Cold ditto, 1/-
Hot Fresh Water Bath, -/9d
Cold ditto, -/9d
Hot or Cold ditto – Wednesdays and
Saturdays, after 12 noon, -/6d
Special WELL BATH for Invalids, 2s 6d
Hot Sea Water, per dozen Tickets, 12/-
Ditto per half-dozen Tickets, 6/-
Open Daily from 7am to 8pm
Sundays mornings from 7am to 10am
Medical Referees – The Resident Medical Men.

"SEA FISHING"

Tenby from time immemorial has been famed for this sport, than which we are led to suppose there are very few, if any, amusements that give rise to more enjoyment. By no means is any other recreation more healthy and strengthening, in the enjoyment of which, taking for granted that the weather will be clear, which it generally is, you may enjoy those fresh sea breezes, which cannot be sufficiently well imbibed without taking a little airing beyond the precincts of the sea-shore in one of our little Tenby crafts; which done, with an expert boatman on board, you may catch a variety of fish, such, for instance, as salmon, sewin, bass, gurnard, pollock, plaice, whiting, mackerel, etc. The last named are just, now coming in, and by taking a couple of lines and a good boat you may often catch as many as three or four dozen in a few hours. A few days since one man caught two dozen, and we may truthfully say that in a short time, if the season prove as good as it did last year, that same man will catch twenty dozen. Let me entreat then, friends, that you will spend part of your visit to Tenby in the fishermen's boats, by doing which you will enjoy rare sport yourself, and at the same time may be the means of cheering many a poor body's heart with the money so gained. May I mention that through the excursions made by the steamers from this little town our sailors lose a great many of their parties, and seldom has the season been slacker than it is at present. Signed: A Fisherman

A certain Wilfred Rees, from London had obviously seen the potential in Tenby and had moved from London, advertising Riding Habits as a specialty.

"Wilfred Rees"

"London Tailor"

(From LAMB's, Jermyn Street, Piccadilly, W)

Tudor Square, Tenby.

COURT, NAVAL and MILITARY TAILOR.

Ladies' Costumes and Riding Habits (a speciality)

The Largest Stock out of London of First-Class Cloths to select

From, either for Ladies' or Gentlemen's Wear.

W Rees – who has had fifteen years' experience in the best West End Houses, viz., Poole's, Saville Row; Hill Bros, Bond Street; and Rose Bros, Grosvenor Street – possesses numerous testimonials from Ladies and Gentlemen in the Principality, and various parts of the Kingdom, certifying to the satisfaction given by him in. Style, Fit and Wear, of Garments supplied. Very Moderate Prices for first-class Tailoring.

AN INSPECTION IS INVITED.

There were also three high class boot and shoe makers in the town at this time, all making boots and shoes to suit your individual measurements whereas today there is only one retail shop, and one small repair shop in Tenby Market belonging to a Mr D Thomas. However, you do get your shoes repaired the same day, or so I am told.

BOOTS (Opposite the Town Hall) BOOTS

NOTICE!

To the Inhabitants and Visitors of Tenby and its Neighbourhood

C ARKELL, of Swansea

RESPECTFULLY announces that he has purchased the

Business lately and for so many years carried on by

Mr J Jones, Boot and Shoe Maker, High Street, Tenby.

The Business will be conducted on the same principles

Of selling good Articles at Low Prices, and C. A. will have special

Facilities from his large establishments of applying all articles in

The Trade, and hopes to, merit a continuance of confidence and

Favours. Repairs neatly done, and on the Shortest Notice.

R JENKINS & SON
BOOTMAKERS
BANK HOUSE, HIGH STREET, TENBY
Have always in Stock a large and good selection of
LADIES, GENTLEMEN'S and CHILDREN'S
BOOTS and SHOES, from the best Manufacturers.
Ladies' Elastic Side Boots, from, 3s 9d
Gentlemen's ditto, 6s 9d
Agent for the "Singer" Sewing Machine, £6 10s
Undoubtedly the best in the market for all kinds of Sewing.
Thomas's Machine, from, £2 15s
Weir's Machine, £2 15s
The "Globe", £2 0s

JOHN F DAVIES
BOOT AND SHOE MAKER
18 NORTON TENBY

Respectfully begs to inform the Gentry, Inhabitants and Visitors of Tenby
and its neighbourhood, that he intends for the future, in addition to the
Bespoken Trade, carried on for so many years past, to keep always in stock
A good supply of Homemade and Ready-Made Ladies, Gentlemen's and
Children's BOOTS and SHOES, in every size, price and quality.
JOHN F DAVIES returns his sincere thanks to his numerous friends
for the kind support they have hitherto done in patronising him.
Agent for the Star Life Assurance Society.

During the summer months steamers crossed the channel from Bristol to Tenby, bringing families for their annual holidays, who brought their own transport and horses with them, because most of the hotels in the town had their own coaching houses and stables and also the grooms to look after the horses.

STEAM COMMUNICATION
BETWEEN BRISTOL AND TENBY

The Bristol General Navigation Company's powerful Steamers
Briton or Juverna, or other suitable Steam Vessels, are intended
to sail from Cumberland Basin, Hotwells (unless prevented by
any unforeseen occurrence, and with liberty to Tow Vessels), as follows:

May - Bristol to Tenby.
Friday 2nd, 9am, Friday 9th, 4 pm, Friday 16th, 8 am,
Friday 23rd, 3 pm, Friday 30th, 8 am

FARES: Saloon 8s. Deck 4s.
Fares, 42s; pair-horse Phaeton,
One-horse ditto, 25s; Gig, 20s; Horse, 25s; Dog, 3s.
All Goods in Craft to be at the risk of the Shipper
Or Consignee, whether conveyed at expense of Ship
Or Freighter. Not accountable for any goods without
Shipping Notes.

My grandfather, John Martin Lawrence, was one of the local milkmen
who delivered to many of the businesses in the town as well as to private

houses. He had a farm in New Hedges with his own small herd of dairy cows, so he would have to milk the cows himself, and deliver quite early, so as to miss the warmer weather of the latter part of the morning. The milk was delivered by pony and trap, with a large copper churn in the back, into which you would put a ladle and fill a copper jug to take to the client's house or hotel. In many cases, the client would come to the trap with their own jugs or containers, which would be filled by my grandfather using the imperial pint, quart, and gallon measures, which were always carried on the trap. His last calls would be coming up Crackwell Street from the harbour, his final call being John James the saddler, where he could sit down and have a chinwag, and a pipe full of Ringer's Shag. He would often meet Dick Francis's grandfather in there, where between them they would discuss what horse to have a bet on that day. My grandfather would then drain the copper churn, with maybe a pint or two left in it and take it into the Sun Inn and give it to the landlord, in exchange for his two daily pints of beer, the first one he drank very quickly and would say, "That's a cutter", the second he drank slowly, again smoking his pipe, and saying, "Ah! That's a healer". He would arrive back at the farm about 1pm for his dinner, and then at 4.30pm it was time for the second milking session, which was mainly for hotel deliveries that evening during the summer months only.

He was also a steward at the Racecourse and on race days he would collect the entry money at the gate of Rumbly Way farmhouse by selling the race cards to the horse-drawn phaetons and carriages coming from the Tenby direction, as it was the only property on the same side of the road before the racecourse. This made sense, as it would take a great workload off the main gate where everyone would be travelling from the Haverfordwest, Narberth and Carmarthen directions, and would mainly be travelling by motor car from those distances, especially as the horseless carriage and the horse-drawn carriage were not yet the best of friends. At about 1 pm he would walk to the course and give his takings to the treasurer and resume other duties. In fact, it was about this time in 1900 when a motor car coming out of the indoor hotel garage of the Imperial Hotel in Lower Frog Street backfired very loudly, just as a pony and trap was passing by; the pony bolted and raced straight through the railings at the Paragon, landing upon the rocks below, killing both the pony and the person driving the trap.

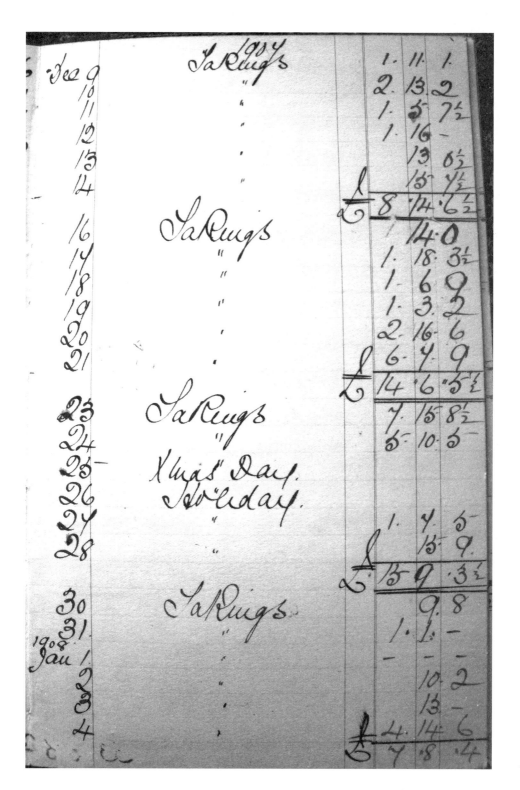

				£	s	d
Dec	9	Takings		1	11	1
	10	"		2	13	2
	11	"		1	5	7½
	12	"		1	16	–
	13	"			13	6½
	14	"			15	4½
			£	8	14	6½
	16	Takings			14	0
	17	"		1	18	3½
	18	"		1	6	0
	19	"		1	3	2
	20	"		2	16	6
	21	"		6	4	9
			£	14	6	5½
	23	Takings		7	15	8½
	24	"		5	10	5
	25	Xmas Day.				
	26	Holiday.				
	27	"		1	4	5
	28	"			15	9
			£	15	9	3½
	30	Takings			9	8
	31	"		1	1	–
1908 Jan	1	"		–	–	–
	2	"			10	2
	3	"			13	–
	4	"		4	14	6
			£	7	8	4

Milk Round Takings

Local Race Ball Theatrical Group. circa. 1898
Main characters Mr and Mrs George Ace.

CHAPTER THREE
"TENBY STABLES ARE BORN"

David Harrison now had itchy feet, he had run third with Rascal in the Tenby Hurdle, ridden by his close friend Robert Weaver Smith, and now felt that he would like to set up on his own. Even at the young age of twenty-three he had decided that his future was to be that of a successful racehorse trainer. He had gathered around him a team of young men all eager to succeed in the racing world, and he had discussed the financial situation with Mr Brychan Rees, who owned both yards, which belonged to the Lion Hotel. The outcome was a partnership. Mr Rees would remain owner of both yards, with David Harrison in control of all training. All horses and staff would be split between the two yards, and Brychan Rees would give his veterinary services to all horses trained there. David Harrison was in control of collecting all monies due from the owners, and ensuring that all veterinary bills were paid promptly. Also the staff were to be paid promptly. David Harrison then approached his father for financial help.

Harrison's father, being a keen follower of racing, was willing to help his son with enough finance to get his business up and running, and also an allowance paid annually. But on 24th July 1899, David Harrison's father died, at the age of 63. The funeral was held on 27th July. He had left his son David a substantial sum, but not enough for him to set up as he had wished. However, his aunt from Ashton-under-Lyne came to the funeral, and he approached her with his idea. At first, his aunt was against it because she did not want David endangering his life by riding in races. However, if he promised not to compete in races and just manage the stables as a business, she would agree. Reluctantly, he agreed, and the funds available were a bottomless pit of cash. She agreed to give him a monthly allowance, which was far beyond his wildest dreams. He now had money, a racing stable, a vet and employees. What he did not have was a license, and this is where his "right hand man", came in; Robert Weaver (Bobby) Smith would hold the license and it would be registered in that name. Harrison's friend and Solicitor George Stokes, of Stokes and Stokes, Tenby, drew up the paper work and a duplicate of the Racing License in the name of R W Smith, with D Harrison as Racing Manager. The document was sent to his aunt in Ashton-under-Lyne. Everything was signed and sealed and the cash rolled in. Harrison was now in business, so, 'Look out world'!

David Harrison was soon to break his promise to his aunt not to ride, by registering the pseudonym of Mr Deer, probably taken from Deer Park, where he lived. He was now well on the way to developing expensive tastes, which were soon to lead to the best of everything, from Saville Row suitings to champagne and cigars and the high life in general. He was to become an established trainer in Wales, and also well respected in England. At the height of his career in the 1920's he had over 40 horses in training, a lot of them owned by famous people whose names ring out clear in the Who's Who of National Hunt Racing. His horses were trained along the two mile stretch of firm golden sands of the south shore. He also rented gallops at Cornishdown, just on the outskirts of the town towards New Hedges. His stable lads slept in lofts above the stables, rolled up in horse blankets on the wooden floor. Their fear of Harrison's brutality was well founded; he kept a Staffordshire Bull Terrier in the yard as a guard dog, and on his arrival he would kick the dog and the dog's howls and yelps would alert the lads and have them scrambling out from under their blankets and rolling them up to hide them, for Harrison would use them to protect his horses. These to him were a precious commodity, the stable lads weren't; they scarcely mattered.

Of local people who worked for him in Tenby, none had a good word. He was arrogant, and drove himself and his workers in the stables of Upper Frog Street to the limits. He was nevertheless also extremely handsome and charismatic and had the gift of infinite charm. He two-timed women, but by all accounts, while his affairs were in progress, he treated them well enough. He certainly lived with passion and strong motivation. He was a big man well over six feet with rounded shoulders and a deep gravely voice. He was considered by his fellow professionals to be a very good trainer, he was always well dressed, and loved to play a game of polo.

By 1900, the Tenby Stable of David Harrison was up and running, and if the reader follows the pseudonym of Mr Deer very closely, you will soon see the connection with David Harrison, also the connection of R W Smith as jockey and trainer, as we follow the next decade with much intrigue and fascination for this man, who seemed to know exactly what he was doing, but he was doing it so blatantly that it perhaps blinded a lot of those close to him, or perhaps it was too obvious and nobody was bothered anyway. He had certainly not broken any law or deceived the racing's governing body in any way, but this seemed to be the way he intended to carry on.

1900

At the race meeting of 1900, on Wednesday January 31st, a fatal accident occurred on the first day. Tom Phillips, whose name you should be familiar with by now from the recent race meetings that I have spoken of, was riding St Anne's, belonging to Mr Morris of Chapel Farm, Castlemartin, in the Cresselly Banking Steeple Chase. Whilst taking the bank on the south side of the course, nearly opposite the Grandstand, he was thrown, with his horse rolling over on him. Dr J B Hamilton, who was close at hand, had Tom Phillips removed by stretcher to the committee room, but he died within half an hour of the fall due to a severe rupture of the liver. Tom had been heard to say on previous occasions that when he died he should wish "to die in his colours". This he unfortunately did.

At the inquest, Mr John Morris of Chapel Farm said that Tom was about 46 or 47 and had been in his employment for some years, and lived for his racing. When asked if Tom Phillips was sober, he replied, "Yes, definitely". Dr Hamilton who was a witness to the accident, said that "Phillips fell off and the horse fell and rolled on top of him". The stretcher bearers, PC's Morgan and Davies, also confirmed this. Dr Hamilton said that there was an accident at the same bank last year when a horse was fatally injured. He said, "It was not long after the start and they were all riding in a bunch together, at a terrific pace". Verdict: Accidental death. John Bull, a valuable bay gelding, belonging to Mr Dan Davies also fell in the same race and had to be shot. The crowds seemed to dwindle away slowly, and the attendance was very thin by the last race of the day.

On the second day, the victory of Mr F Bibby's Lady Lovelace from the Lawrenny Stable of Mr Lort Phillips was a very popular one and a good one for the backers at 3-1. In the Knightston Selling Hurdle, Keymer, an outsider, challenged the favourite and won a good race by three quarters of a length. The winner was sold to Mr Sheehan, for 120 guineas. An objection had been lodged to the winner, on the grounds of the horse being in the forfeit list, was over-ruled, with the £5 deposit being forfeited, the objection being declared as "frivolous".

At the Race Ordinary, they were pleased with the result of the Tenby Meeting, as Hunt Steeple Chase meetings were in a depressed state all over the country, and in many places they had been abandoned altogether, because of the War in South Africa. There was a one minute silence for the death of Tom Phillips, and then a toast to his memory as a gallant horseman. Mr J F Lort Phillips, had already collected £31 at the race meeting, for his widow, and it was decided that further monies should be made available for her terrible loss. It was also decided to build an ambulance shed, to incorporate a mattress and the necessary medical supplies, that Dr Hamilton had suggested previously. Also, an ambulance was to be available at the future meetings, for conveyance, if necessary, to Tenby Cottage Hospital. I have not found any evidence of this in my research, but I do know that "Diments Steam Laundry Van" was used as an ambulance on race days, by kind permission of Mr Diment, who also supplied the driver for the necessary days.

In the autumn of 1900, David Harrison and Brychan Rees travelled over the South Wales area and bought about six horses between them. Most were bought by David Harrison, but Brychan Rees was secretly keeping him under his wing, so to speak, and to make sure that the animals were 100% sound, when purchased. As far as jockeys were concerned at this time, they mostly rode their own horses, with Robert Smith also riding, who was a very good jockey in his own right. Brychan Rees would ride point-to-point every day if he possibly could. He was a master of the art of horsemanship, which of course would later be proven by his sons Fred and Lewis Bilbee Rees. In fact, Brychan Rees was still riding at local point-to-point until he was well into his 60's. The stable lads were all local, apart from one or two who had come over from Ireland to look for work. The names that come to mind, are Oscar Thomas, Norman Pilsen, Charlie Goodridge, Affy Smith, Clem Hooper, William John, Drifter Harris, and of course Arty 'Royal' Smith, who became travelling head lad. Arty was responsible for breaking in any horses that Harrison had bought as two year olds. It was said amongst the stable lads that after Arty had broken in and schooled a horse, that you could guide it by holding one hair of its mane.

1901

A report from the Tenby Observor:

The whole country was of course saddened by the death of Queen Victoria in January 1901, and at the Tenby Meeting of February 5th and 6th, everyone wore a black armband and there was a one minute silence before the start of the first race. The Prescelly Mountains in the background were covered in snow, as was most of the country, but in "Little England beyond Wales" the sun shone brilliantly. Every precaution had been taken for the prevention of accidents, and thankfully there were none, mainly due to the abolition of the banking races, apart from one at the whole of the meeting, which attracted only four entries, and hopefully this race will disappear altogether after this season. The committee had again placed the management of the race meeting in the hands of Messrs Smith and Page of Hereford, whose organisation gave every satisfaction, and this year they were also the official handicappers.

On the first day, Wednesday February 5th, in the Penally Selling Steeple chase, one entry had somewhat of an unusual ring about it. It read as follows:

Mr Deer's (late Mr Harrison's) , Fairy Light,
Aged, 12st, ridden by Mr Deer.
The horse was not placed.

On the second day, Thursday February 6th:
The Tenby Hurdle 40 sovereigns 2 miles
Mr Deer's Sweet Moments, 4 years, 10st 5lb, R W Smith (0)
Also unplaced.
The Lawrenny Selling Steeple Chase 40 sovereigns 3 miles.
Mr Deer's (late Mr Harrison's), Fairy Light, 12st, ridden by Mr Deer.

This was Mr Deer's first winner. Mr Deer also rode the horse. So who was the late Mr Harrison? There is no evidence in my research of David Harrison's father ever owning a horse, and David Harrison would surely not use his father's name in this way, so the only explanation that I can give is that Mr Harrison had bought Fairy Light, and then sold it to Mr Deer before the Tenby Meeting, assuming that Mr Harrison was the owner of late, before the purchase by Mr Deer. So, in effect, he had sold his own horse to himself, and probably for a profit. It was a selling chase, so it will be interesting to see who the new owner is, if we ever come across it.

There was further controversy concerning the winner of the Penally Steeple Chase on the first day, on the grounds of insufficient description and was allowed to be withdrawn, but on the second day a further objection was laid against the same horse, Glenduff, on the grounds that the jockey, Mr P Sheehan, had no license to ride, as it had been proven that he had received fees for riding whilst pretending to be an amateur. Glenduff was disqualified and the race was awarded to the second horse Lady Lovelace. Mr P Sheehan (IRE) was reported to the National Hunt Committee.

1902
In January of 1902, David Harrison had fallen from a horse and had broken his collarbone and was concussed, whilst following the Local Hunt Meeting. At the race meeting on January 23rd, the weather was terrible and the course was in a deplorable condition. Smith and Page were again the organizers, although the attendance was good and so were the entries. David Harrison having no entries, (and neither did Mr Deer), perhaps because of his injury. It is interesting to note a few of the races.
The first race of interest is the:

LICENSED VICTUALLERS' HURDLE
40 sovereigns, 4 yr upwards, 2 miles over 8 hurdles.
1st, Mr JW Philipps's*, David Grieve, F Davies
2nd, Mr F Bibby's, Kirkland, 6 yo, E Thomas (stud groom for Lort Phillips)
3rd, Mr O'Geran's, Bob the Devil, Mr Buck
*Mr JW Philipps, brother to Lord Kylsant Owen Cosby Philipps, was to become Lord St Davids.

The distance between the first and second was a distance, with the third horse a neck away. Kirkland, of course, going on to win the 1905 Grand National as a 9 year old, but later

61

this year was to win 'The Grand Sefton Chase' at Liverpool, yet running here in a two mile hurdle race.

THE TOWN STEEPLE CHASE.

4 year old up. 2 miles over flying course.

For some reason the most expensive prize money to date of 100 sovereigns

Mr J Widger's, (IRE) Venetian Monk, Owner, 1

Mr E P Ryan's, Extinct, Sullivan 2

Mr A Scott's, Premier II, Owner 3

IN THE PENALLY SELLING STEEPLE CHASE.

40 sovereigns. 4 years old. 2 miles.

Mr Roger's, Rosegarland II, Owner 1

Mr Sheehan's (IRE), Lady Alice III, Sheehan 2

Notice Sheehan not riding as Mr P Sheehan, after being reported last year to The N. H. Committee.

Two very valuable horses were destroyed after falling badly.

Robert Weaver Smith

On July 31st 1902, Brychan Rees and David Harrison had organised "Tenby Horse Show", perhaps to recoup some losses from Mr Harrison's injury, or to pay for Mr Deer's hospital bills.

It was advertised as follows:

Come to TENBY
THE NAPLES OF BRITAIN
LONDON 276 miles – Population 4,700
TENBY HORSE SHOW
BANK HOLIDAY AUGUST 4TH
At THE SPORTS FIELD, HEYWOOD LANE

Admission to show: 1s. Single horse and carriage 2s.
Pair horse and carriage 3 s. Occupants 1s. each extra.
Judging starts 11.30am
Jumping Competition 2.30pm
Luncheons and Teas available.

There was beautiful sunshine throughout the day and the Tenby Town Band provided the entertainment.

Best Brood Mare £5 Delightful Lady, Mr Howell Thomas Carmarthen
Best Foal £2 Prudence J W Philipps MP Lydstep Haven
Best Yearling Colt or Filly, £3 J W Philipps MP Lydstep Haven*
Best Two Year Old Colt or Filly, £5 J W Philipps MP Lydstep Haven
Best Hunter Colt or Filly £5. Flyaway 3 yrs old. J W Philipps MP Lystep Haven
Best Hack to be ridden £3. Lucky Jim W Parcell, Manorbier
Best Harness Horse to be driven £3. Lady Athol. E Jones Landeilo
Best Jumper £7. Officer. J Rees, Nantgaredig
Best Jumper, Resident in Pembrokeshire £5. Hard to Find,
    Mr H Seymour Allen,Cresselly
*At this time J W Phillips was MP of Pembrokeshire

Well, I think that they may have recouped a pound or two there, and got to know the Member of Parliament at the same time. It was in fact a successful show, which was held for many years, having first been held in 1898.

1903

In 1903 the meeting at Tenby was again in January on the 22nd and 23rd. The entries were excellent and the weather fine with the going good.

First Day

2.15 PENALLY SELLING STEEPLE CHASE PLATE.
Two miles. 40 Sovereigns, weight for age, winner to be sold for 50 sovereigns.
My Byrone's, Ravanette, E Sullivan 1
Mr Dixon's, Bunthorne, Mr J T Rogers 2
Mr Bassett's, County Clare, Mr Deer 3

2.50 VISITORS SELLING HURDLE RACE.
40 Sovereigns. Weight for age.
Winner to be sold for 50 sovereigns. Two miles over eight hurdles.
Mr Lawrence's, Weidersehen, Davies 1
Mr Bassett's, Bird on the Wing, Mr Deer 2
Mr Harty's, Old Tim, Rattle 3
Mr Deer's, Lady Langford , Mr Wood 0

At this meeting, you can see that Mr Deer is riding for Mr Bassett and Col Lindsay, and is also the owner of the fourth place horse, in the 2-50 and the 3-25.

3.25 TOWN MAIDEN STEEPLE CHASE
of 40 Sovereigns. Two miles.
Capt Collis's, Carnroe, Owner 1
Mrs Elliott's, Bally Mountain, F Parker 2
Mr Parker's, Red Briar, A Parker 3
Mr Deer's, Reversed, Owner 0

4.0 CRESSELLY STEEPLE CHASE.
40 Sovereigns. Three miles.
Mr Partridge's, Ferry Lass, Mr Rogers 1
Mr Stuart's, Red Sea II, Horton 2
Col Lindsay's, Laarnce, Mr Deer 3
Mr Stuart's young chaser fell and broke his back at the water jump and was shot.

Second Day

1.30 STEWARD'S STEEPLE CHASE.
40 Sovereigns. 3 miles.
Capt Collis's, Talleyrand , walked over, Owner 1

2.0 KNIGHTSTON SELLING HURDLE.
40 Sovereigns. 2 miles.
Mr Harty's, Old Tim, Rattle, 1
Mr Hobbs's, Witch o' the hills, F Parker, 2
Mr Cave's, Worcester Sauce, R Morgan, 3
Winner trained by R W Smith, Tenby
'David Harrison's stable'

3.40 DEER PARK STEEPLE CHASE.
40 sovereigns. 12st each. 3 miles.
Col Lindsay's, Laarnce, Mr A Wood 1
Mr Hobbs's, Frieze, F Parker 3
Mr Deer's, Reversed, Owner 0

Smith and Page again successfully managed the meeting.
Judge – Major Glascott
Clerk of Scales - Col Denne
Clerk of Course – George Chiles
Starter – Thomas Gwyther
Auctioneer – Mr E Grabham
Hon Secs – C W R Stokes and B J Rees

Two races missing on second day. Lost?

1904

"COURT CASE"

On 21st January 1904 a claim for damages was made by the plaintiff Mr C W R Stokes against the defendant Mr T D S Cunninghame of the Abbey, Penally. The case was heard at the Pembrokeshire Assizes and lasted for four hours. Mr Stokes was out for a jaunt, in his horse and trap through the quiet lanes around Penally, when the defendant was driving a horseless carriage towards him, which caused him some concern as to the passability of this noisy thing in the narrow lane. The defendant's carriage forced Mr Stokes's trap off the road, tilting it and causing the horse to bolt. The horse fell and sustained such injuries that its value was so now depreciated from that of 'almost a thoroughbred', to an animal worth no more than £1 for dog meat. Mr Stokes was also thrown into a gateway and sustained cuts and bruises. The case was found proven, and Mr C W R Stokes was awarded £120 in damages, in favour of his son and partner Mr George Stokes, who was driving the trap.

Horseless carriages were obviously not very popular in Penally or the Pembrokeshire Assizes at this time. Although you could buy a horseless carriage for about £80 from George Ace in Tenby, at that time, I am sure that one could buy a fine, 'almost a thoroughbred', for 120 guineas. Perhaps we should see if Mr Stokes does buy a horse of some note, in the near future.

The meeting for 1904 took place at the end of January.

First Day

LICENSED VICTUALLER'S NOVICE HURDLE
40 Sovereigns. 2 Miles.
*Mr J Anthony's, Gleninch, Mr Ivor Anthony, 1
Mr F Bibby's, Comfit, Capt Rasbottom, 2
Mr J W Philipps's, Varsity Lass, A Cooke, 3
Won by 4 lengths at 2-1
*The father of the Anthony brothers, John (Jack) Anthony.

PENALLY SELLING STEEPLE CHASE.
40 Sovereigns. 2 Miles.
Mr Downing's, Elton II, E Sullivan, 1
Mr Deer's, Everleigh, Owner, 2
Mr Ryan's, Carrigeen, Mr N Cuthbertson, 3
Won by 6 lengths at 2-1

VISITORS SELLING HURDLE.
40 Sovereigns. 2 miles over 8 hurdles
Mr Deer's, Pepper, Owner, 1
Mr Roger's, Elfleet, Mr Ivor Anthony, 2
Miss Hunt's, Liberty Bell, Horan, 3

CRESSELLY STEEPLE CHASE.
40 Sovereigns. 3 Miles.
Mr T E Gilbert's, Lawrence, 1
Mr M Crowther's, Nahillah, 2
Lieut-Col Lindsay's, Laarnce, 3
20-1 won easily.
2nd Day not reported, not available, probably lost.

David Harrison had noticed a very promising young eighteen-year-old jockey at this meeting, riding a winner for his father in the first race, and later a very close second to his own horse Pepper in the third race. His name was Ivor Anthony. As David Harrison was now beginning to get more owners bringing horses to his stables, he needed a good young jockey, and both he and Brychan Rees agreed to employ him as the first jockey. Ivor Anthony accepted and moved to Tenby. He came from a big racing family in South Wales and all were good horsemen. David Harrison was not yet to know it, but he had just employed one of the finest jockeys over the sticks of the 20th Century.

At this stage, it would be a good idea for the reader to be introduced to the famous Anthony Brothers, as it can become somewhat confusing at a later stage. There were four brothers, the sons of John (Jack) Anthony, a Carmarthenshire farmer of Cilveithy, Kidwelly, near Carmarthen.

Firstly, not to be confused with a relation of the Anthony Brothers, Algernon (Algy) Anthony, was an Irish jockey and later a trainer from the Curragh. He rode and trained Ambush to win the Grand National in 1900 for the Prince of Wales. He also trained the brilliant Troytown to win the Grand Steeplechase de Paris in 1919 and the Grand National in 1920 and was also responsible for putting Master Robert in a plough, to try to cure his breathing problems.

The four brothers were all successful in the racing world. The eldest was Owen Anthony, then Ivor, then there was perhaps the least well-known, Major-General Anthony of the Royal Army Veterinary Corps (who owned the two mile chaser Clashing Arms), and the youngest was John Randolph (Jack) Anthony.

Owen rode 110 winners, and was second in the 1913 Grand National on Irish Mail. In 1921 he took out a trainer's license and in 1922 he trained Music Hall to win the Grand National. In 1929, he took the horses of the well known Newbury based professional gambler, Ben Warner, from David Harrison's Tenby Stable. He then took over the delicate charge of handling Miss Dorothy Paget and her horses, after the fiasco of the 1935 Grand National saw Golden Miller unseat his rider, Jerry Wilson, two fences after Valentine's Brook at the 11th fence on the first circuit, while trained by Basil Briscoe. He won her the 1936 Gold Cup with Golden Miller and in 1940 trained the Cheltenham double with Roman Hackle in the Gold Cup and Solford in the Champion Hurdle. He died suddenly in 1941, from pneumonia.

Brychan's Yard (left to right)
Brychan Rees, David Harrison and Ivor Anthony.

Second was Ivor, who joined David Harrison after the January meeting of 1904, becoming top amateur and also winning the National Hunt Chase on Timothy Titus only shortly after joining the stable. He was only eighteen. In 1908, he won the Scottish Grand National for the stable on Atrato, owned by Mr J W Philipps, Lydstep (remember him at the horse show). He won the Welsh Grand National in 1911 on Razorbill and became champion jockey in

1912, having already turned professional. He was badly injured in 1924 and had to retire from riding. He later took over from Aubrey Hastings at Wroughton as trainer.

John Randolph (Jack) Anthony, was the youngest, and won the Grand National on the one-eyed Glenside in 1911, when Tich Mason could not ride because of a recently broken leg. He rode his first winner at Tenby Races in 1906 at the age of sixteen. He was amateur champion jockey in 1914 with 60 winners. In 1915 he rode the Grand National winner Ally Sloper, and again won the Grand National in 1920 on Troytown. He turned professional in 1921. He was again champion jockey in 1922 with 78 winners. He retired in 1927 and took out a trainer's license, to train at Letcombe Regis on the Berkshire Downs.

David Harrison's string on South Sands, Tenby. circa. 1905

RW Smith in front, others are possibly Clem Hooper, Arty 'Royal' Smith,
Affy Smith, Norman Pilsen, William John, Charlie Goodridge,Oscar Thomas
and Vincent Francis.(Dick Francis's father)
"Look closely at the blankets on the horses".

In the autumn of 1904, Harrison was approached by a certain Mrs Mundy with a view to having some of her horses trained by him, firstly if successful, then more would follow. She was a sister to Lord Tredegar. She married Major Basil St John Mundy in 1894, but he was very badly wounded in the

Boer War, and died in 1926. Both Violet Mundy and her sister, Blanche, lost their only sons in World War I. Needless to say she was always dressed in black. She would always tell her jockeys to take care of themselves, as horses could always be replaced, jockeys could not. She farmed at Thornbury on the Severn and was held in great respect by jockeys and trainers alike. A great woman for country pursuits including ferreting and shooting, she was also a fine horsewoman and was soon to become known as "Hellcat Mundy". At her farm near Thornbury, she could be seen coming up the lane on an old donkey, with a sheaf of corn across her saddle, which she did on a regular basis, to feed her magnificent strain of white turkeys. One thing was sure, she would put up with no nonsense from David Harrison, although she admired him for his horsemanship and training ability.

1905

The meeting of 1905 was held on January 26th and 27th. The weather was very mild, as it had been all winter so far, and there was a larger than normal Irish following, mostly due to the stables of Mr Hobbs and Mr Sheehan, almost bringing with them a raiding party. However, proceedings were marred by two fatal accidents, both at the water jump.

First day

LICENSED VICTUALLERS NOVICE HURDLE.
2 Miles.
Mr Deer's, Lydstep Girl, 4 year old, 10st, Mr Ivor Anthony, 1
Mrs T Morgan's, Wet Sail, Aged, 1 2st 5lb, F Morgan, 2
Mr Deer's, Alcaeus, 5 year old, 11st 4lb, Owner, 3
Winner trained by R W Smith, Tenby.

VISITORS SELLING HANDICAP HURDLE
Mr W Bird's, Geneso, 5 year old, 11st 2lb, Mr Billyeald, 1
Mr J Anthony's, Plato, 4 year old, 10st 3lb, Owner

PENALLY SELLING STEEPLE CHASE.
2 Miles.
Mr J Widger's (IRE), Hubble, Bubble, Aged, 12st 3lb, Mr J Widger, 1
Mr Deer's, Reversed, Aged, 11st 3lb Mr Ivor Anthony

TOWN HANDICAP STEEPLE CHASE.
2 Miles.
Mr Deer's, Rarograph, 5 year old, 11st 12lb, Mr Ivor Anthony, 1
Mr F Bibby's, Marchalong, 6 year old, 10st 10lb, F Mason
Winner trained by R W Smith, Tenby

CRESSELLY STEEPLE CHASE
Mr F Bibby's, Shoot, 5 year old, 10st 7lb, F Mason, 1
Mr Deer's, Laarnce, Aged, 11st 7lb, Mr O Anthony, 2
Second Day

THE CORPORATION HANDICAP HURDLE.
2 Miles.
Mr Deer's, Booty, Owner, 1
Mr D Ebsworth's, Tiara, J Rees, 2
Mr J W Philipps's, Varsity Lass, Mr Ivor Anthony, 3
Winner trained by R W Smith, Tenby

LAWRENNY SELLING STEEPLE CHASE.
2 Miles.
Mr J Widger's (IRE), Hubble Bubble, Mr J Widger, 1
Mr Hobbs's (IRE), Kilgrogan, Mr Billyeald, 2
Mrs Mundy's, Caviare, Mr O Anthony, 3

THE TENBY HURDLE.
2 Miles.
Mr Lort Phillips's, Carolus Rex, F Mason, 1
Mrs T Morgan's, Wet Sail, F Morgan, 2
Capt Elwes's, Gangbridge, W Morgan, 3

CRESSELLY STEEPLE CHASE.
3 Miles.
Mr R Lawrence's, Off Hand, J Rees, 1
Mr J Harty's, David Grieve, S Moran, 2
Mr W Bird's (IRE), Consistent, Mr Billyeald, 3

THE DEER PARK STEEPLE CHASE.
3 Miles.
Mr Barclay Walker's, Skamo, F Mason, 1
Mr L V Colby's, All Hampton, G Clancey, 2
Capt H C Elwes's, Killerby, W Morgan, 3

Lydstep Girl ridden by Ivor Anthony was a very well backed and popular winner in the first race of the meeting. Mr Hobbs's Irish party were very upset when his well fancied horse, Bribery, fell and broke its back at the water jump and had to be shot. Mr Deer's Rarograph was well backed at locally 2-1, and ridden by Ivor Anthony in the Town Chase, he beat the well fancied Marchalong for which Mason had made a very long journey to ride him. However, Mason picked up some other fine winners, which made his trip worthwhile. Also, he was soon to ride Kirkland to victory in the Grand National. Mr T Sheehan had bad luck when his well fancied horse, Croom, fell and broke its back at the water the second time around in the Cresselly Steeple Chase and had to be shot, a great shame, as he had big hopes for him in the Grand National. Again on the second day the sun was shining in an almost cloudless sky with scarcely a breath of air stirring. In the Handicap Hurdle, which opened the day's proceedings, Booty was looked upon as a good thing for the Tenby Stable, and so it proved. Varsity Lass deposed Booty of the leading position in the market and early backers took advantage, for Booty, in the hands of her owner, scored cleverly from Tiara in a good finish. Hubble Bubble was again an odds on medium, though there was lots of money for Kilgrogan. The Tenby Hurdle looked a good thing for Wet Sail, though many backers followed Mason, who bestrode Carolus Rex for the Squire of Lawrenny, with great success.

'KIRKLAND'

Two days before the 1905 Grand National, Edward Thomas and Jack Smith walked Kirkland to Narberth Railway Station to catch the train to Liverpool. Kirkland won the Grand National by three lengths at 6-1, carrying 11st 5lb and ridden by champion jockey F. (Tich) Mason. A photograph of Kirkland, F Mason in the saddle is shown above. On returning from the 1905 Grand

National, Kirkland was stabled at the Commercial Hotel, Narberth overnight. Crowds of people were already celebrating their victory, having backed the local hero. Jack Smith's niece remembers Mr J F Lort Phillips was met at the Commercial Hotel by his wife, Maud and their chauffeur Mr C Absolam, whereupon Mr Lort Phillips gave Edward Thomas a white £5 note printed by the Bank of Pembrokeshire and told him and Jack Smith to bring Kirkland back the next day 'at their own leisure'. Needless to say a good night was had by one and all. The only person who was sober the next morning was the hotelier, Mr Fred Thomas, who, upon finding out when the horse was leaving, charged 6d for anyone to go into the back yard to see the horse. The two young lads from the Lawrenny stable had ridden to the Commercial on horseback, and on their return one of them was so drunk that he knew he would have the sack, turned his horse loose at the turn of Lawrenny Hill and disappeared up the valleys for a number of years, before returning to become landlord of the Railway Inn, Pembroke.

(left to right) Edward Thomas, trainer and Mr JF Lort Phillips

Jack Smith's niece recalls how Jack always spoke of how he went to Liverpool with Kirkland, and how he slept in the stable with him. He used to call him 'his horse'. "He loved that horse", she said. Jack Smith was the brother of Robert Weaver Smith, who held David Harrison's license at Tenby. He worked at Lawrenny Stables until he joined the Royal Artillery in 1914, where he looked after the horses that pulled the massive gun carriages. He returned safely after the war and can be seen in the Grandstand photograph of 1920. He was known as Jack Smith 'the Green' because he lived with his sister Serepta Smith, at 'The Green', Tenby.

The Commercial's name was changed in the late 1950's or early 1960's to 'The Kirkland Arms', by the licensee, Mrs Irene M Thomas, maybe after discovering the story which had lay dormant for so many years.

George Legge, groom, with Kirkland at the Lawrenny Stables.

Kirkland, a chestnut gelding, was foaled in 1896 in Ireland, bred by the Rev. E. Clifford. He was bought out of Ireland as a two year old by the Liverpool born manufacturer, Mr Frank Bibby, who put him with the Lawrenny Stable of Mr J F Lort Phillips, along with some of his other horses. Kirkland started his career in auspicious fashion and before his sixth birthday he had won ten chases, including the 1902 Grand Sefton Chase. All these victories seemed to have sapped his strength and he won nothing for the next two years. However, he was fourth in the 1903 Grand National, beaten a head for third place by the great Manifesto, and in 1904 he was second by eight lengths to Moiffa. Although he started favourite at numerous chases after his 1905 victory, he was not to win again. In the 1908 Grand National he fell, was remounted and finished seventh, having started favourite. His career was in decline. The staff at the Lawrenny Stables at the time consisted of Edward Thomas; stud groom Jack Smith; groom George Legge; and two lads, William Bowen aged 16, born Reynoldston, Pembs, and William Hooker aged 18 from Bath, Somerset. The blacksmith was William Thomas aged 44, born Rhoscrowther, his daughter Mary, 20, was the village schoolteacher. He also had two sons Arthur aged 12, and Percival aged 9. George Legge aged 23 was born at Nash, and Jack Smith aged 27, born The Green, Tenby.

By the end of the 1905 season, three owners who were great stalwarts of Tenby Races and National Hunt Racing in general had been elected to the National Hunt Committee. They were as follows:

Mr Frank Bibby	October 10th 1898
Lieut-Col J F Lort Phillips	December 12th 1898
Sir John Wynford Philipps (1st Viscount St David's)	December 11th 1905

1906

In 1906 the meeting at Tenby was on January 24th and 25th. The entries were very scarce for both days, although the weather and crowd attendance was good. During the previous months, Mr Ivor Anthony, David Harrison's new jockey, had bought a horse of his own, which was stabled with David Harrison.

Some of the races are missing, lost?

First Day

LICENSED VICTUALLERS NOVICE HURDLE.
40 Sovereigns. 2 Miles.
Mr R de Wend-Fenton's, Gold Band, E Davis   1
Mr Lort Phillips's, Huntley, T Moran 2
Mr J W Philipps's, Wolsingham, Mr Ivor Anthony 3
In the Penally Selling Steeple Chase Mrs Basil Mundy's Bow
Ridden by Ivor Anthony, walked over.

VISITORS SELLING HURDLE.
40 Sovereigns. 2 Miles.
Mr J W Philipps's, Lady Pottery, Mr J R Anthony 1
Mr G W Gittins's, Taboo, Mr O Anthony 2
Mr J Delaney's, Australian Homer, T Moran 3

CRESSELLY STEEPLE CHASE.
40 Sovereigns. 3 Miles.
Lord Grosvenor's, Noble Lad, J Conway 1
Mr T Longworth's, Royton, S Evans 2
Mr Barclay Walker's, Apollina, T Moran 3

LAWRENNY NOVICE STEEPLE CHASE.
40 Sovereigns. 2 Miles.
Mr F Bibby's, Aerostart, T Moran 1

Mr I Anthony's, Bacton Lad, Mr Ivor Anthony 2
Mr Deer's, Kelston, Mr O Anthony 3

No other reports available.

On April 18th 1906, David Harrison married Grace Morris, the daughter of a clergyman Henry Morris of the Norton, Tenby. Mr & Mrs Harrison moved into The Grove, in Heywood Lane, Tenby, to live. Grace was not a horse-woman, but she was soon to learn, and also to have a keen eye for the purchase of her own horses, to be trained by her husband.

1907

In 1907 the meeting was on January 24th and 25th. The weather was inclement and the hard frost of last week had gone, with the going as good as could be expected. During the first day, Mrs Wynford Philipps of Lydstep Haven, wife of Mr J W Philipps MP, horse breeder and owner, invited a large party that occupied a considerable portion of the Grandstand. Tea had been specially arranged for the occasion by Mrs Philipps herself*. What the occasion was, I have no idea. Mr John Anthony of Cilveithy, father of the yet to be famous Anthony Brothers, bought a fine horse, Mar Lodge II, by Deeside, for 500 guineas as a present for his youngest son, Mr J. R. Anthony. It in fact gave Mr J. R. Anthony a winning mount at Ludlow, and was sold to Mrs Mundy. She won some fine steeplehases with Mar Lodge II and had great hopes for him at Liverpool in the very near future.

On the first day, in the Cresselly Steeple Chase over three miles, there were only two runners: Mr F Bibby's Leamington ridden by F Mason, and Mrs Mundy's Mar Lodge II, ridden by Mr J. R. Anthony. The two horses kept company until the final water jump when Mar Lodge II fell and broke his back, having to be shot; Leamington also fell but was re-mounted and went on to win. Mrs Mundy was inconsolable, but the first thing she did was to go and see if Mr J. R. Anthony was all right. Such was Mrs Mundy's concern for her jockeys. *William John shown left.*

75

*She was to die as Lady St Davids on 30th March 1915, only to be followed by the death of her eldest son in June during the World War. Her other son was also soon to die in the War. Lord St Davids remarried within twelve months of her death. Viscount St Davids' second wife was Lady Elizabeth Rawden Hastings, Baroness Strange of Knockyn and Hungerford.

First Day

PENALLY SELLING STEEPLE CHASE.
40 Sovereigns. 2 Miles.
Mr T J Longworth's, Greenfinch, Mr Ivor Anthony 1
Mr F Beauchamp's, Celebration, J Hunt 2
Winner trained by R W Smith, Tenby.

LICENSED VICTUALLER'S NOVICE HURDLE.
40 Sovereigns. 2 Miles.
Mr L Beauchamp's, Little Prince, J Hunt 1
Mr F Bibby's, Pharmigan , F Mason 2
Mr J Roger's, White Belle, Watkins 3

LAWRENNY NOVICE STEEPLE CHASE.
40 Sovereigns. 2 Miles.
Mr F Bibby's, Castle Treasure, F Mason 1
Miss H G Studd's, Spinning Coin, Mr J Anthony 2
Mr E Morris's, Flattery, G Morris 3

Second Day

TENBY HURDLE RACE.
40 Sovereigns. 2 Miles
Mr N Cuthbertson's, Booty, Owner 1
Mr J W Philipps's, Woodstone, Mr J R Anthony 2
Also ran Merlin's Hill ridden by Mr J R Anthony 0.

CORPORATION HURDLE.
40 Sovereigns. 2 Miles.
Mr L B Beauchamp's, Little Prince , J Hunt 1
Mr J W Philipps's, Hyacinth, Mr J R Anthony 2
Mr R Whittindale's, Chranas, Mr Whittindale 3

TOWN SELLING HANDICAP STEEPLE CHASE.
40 Sovereigns. 2 Miles.
Mr R Lawrence's, Hungarian, Mr O Anthony 1
Mr Deer's, Lydstep Girl, Mr I Anthony 2
Mr L B Beauchamp's, Celebration, J Hunt 3

DEER PARK STEEPLE CHASE.
40 Sovereigns. 3 Miles.
Mr J W Philipps's, Dathi, Mr I Anthony 1

F (Tich) Mason was again champion jockey in 1907 but for the last time. He was champion jockey six times. 1901 – 58 winners; 1902 – 67 winners; 1904 – 59 winners; 1905 – 73 winners, 1906 – 58 winners; 1907 – 59 winners.

His big victories included:

1   The Grand Sefton Shaker – 1898, Kirkland 1902, Caubeen 1908
2   The Champion Chase – Killmallog 1902
3   The Lancashire Chase – Seisdon Prince 1905
4   The Grand National – Kirkland 1905
5   The Imperial Cup – Black Plum 1910
6   The Welsh Grand National – Caubeen 1910

F (Tich) Mason rode at Tenby during these championship years, and for many years afterwards well into the late 20's, which proves the importance of the Tenby Meeting in the Racing Calendar. Both Kirkland and Caubeen were owned by Mr Frank Bibby.

On 14th October 1907, Grace Harrison gave birth to a son, David. On 22nd August 1945 David married Miss Auriol Joan Bartlett Allen of Cresselly, Pembrokeshire, taking the name Harrison-Allen. They divorced in 1960.

1908

The meeting of 1908 was held on Wednesday January 23rd & Thursday 24th. The entries were excellent and the spring-like weather over the two days ensured a very good attendance.

First Day

2-0 LAWRENNY NOVICE STEEPLE CHASE
40 sovs Two miles
Old Silver, 11st 2lb, Vincent Francis*, 1
Capacity, 11st 7lb, F Mason, 2
General Killian, 11st 3lb, Mr J R Anthony, 3
Winner trained by Donnelly, Lawrenny

* Dick Francis's father, seen here beating the great F 'Tich' Mason into second place, whilst riding for John Donnelly the other Lawrenny trainer. For some reason the names of the owners were not reported for this meeting

2-40 VISITORS SELLING HANDICAP HURDLE
40 sovs Two miles
Little Tom, J Hunt, 1
Edie Violet, R Burford, 2
Funny Wag, Mr J R Anthony, 3
Winner trained by Hunt

3.20 LICENSED VICTUALLERS' NOVICE HURDLE
40 sovs Two miles
(Mr Wynford Philipps's)Atrato, 12st, Mr J R Anthony, 1
Creamgate, 11st 4lb, F Mason, 2
Bedgrove, 10st 10lb, J W Rees, 3

Winner trained by R W Smith, Tenby
4.0 CRESSELLY HUNTERS STEEPLE CHASE
40 sovs Three miles
Bucknell, 11st, A Clay, 1
Red Cardinal, 11st 2lb, Mr J R Anthony, 2
Bosphorous, 10st 12lb, Mr C H R Crawshay, 3
Winner trained by Cundall

Atrato, running here in a two mile Novice Hurdle, went on a few months later to win the Scottish Grand National over 4 miles 120 yards, ridden by Ivor Anthony and trained by David Harrison.

Second Day

1-15 TOWN SELLING HANDICAP STEEPLE CHASE
50 sovs Two miles
Roman Fruit, R Burford, 1
Eascene, Mr O Anthony, 2
Funny Wag, Ivor Anthony, 3
Winner trained by Dudley Hill, Ross

2-0 CORPORATION HURDLE RACE
40 sovs Two miles
Motapo, 11st 1lb, Ivor Anthony, 1
Shelsey, 11st 1lb, G Green, 2
Kirkland, 10st 11lb, F Mason, 3
Winner trained by R W Smith, Tenby
Also ran Lara (V Francis)

2-40 KNIGHTSTON SELLING HURDLE
40 sovs Two miles
Reptile, 11st 6lb, Ivor Anthony, 1
Jodella, 11st 10lb, J Hunt, 2
Edie Violet, 11st 5lb, Mr J Walker, 3
Winner trained by R W Smith, Tenby

3-20 TENBY STEEPLE CHASE
40 sovs Two miles
Loop Head, 11st 11lb, F Mason, 1
Dathi, 12st 7lb, Ivor Anthony, 2
Fidessa, 10st 7lb, Owner, 3
Winner trained by Donnelly, Lawrenny

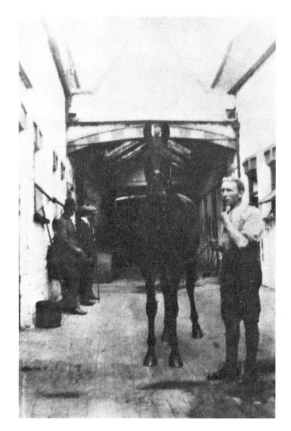

Arty "Royal" Smith

David Harrison's Stables

3-50 DEER PARK HUNTERS CHASE
40 sovs Three miles
Borodino, 11st 2lb, Mr C H R Crawshay, 1
Whitecliff, 12st 5lb, Ivor Anthony, 2
Winner trained privately

Kirkland running here as a 12 year old in a two mile hurdle; was to be favourite for the Grand National this year, finishing seventh after falling and being remounted by F (Tich) Mason.

1909

In 1909 the weather was as that of a summer's day, encouraging a large crowd and large entries for the race meeting held on 21st and 22nd of January.

LICENSED VICTUALLER'S NOVICE HURDLE.
40 Sovereigns. 2 Miles.
Mr F Bibby's, Sweet Cecil, F Mason, 1
Lord St David's, Marmaduke, Ivor Anthony, 2
Mr L B Beauchamp's, Easter Monday II , J Hunt, 3

PENALLY HOUSE SELLING STEEPLE CHASE.
40 Sovereigns. 2 Miles.
Mr T Sheehan's (IRE), Ireland's Eye II , Cuthbertson, 1
Mr S J Bell's, Genuine, Bell, 2
Mr Dudley Hill's, Roman Fruit, Hill, 3

VISITORS SELLING HURDLE RACE.
40 Sovereigns. 2 Miles.
Mr T W Hay's, Silver Fern, W Bulteel, 1
Mr H A Fenton's, Bel Or, R Gordon, 2
Mr R Carpenter's, Jilted, Owner, 3

LAWRENNY NOVICE STEEPLE CHASE.
40 Sovereigns. 2 Miles.
Mr F Bibby's, Petar, F Mason, 1
Lord St David's, Oarion , Mr J R Anthony, 2

CRESSELLY STEEPLE CHASE.
40 Sovereigns. 3 Miles.
Mr Harries's, * Glenside, Mr J R Anthony, 1
Capt Foster's, Springate, Owner, 2
Mr J Lewis's, Greenhorn, Owner, 3

Springate was the hot 3-1 on favourite, but was well beaten by the 7 year old Glenside, who had only one eye.

Glenside would be later to win the 1911 Grand National having been sold in the meantime to Mr F Bibby.

In the opening race Marmaduke was well backed, having won a week earlier at Carmarthen, in the Llanelly Maiden Hurdle £40 over 2 miles with Ivor Anthony aboard and trained by R W Smith, Tenby, although the finish was close, Sweet Cecil drew away in the finishing straight. Four races from the previous week's meeting at Carmarthen are of interest, and are shown here:

THE HARKFORD STEEPLE CHASE.
£40 over 2 miles.
Mr F Bibby's, Denmark, aged, 11st 13lb, Vincent Francis, 1
Mr S P Hogan's, What's Up, aged, 12st 13lb, A Hogan, 2
Lord St David's, Crautacaun, aged, Ivor Anthony, 3
Winner trained by John Donnelly, Lawrenny.

UNITED COUNTIES STEEPLE CHASE.
£40. 3 Miles.
Mr T Sheehan's (IRE), Glencorrig, P Sheehan, 1
Mr F Bibby's, Petar, Vincent Francis, 2
Mr S P Hogan's, Crown Receiver, A Hogan, 3
Winner trained by Owner in Ireland.

*[1] F Mason is riding for Mr Frank Bibby on the first day, winning two races.
*[2] Dick Francis's father, Vincent, is riding for Mr Frank Bibby on the second day, also winning two races, plus having a second place.

THE MAESYPRIOR STEEPLE CHASE.
£30. 3 Miles over banks.
Mr G Stokes's, Pembroke Lad, 11st 7lb, Owner, 1
Mr G Stokes's, Topthorne, 11st 12lb, Ivor Anthony, 2
Winner trained privately.

I cannot comment on the winner being trained privately – but Mr Stokes has certainly spent his money very wisely from the compensation court case at the earlier mentioned Pembrokeshire Assizes, by purchasing two 'almost thoroughbred' horses.

THE TALLY HO OPEN STEEPLE CHASE.
£30. 2 Miles over the flying course.
Mr F Bibby's, Petar, aged, 11st 9lb, Vincent Francis, 1
Mr Cooper's, Egerton's Price, aged 11st 2lb, Mr J R Anthony, 2
Winner trained by John Donnelly, Lawrenny.

Robert Weaver Smith

1910

Tenby races are not mentioned anywhere for this year, but there were reports of very heavy snowfalls for long periods; however, the Carmarthen meeting was put forward because of snow and was run at the end of January, so I have included this.

First Day

1-15 MAESYPRIOR MAIDEN STEEPLE CHASE
40 sovs Three miles

Mr D Harrison's, Sloe Gin, George Stokes, 1
Mr T Sheehan's (IRE) , Miss Slattery, P Sheehan, 2
Mrs R Harries's, Merry Widow, V, Mr Kelly, 3
Winner trained by R W Smith, Tenby

2-0 TALLY-HO SELLING STEEPLE CHASE
40 sovs Two miles

Mr Barclay-Walker's, Hackmount, Vincent Francis, 1
Mr J F Lloyd's, Rosethorpe, Mr O Anthony, 2
Mr Beauchamp's, Grey Diamond, D Naish, 3
Winner trained privately

2-40 DERRHYS SELLING HANDICAP HURDLE
40 sovs Two miles

Mr Hereford's, Usher, G Nash, 1
Mr D Harrison's, The Lieutenant, Mr J R Anthony, 2
Mr C F Bruce's, Happy Child, Owner, 3
Winner trained by Stanley, Punt

3-20 LLANELLY HUNTER'S HURDLE
40 sovs Two miles

Mr W H P Rees's, King's Colour, Mr O Anthony, 1
Mr Colwyn Philipps's, Starlight VII, Owner, 2
Mr J M Ridge's, Jack Spraggon, B Roberts, 3
Also ran Lucky Jim (V Francis)
Winner trained by Lucy, Cheltenham

3-55 HARKFORWARD STEEPLE CHASE
40 sovs Two miles

Lord St Davids', Oarlon, Mr J R Anthony, 1
Mr W E Sharp's, Dying Duck, Mr A M Brogden, 2
Winner trained by R W Smith, Tenby

Second Day
First Race

1.15 TOWY SELLING HURDLE
40 sovs Two miles

Mr D Harrison's, The Lieutenant, Mr J R Anthony, 1
Mr T Rudge's, Jack Spraggon, B Roberts, 2
Mr F Sikes's, Usher, P Sheehan, 3
Mr Sikes obviously purchasing Usher from the previous day's Selling Race
Winner trained by R W Smith, Tenby

2-0 TOWY MAIDEN STEEPLE CHASE
40 sovs Two miles
Mr W E Sharp's, Dying Duck, Mr A M Brogden, 1
Mr Beauchamp's, Grey Diamond, D Naish, 2
Winner trained by Brogden, Banbury

2-40 CARMARTHEN TOWN SELLING HANDICAP STEEPLE CHASE
40 sovs Two miles
Mr J F Lloyd's, Rosethorpe, Mr J R Anthony, 1
Mr C S Smith's, Cilwendeg, Mr A Smith, 2
Mr Dudley Hill's, Loughmoe, J E Walker, 3
Winner trained by Cuthbertson

3-20 BRONWYDD HURDLE RACE
40 sovs Two miles
Mr D Harrison's, Maudberg, Mr J R Anthony, 1
Mr F G Sikes's, St Remi, P Sheehan, 2
Mr H Feathersonhaugh's, Petit Tor, Mr A Smith, 3
Winner trained by R W Smith, Tenby

3-50 UNITED COUNTIES OPEN HANDICAP STEEPLE CHASE
40 sovs Three miles
Mr R Carpenter's, L'Abbe Royal, Mr A Smith, 1
Mr B O'Donnell's, Silent Bird, J Macormack, 2
Winner trained by Dudley Hill, Ross

January 1910

Mr Frank Bibby won the Welsh Grand National with Caubeen ridden by F (Tich) Mason, and trained by Edward Thomas, for the Lawrenny Stable. The Welsh Grand National was then run at Cardiff.

It seems that Mr Deer's aunt in Ashton-under-Lyne has passed away, and so it seems has Mr Deer. So I suppose Mr David Harrison will have to purchase Mr Deer's horses, at a bargain price, I have no doubt.

This is a short report of the 1910 Hunt Point to Point, held in early January:

3 MILE HUNT CUP
Mr D Harrison's, Sloe Gin 13st 3lb, G Stokes, 1
Mr Hugh Allen's, Parchunk 13st, Mr H Allen, 2

Winner to receive the cup presented by Mr Seymour Allen, M.F.H.
Second horse to save his stakes.
Mr Seymour Allen's, Daisy, 13st 7lb, Owner, 1
Mr Seymour Allen's, Careful, 12st 7lb, G Stokes, 2
Mr Seymour Allen's, Dorothy, 12st 7lb, Hugh Allen, 3

Mr David Harrison at The Grove, Heywood Lane, with Grace and young David.

1911

The Tenby meeting of 1911 was held on January 12th and 13th. There was persistent rain on the opening day, although the attendance was good. There were two successes by Capt Hughes Morgan, the popular Mayor of Tenby. Both horses were well backed by locals especially Capt Hughes Morgan himself, whose equine ventures have hitherto been on the flat, as past owner of Willonyx and other good horses, he has certainly made a distinctly promising start, on his debut at cross-country. Sweet Peach, which he acquired at Caerleon for 110 guineas, satisfied his owner. His second victory was with Rex, which previously ran in the Lawrenny interested party, without gaining winning brackets. He purchased him at Cheltenham, entirely with a view of running at this meeting, and always lying handy, the well bred son of Lavero, came out at the distance, full of running, and won by six lengths amongst a great uproar of applause.

These are the only existing results.

LICENSED VICTUALLER'S NOVICE HURDLE.
40 Sovereigns. 2 Miles.
Mr S J Bell's, Shadow Glance, Mr J Anthony, 1
Lord St David's, Valencian , Ivor Anthony, 2

TOWN SELLING STEEPLE CHASE.
40 Sovereigns. 2 Miles
Capt D H Morgan's, Sweet Peach, Ivor Anthony, 1
Mr T Lewis's, Greenhorn, Mr J Anthony, 2
Winner trained by R W Smith, Tenby.

VISITORS SELLING HANDICAP HURDLE.
40 Sovereigns. 2 Miles.
Mr C S Smith's, Night Wing, Mr Arthur Smith 1
Mr D Harrison's, Maudburg, Ivor Anthony 2

LAWRENNY NOVICE STEEPLE CHASE.
40 Sovereigns. 2 Miles.
Capt D H Morgan's, Rex, Ivor Anthony, 1
Mr D C Pratt's, Carmatton, E Pratt, 2
Winner trained by R W Smith, Tenby.

THE GROVE STEEPLE CHASE.
40 Sovereigns. 3 Miles.
Mr C Philipps's, Bushey Park, Owner, 1
Others fell.

The amount of horses now in the Tenby area proved that there was business enough for another Blacksmith and Mr J Richards opened a new smithy in the town, in South Parade. On 26th January, the Tenby Race Committee, had a fright when they received a letter from the Ministry of Defence. The letter stated that Tenby Racecourse is favourably regarded for the Welsh Territorial Divisional Army Camp, with it being 300 feet above sea level, making it of extra importance. However, before a definite decision was to be made, other preliminary facts would have to be taken into account. I know no more than this, except that it obviously did not happen, especially when there was an established camp at Penally that had been there for many years.

On 2nd February 1911, Mr Brychan Rees, whilst out hunting with Seymour Allen's Hunt, was taking a bank near Hayes when the mare he was riding suddenly turned a somersault and fell, luckily throwing Mr Rees clear of her, however she did not rise again and was instantly shot. The mare belonging to Mr Villiers was of a great value and a sad loss to him.

In the same year, Ivor Anthony rode Razorbill to win the Welsh Grand National, by a short head, with his brother Jack 15 lengths away in third.

In the 1911 Grand National, Ivor Anthony's brother, John Randolph Anthony rode the winner, Glenside, who only had one eye. Glenside had recently been purchased by Mr Frank Bibby, and was now trained by Captain Collis at Kinlet, Worcestershire. It is interesting to note that Captain Collis rode Comfit for Mr Frank Bibby to win the 1903 National Hunt Chase. Mr J. R. Anthony also won the 1915 Grand National on Ally Sloper and again in 1920 on Troytown, winning all three as an amateur. It is a trophy that any professional would be more than proud of, especially riding all three within a space of ten years. However this feat had been achieved previously by Mr Tom Pickernell and Mr Tom Beasley.

Firstly Tom Pickernell (coached by the great Tom Olliver) won on Anatis in 1860, The Lamb in 1861 and Pathfinder in 1875; he was very unlucky not to complete the treble in 1862 on Cyrus, when he was beaten by a head. Secondly Tom Beasley won on Empress in 1880, Windbrook in 1881 and Frigate in 1889, winning three Grand Nationals in nine years. Tom Beasley was also a high-class flat jockey and rode two Irish Derby winners Tragedy in 1889 and Narraghmore in 1891, thus giving him the unique distinction of winning the Grand National and the Irish Derby in the same year, 1889. Beat that if you can.

A popular race meeting at the time was the "South Wales Derby Day" run at Cowbridge and there was always a large attendance, being run in April, with the weather usually fine. Also His Lordship of Tredegar was more than often present and a big attraction. It gained the name "Derby Day", because of the representation of all those who loved their horses and their racing, from the most expensive Rolls Royce to the Pony and Trap and the humble Coster's Shay, and Romany Caravan, in all its gilded glory, with 'Gypsy Rose Lee' telling your fortune through a crystal ball.

In the first race "The Cardiff Hurdle" of 50 sovereigns, over two miles, Ivor Anthony was riding Sky Pilot for David Harrison, losing by a neck to Colonel Lindsay's Apex, both 5-4 joint favourites. However, in the 3-15 Selling Hurdle of 50 sovereigns over two miles, Ivor Anthony got David Harrison's Queen's Courtier up to win by a head, carrying 12st 9lb, trained by R W Smith, Tenby, at 6-4. On the same day at Carmarthen Point-to-Point, Brychan Rees and George Stokes took two of David Harrison's horses for the three miles Open Race, for Carmarthenshire, Cardiganshire and Pembrokeshire Hunts, Brychan Rees coming in second on Tadpole at 2-1, having been beaten by Jack Anthony on Happy Go Lucky, with George Stokes having a nasty fall on Longridge.

Mr George Lort Stokes riding Pembroke Lad.

1912

In 1912, The Tenby Meeting was held on 11th & 12th January.

First Day

LAWRENNY NOVICE STEEPLE CHASE.
40 Sovereigns. 2 Miles.
Mr D Harrison's, Strangeways, Mr J Anthony, 1
Mr C S Smith, Fleacatcher, W Smith, 2
Winner trained by R W Smith, Tenby.

VISITORS SELLING HANDICAP HURDLE.
40 Sovereigns. 2 Miles.
Mr S E Armitage's, Veno, W J Smith, 1
Mr L Beauchamp's, Can't Sing, J Hunt, 2
Mrs D Harrison's, Davy JonesMr J Anthony, 3

TOWN SELLING STEEPLE CHASE.
40 sovereigns. 2 Miles.
Mr W Murphy's , Saxondon, Mr T Murphy, 1
Mr D H Thomas's, Heather Lad, Ivor Anthony, 2
Mr T Lewis's, Greenhorn, Mr J Anthony, 3

LICENSED VICTUALLER'S NOVICE HURDLE.
40 Sovereigns. 2 Miles.
Mr L Beauchamp's, Barbed Head, R Gordon, 1
Mr T Sheehan's (IRE), Sweet Harkness, P Sheehan, 2
Mr J F Lort Phillips's, Succubus, Vincent Francis, 3

THE GROVE STEEPLE CHASE.
40 Sovereigns. 3 Miles.
Mr Colwyn Philipps's, Tempo Belle, Owner, 1
Mr D Harrison's, Howth Park, Mr J Anthony, 2

Second Day

PENALLY MAIDEN STEEPLE CHASE.
40 Sovereigns. 2 Miles
Mr D Harrison's, Strangways, Ivor Anthony, 1
Mr L Beauchamp's, Arable, R Gordon, 2
Winner trained by R W Smith, Tenby

KNIGHTON SELLING HURDLE.
40 Sovereigns. 2 Miles
Capt H Morgan's, Rex, Ivor Anthony, 1
Mr P Sheehan's, Flourens, P Sheehan, 2
Mrs D Harrison's, Davy Jones, Mr A Smith, 3
Winner trained by R W Smith, Tenby.

TENBY SELLING HANDICAP STEEPLE CHASE.

40 Sovereigns. 2 Miles.
D H Thomas's,   Heather Lad, Ivor Anthony, 1
Won by distance.

DEER PARK OPEN HANDICAP STEEPLE CHASE.
40 Sovereigns. 3 Miles.
Mr Colwyn Philipps's, Tempo Belle, Owner, 1
Mr J F Lort Phillips's, Scarborough, Vincent Francis, 2

There was fine weather and large crowds on both days, with Ivor Anthony having a very popular win on his second winner Rex, who bore the Orange and Oxford blue of Capt D Hughes Morgan, the Mayor of Tenby. Rex, being the son of Lavens-Reigning Queen, has added quite a number of wins for this popular local sportsman. Rex won by 15 lengths, and was about to leave the Tenby Stable, being purchased by Mrs Sheehan from Ireland. In the Tenby Selling Handicap Steeple Chase, Heather Lad, who made all the running won by a margin of 40 lengths. Mrs D Harrison also should be congratulated for running her Davy Jones into a place on both days, having chosen two horses earlier in the winter that she purchased with her husband's help and guidance.

The races were marred, however, by an unpleasant and unfortunate incident involving the loss of £195, of which Mr Tom Sherwell, a well-known Swansea Turf Commission Agent, was most mysteriously relieved on the first night of the meeting. Mr Sherwell, previous to coming down to Tenby, went to a Swansea Bank and drew out £195 in Bank of England notes, the numbers of which are known. On Wednesday night he was in the company of other bookmakers in one of the local hotel bars, and it was upon leaving that he discovered his loss. The matter is in the hands of the local constabulary, and as the numbers are known, it is hoped that the money may be recovered. All are in £5 notes.

On 18th January 1912, an application was made to the Planning Authority by Mr David Harrison of The Grove, Heywood Lane, for a purification scheme on land adjoining The Grove. In connection with the plans for The Grove residence of Mr Harrison, two letters were read out at the Corporation Sanitary Meeting; one from Mr Harrison making an application for a portion of the field tenanted by Mr J Mabe, of Tenby, for a purification tank. It was stated that Mr Mabe held the field from the Corporation as a yearly tenant at £8 per year. After further discussion, the plans were passed and it was agreed that Harrison be granted permission to use an eleventh part of an acre of the field, occupied by Mabe at a rent of thirty shillings a year, and that he be given a lease on the same terms as that on which The Grove was rented to him by the Corporation. I had quite a shock when I read this only recently (May '02), as up until now, I was led to believe that he owned The Grove.

Later in the year, the Lord Chancellor, Lloyd George, visited Penally Camp to present medals to the troops. After inspecting the Yeomanry at Penally Barracks, he spent the weekend with Lord* and Lady St Davids at Lystep Mansion. Some suffragettes, who were aware of his visit, took advantage of the opportunity to cause a disturbance and called Lord St Davids' "you traitor". So PC Nash, the Penally village policeman was sent for and ordered to spend the night patrolling the property.

* Lord Kylsant's brother.

David Harrison's Yard.

(left to right) Ivor Anthony, Brychan Rees (the lads) and R W Smith.
Lads include: Arty 'Royal', Clem Hooper, Oscar Thomas, Drifter Harris, Norman Pilsen,
Charlie Goodridge, Affy Smith and William John.

1913

In 1913, at the Seymour Allen Hunt Point-to-Point, David Harrison won the Seymour Allen Hunt Cup over 3 miles, with Longridge carrying 13st 7lb ridden by Mr G Stokes, and backed in to 2-1 on. Second was Mr Mathias's Lukie ridden by the owner, the Hon Colwyn Philipps rode his own Lop Ears into third place. In the farmer's and tradesmen's race, with a first prize of £8, Brychan Rees won easily, riding Greenhorn for Mr T Lewis, at 2-1 on.

January 16th and 17th saw the Tenby Races of 1913 very well attended, despite the rain and bleak weather. £450 was offered as the prize money for both days, and entries for the races were good, apart from two races where there were walkovers.

LICENSED VICTUALLERS NOVICE HURDLE.
40 Sovereigns. 2 Miles.
Mr D Harrison's, Fleacatcher, Ivor Anthony*, 1
Mr Tyrwhitt Drake's, Snap, Mr O Anthony, 2
Mr D Harrison's, Watchman, Mr Drake, 3
Winner trained by R W Smith, Tenby.
5-2 on.
*Ivor Anthony headed the jockey championship table in 1912, and had turned professional

VISITORS SELLING HANDICAP HURDLE.
40 Sovereigns. 2 Miles.
Mr L Beauchamp's, Deche, J Hart, 1
Mr D Harrison's, Chickabiddy, Mr F B Rees, 2
Mrs Sheehan's (IRE), NCR, P Sheehan, 3
Winner trained by Hunt.
Notice the jockey in second place is the elder of the Rees brothers, Frederick Brychan Rees, one week before his eighteenth birthday.

THE LORD-LIEUT PLATE.
40 Sovereigns. 2 Miles.
Mr D Harrison's, Strangways w o, Ivor Anthony, 1
Winner trained by R W Smith, Tenby.

TOWN STEEPLE CHASE
Mr Rhys Williams's, Veglor w o, Ivor Anthony, 1

GROVE STEEPLE CHASE.
40 Sovereigns. 3 Miles.
Mrs Harrison's, Tempo Bello, Ivor Anthony, 1
Mr J M Brace's, Ballymadon, W Smith, 2
Winner trained by R W Smith, Tenby.
Grace Harrison has her first winner, Tempo Bello, ridden by the champion jockey Ivor Anthony.

On the second day, the weather had improved but the attendance was slightly down due to the scarcity of runners in some of yesterday's races. Backers, as a whole had the worst of the argument, as three out of the five favourites were beaten. There was a run of money on St Ethel, just before the off, but Mr Brace's horse was never really in the race. Veglo and Battleground were each in turn favourite for the Tenby Steeple Chase, and after jumping the water jump Battleground drew away for a convincing victory. In the

Coronation Hurdle there was a lot of money and a great deal of excitement as Mr J F Lort Phillips "declared to win" on his horse Succubus, well ridden by Vincent Francis, he saw that the local backers again followed him for a fine victory, to win from David Harrison's Flicker. A lot of stable money went on David Harrison's Howth Park in the last race, but he was well beaten by Yonder.

David Harrisons Stable.

(left to right) Norman Pilsen, Clem Hooper, Oscar Thomas and Arty 'Royal' Smith

LAWRENNY MAIDEN STEEPLE CHASE.
£40. 2 Miles.
Mr D Harrison's, Royal Demand, Ivor Anthony, 1
Mr D Harrison's, The Fly III, Mr Drake, 2
Won by 3 lengths 5-2 on. Winner trained by R W Smith, Tenby.

TENBY SELLING HANDICAP STEEPLE CHASE.
£40. 2 Miles.
Mr J Brace's, Battleground, W J Smith, 1
Mr Rhys Williams's, Veglor, Mr F B Rees, 2
Winner trained by Bulteel, Portslade.

CORONATION HURDLE.
£40. 2 Miles.
Mr J F Lort Phillips's, Succubus, Vincent Francis, 1
Mr D Harrison's, Flicker, Ivor Anthony, 2
Mr Lort Phillips's, Carew, A Griffiths, 3
Won by 3 lengths at 3-1. Winner trained Privately, Lawrenny.
Mr J F Lort Phillips declares to win.
It takes some doing to declare to win and finish with an SP of 3-1. Mr Lort Phillips certainly knows when to have a good bet, and look who the jockey is. One can now see where Dick Francis got his riding skills.

KNIGHTSTON SELLING HURDLE.
£40. 2 Miles.
Mr Beauchamp's, Prince of Tyre, J Hunt, 1
Trained by F Hunt, Winchester.
This was Prince of Tyre's third successive win, in a short time, and J Hunt had a big struggle to get him home in front.

In the last race, David Harrison's Howth Park was well beaten by Yonder. I have found no other details on the last race. The main problem when doing research of this nature is that years ago people actually tore part or whole pages out of the newspaper, maybe for something which was printed on the other side of the sheet, little realising that in a hundred year's time someone might want to know the winner of the race, or what happened. It is very disheartening sometimes, especially when a whole year has gone missing, and it is exactly that year that one is looking for. This is probably one of the reasons why it has taken me so long to complete this book as I just shelved the whole project until I could find another avenue of researching the parts that are missing.

1914
In 1914, Tenby Races were held on 15th and 16th January. There had been a very hard and keen frost for some days before the meeting, but the days were bright enough, it was the going that was the worry. Many owners were telegraphed with the information and withdrew their horses, not willing to risk them, which is understandable. Straw had been laid down over many parts of the course, and on the morning of the meeting it was set alight. It burnt for hours, and although it did help a lot, it was decided that the first three races should be restricted to matches.

CORONATION HURDLE.
40 Sovereigns. 2 Miles.
Mr L Beauchamp's, Loch Maree, F Hunt, 1

TOWN SELLING STEEPLE CHASE.
40 Sovereigns. 2 Miles.
Mr D Harrison's, Royal Birthday, Mr P Roberts, 1
Trained by R W Smith, Tenby.

GROVE STEEPLE CHASE.
40 Sovereigns. 3 Miles.
Mr D Harrison's, Fly III, Mr J Anthony, 1
Trained by R W Smith, Tenby.

LICENSED VICTUALLERS SELLING HANDICAP HURDLE.
40 Sovereigns. 2 Miles.
Mr H T Young's Little Wave, F Dainty, 1
Mr D Harrison's, Watchman, Mr J Anthony, 2

The rest of the meeting was abandoned due to frost. Because of the war, there was no racing at Tenby until 1920.

Left, Arty 'Royal' Smith and Right, Brychan Rees.

At the last meeting of the Welsh Grand National before the war in 1914, only four horses out of the eleven entries came to the start, with the outsider being Mr J F Lort Phillip's Succubus. It was a hard fought race, with Mr F Parker's Dick Dunn the favourite, landing ahead of Succubus at the last, but was pressed so hard by Succubus on the run in that a dead-heat was given.

"Mr Lort Phillips was wishful to divide", reported the Western Mail, but Mr Parker, who had bet odds on his horse, could not be brought to this way of thinking, and insisted on a run-off, after the last race of the meeting and Mr Lort Phillips agreed. Again, odds were bet on Dick Dunn, but after the two horses had practically walked for the first furlong, Succubus, at the turn past the stands, made a sudden burst for home, and quickly opened up a fifteen lengths lead, and making the whole of the running, won a hugely popular victory for Pembrokeshire, and the Lawrenny Stable. Succubus was ridden by C Kelly.

* * * * * * * * * * *

David Harrison's string, in front of the Grandstand at Tenby Race Course

Penally House had been for sale since the death of Mr C J Williams in 1912, and was this year purchased by Sir David Hughes-Morgan and his wife, Lady Blanche. Sir David was Chairman of the Western Mail and Echo, and had already had considerable success with his horses, trained by David Harrison at Tenby. This also seemed to be the year when Augustus John was reported in many of the national newspapers as a "great artist in his own lifetime".

1915
David Harrison took some horses to the Cardiff meeting on Easter Saturday, 6th April 1915, one of which was Mrs Mundy's First Smoke, a recent

winner at Manchester *, where Harrison won many times and was well fancied and well backed. There is also another jockey's name to note in the frame of the first race, F B's younger brother L B Rees.
* ref. 1927

The attendance was probably the largest that has ever been seen at Ely, for there was a huge crowd outside where wagering was allowed. The small ring was absolutely packed, whilst Tattersalls and the members enclosures were both comfortably full. Backers made no mistake by following the West Wales jockey, John Randolph Anthony, after his second Grand National win recently on Ally Sloper.

EASTER SELLING STEEPLE CHASE.
50 Sovereigns. 2 Miles 1f.
Mr C Wilson's, Victor Felicitas, F G Lynch, 1
Mr L B Beauchamp's, Meadow Lark, J Hunt, 2
Mr D H Thomas's, Heather Maid, Lewis Bilbee Rees, 3
Winner trained by Kemp 7-4 on Won by 30 lengths.
Lewis Bilbee Rees, younger brother of Fred B. Rees is only 17 years old here.

WINDSOR SELLING HURDLE.
40 Sovereigns. 2 Miles.
Mr H Law's, Usilyas, Mr J R Anthony, 1
Mr L B Beauchamp's, B and S, J Hunt, 2
Mr Franklin's, Galtham, Owner, 3
Winner trained by Gillett 5-4 on Won by 5 lengths.

THE STEWARDS HANDICAP STEEPLE CHASE.
60 Sovereigns. 3 Miles 1f.
Mr W Rees's, King's Colour, Newley, 1
Mr H Wernher's, Bruce, E Smith, 2
Mr E Robinson's, Meiktila, T Willmott, 3
Winner trained by Newey 3-1 Won by 4 lengths.

CARDIFF MAIDEN HURDLE.
200 Sovereigns. 2 Miles.
Lord Londonderry's, Tremolite, Mr J R Anthony, 1
Sir Robert Willmott's, The Bore Gelding, E Metcalf, 2
Winner trained by Whittaker 9-4 on Won by 20 lengths.

LLANRUMNEY HANDICAP STEEPLE CHASE.
70 Sovereigns. 3 Miles. 1f.
Mr H Wernher's, Piper's Hill, P Smith, 1
Mr P Whittaker's, Lord Rivers, Mr J R Anthony, 2
Winner trained by Hallick 6-4 Won by 5 lengths.

David Harrison had no luck at all, and the fancied First Smoke, owned by

Mrs Mundy, was well beaten out of the frame. In 1915, the Grand National was run at Aintree for the last time, until its reappearance in 1919. In the meantime it was run at Gatwick.

The meeting of March 1915 had a garrison town-naval base station look and feel about it, for obvious reasons, but none had dreamt that they would be at Aintree on Grand National Day, most being from the Dominions of many thousands of miles away. Jockeys took off their service jackets to don their silks. Munition workers, off for the day, were thought to be in a position to do themselves well, and the name "Silver Ring" was an anomaly, with so much betting in the new ten-bob notes, and with silver being scarce anyway. The "Jimmyogoblin" sovereign was brought forth only if there were no more treasury notes to bet with. Railway companies and race card sellers were alike stigmatised with the new word "profiteers". Irish Mail was top of the handicap and ridden by Mr Leslie Brabazon and was also favourite, in a field of twenty. Ally Sloper, who had already won over the course, was 100-9. But he was a grand young horse and "some jumper". With the lost 5lbs of Mr John Randolph Anthony, he won in a good finish to beat Jacobus, who was bred for speed (from Wavelet's Pride and Kendaline). Ally Sloper was Hon. Aubrey Hasting's second Grand National winner, his first being Ascetic's Silver in 1906, which he rode to victory himself.

It was significant of the part that women were now playing in public and industrial life, that a woman-owner captured the Grand National prize for the first time. Miss Norris had run the Wild Man from Borneo in the 1897 Grand National, but when he won it in 1895 he was owned by Mr J Gatland and ridden by Mr J Widger (whose name was regularly seen on the Tenby Race Cards). Mrs Widger ran Sunny Shower in 1901 and Lady Torrington ran Circassian's Pride in 1911, but that was the entire female contribution to Grand National ownership, until Lady Nelson won with Ally Sloper in 1915. Women now had the vote, and Miss Emily Davidson threw her life away by running in front of the King's horse Anmer in the Suffragette Derby of 1913. Women now played an active part, not only in general work, but in their own forces, and as nurses during the war; their increasing visibility upon the racing scene in general was significant enough to show that this would be repeated on a larger and wider scale, sooner rather than later.

Shown opposite: Top - Glenside, Below - Ally Sloper.

Glenside
Winner of the Grand National, 1911

The Grand National "The Canal Turn"

CHAPTER FOUR
AN ECCENTRIC MOVES TO TENBY

In 1889, "Trayles", a four year old chestnut colt by Restless out of Miss Mabel, won four of his five races, ridden by (Jack) W Robinson. Robinson rode many classic winners and was very often in the same frame as the great Fred Archer and George Fordham. (Fred Archer unfortunately shot himself through the brain on 8th November 1885, aged twenty-nine suffering from severe depression.) Trayles won the Ascot Gold Cup, Alexandra Gold Plate and the Goodwood Cup – a feat never before accomplished. His other victory was the Newmarket Challenge Whip.

The proud owner of Trayles was Mr Warren de la Rue, of Regents Park,

Trayles, ridden by (Jack) W Robinson.

London. He was the grandson of Thomas de la Rue, the founder of the de la Rue printing company. He had taken over the family firm at the age of twenty-two, and had more than quadrupled its size, before retiring twenty years later to lead a social life in London. He kept a string of racehorses on his 10,000 acre stud farm in Chippenham, a stables in Newmarket, and a house at 43

York Gate. His brother invented the papier mache splint, which was used with great success in the 1914-18 war. His brother also designed the décor for the Albert Hall, London.

From 1880, de la Rue's supplied all the surface-printed Great Britain stamps, all of India's postal needs, all the colonial stamps, and had a consolidated contract with the Board of Inland Revenue to the effect of giving them a monopoly. For the Golden Jubilee of Queen Victoria, de la Rue's went to endless trouble to produce the first bi-coloured stamps to mark the occasion, the "Jubilee" issue of 1887-1900. In 1890, the Post Office asked de la Rue's to produce an envelope to mark 50 years of uniform penny postage. Ten thousand of these are said to have been sold within three hours of being put on sale outside the Guildhall in London. By 1882, Warren William de la Rue had divorced his wife and reverted to a splendid bachelor existence.

At his town house at York Gate, Regents Park, he had a special lift installed for sending his false teeth down to be cleaned by his valet. A total eccentric, he had bought two houses in Tenby in 1913, and having previously fallen from his horse in Hyde Park, his eccentricity became almost alarming and he was persuaded to move to Tenby to live (along with the rest of the eccentrics that were already living there). The property that he bought was on the Esplanade, but not liking either the style or quality of the two fifteen bedroomed gentlemen's residences, he knocked them down to build a house to his own specifications, naming the house 'Trayles' after his famous horse.

On February 13th 1913, the Tenby Observor noted:

"Free and Fair Local News".

"The best news I have to publish this week is that plans for the alteration of No's 5 & 6 the Esplanade into one residence for Mr Warren de la Rue, are in the hands of the Borough Surveyor for the approval by the Town to whom they will be presented next Monday. There will be considerable expenditure upon these houses and also the erection of two dwellings with a garage, small stable and an electric power house on the plot of ground in Picton Road. Altogether Mr de la Rue's purchase of the property in Tenby will result in the expenditure of several thousand pounds in the building alterations and appointments. I understand that building operations will be placed in the hands of an eminent firm of London contractors, but of course a large amount of local labour will be required."

By February 20th plans were presented to the council and passed without discussion.

De la Rue meanwhile changed his mind about the whole project. A delightful editorial by Frank Mason, the then editor of the Tenby Observor, as well as

Sculptured head of Trayles. Warren de la Rue.

the Estate Agent who had put together de la rue's purchase reads:

I am truly sorry to have to announce that the purchaser of No's 5 & 6 the Esplanade and the garden plot in Picton Road has decided not to convert them into a fine Georgian residence for his own use, the news came as a thunderbolt on Friday last. Mr de la Rue's change of mind has arisen through no fault of Tenby or anyone in it, in fact he is still charmed by Tenby and hopes to visit it every year.

De la Rue had found the gardens on the cliff were not part of the deeds and not the property of the vendor Ellen Thomas then 74 years of age. The problem was overcome though by Mrs Thomas, the widow of Thomas Hugh Thomas, a Tenby businessman, swearing a declaration of "squatters rights" and the gardens were incorporated on the deeds of the property. On 10th April work on the demolition of the existing building to make way for a "residence of the 'bungalow' type" was reported as well advanced. Regular progress reports appeared in the paper and various properties were rented and purchased for the season for the de la Rue household. He himself inspected the work on 16th June. A local painter John Lloyd was killed during the construction when he was blown off an unsecured ladder in a September gale.

By 9th October, de la Rue was in residence in the Coburg Hotel making daily visits to urge the workers to complete the work faster. On 23rd October Mason reported:

"A large number of men are working overtime in order to complete the new residence, a fine installation of electric light enables the work to be pushed on without interruption." This was from a coke fired generator, the first to be built into a new building in Tenby, some three years before the town supply. The New Year's Day edition 1914 reviewed the progress of the project:

1st January 1914

"There are not many changes to record in the appearance of Tenby during the last twelve months. No doubt the greatest has been the conversion of No's 5 & 6 The Esplanade into the magnificent house known as Trayles and which is shortly to be occupied by Mr Warren de la Rue who has spared neither time or money in making his new residence cosy and comfortable with every convenience and luxury. In a week or two we hope to see him take possession and for many many years to be a highly popular and valued resident."

The house Mr de la Rue built was a fine Edwardian residence, and included all the old comforts and standards of living such as open fires in every room and wooden shutters. It also incorporated the more modern facilities. The central heating system in the lounge and front bedrooms is original and the house was the first to be built in Tenby that had electricity installed provided by a steam generator. Of particular note are the Spanish mahogany doors and fireplaces in the lounges.

Warren de la Rue was a fitness fanatic and doctors told him to walk a certain distance every day and if fine, he would venture out on to the Esplanade with a pedometer on his leg. He would be wearing several topcoats in the Victorian manner and would station servants at each corner to recover his coats as he cast them off. On longer walks he would have his butler follow him in a pony and trap to accept his cast off garments and to take him home should he become fatigued.

De la Rue was noted in the area for his gadgetry – his bathroom would have done credit to a modern sports centre, with wave-making machines, jets and weight lifting equipment, housed in what now is The Atlantic Hotel, The Esplanade, Tenby. The weather and geographical details fascinated him and he would spend hours in his study working out such interesting details as the visible horizon from the beach (only two and a half miles away whereas from the portico it is eleven and a half miles away). He worked on rainfall and calculated how it is that Tenby can hold records for both sunshine and rainfall in the same year – apparently he discovered that rain fell most at night. As he lay in his bed, he could look through a system of mirrors similar to a periscope and see the direction of the wind from the weather vane on the church.

In various rooms and in the garden one can see evidence of his interest. Ivory plaques on the bay windows show the compass points, a flagstone on the South Terrace in the gardens shows the direction of Ilfracombe and Lundy in lead letters, and a sun dial base shows how to adjust sundial time to Tenby time, which is itself 18.8 minutes behind Greenwich Meantime*.
*The scientific papers he produced may be seen hanging in the Reception Lounge of the Atlantic Hotel today.

De la Rue was a public figure and benefactor in Tenby. He led the movement to preserve the town walls as an ancient monument and developed and donated a part made of aluminium to keep the four clock faces of the church tower in synchronisation. He was ever a thorn in the side of local tradesmen, struggling to install and keep up with every new gadget and piece of equipment, to the highest standards of excellence by which he had always lived. He died at Tenby on 15th April 1921, aged 76, suffering from an incurable gentleman's disease and also the knowledge that de la Rue's was soon to become a public company; Severely depressed by all this, he took his own life. Above the doorway is a fine sculptured stone head of his famous horse "Trayles", which he had specially commissioned. He left the house to his housekeeper, Nancy Burrell.

When the 1939 war broke out, the Esplanade was used as a garrison for troops and Trayles was the officers quarters. The house next door then known as the Carrington Hotel was used for other ranks and during recent renovations a November edition of the 1939 Daily Graphic was found which forecast "Mr Hitler to invade next Spring". A letter from a Wren to her boyfriend, Syd, complained, "life is hell here with three hundred marines and only three Wrens". A rehearsal for the D Day landings code name "Operation Jansen" was held in the bay. It was split into two halves "Wetshod and Dryshod". 'Trayles' was the headquarters of the Wetshod exercise. Captain Entwhistle organised the allocation of accommodation and installed seven hundred telephones in the building to maintain communication. Montgomery, Churchill and Eisenhower all visited the operation at various times.

CHAPTER FIVE
GAMBLING

In the first half of the nineteenth century betting shops flourished all over the country, with more than four hundred in London alone. In order to lay off last minute excessive amounts of cash on one horse, leading book-makers kept hansom cabs at the door to get the money spread as quickly as possible to other bookmakers. However, the Attorney General at the time commented that, "The mischief arising from the existence of these betting shops was perfectly notorious". The 1853 'Betting Houses Act' closed them all down. But all this did was to drive betting underground. A net-work of bookmakers' runners and illegal betting shops operated every-where. There were no books, no income tax and no betting duty. The bookmakers' runners earned 10% commission on all the bets they collected. If the police caught a runner, he had two warnings: the third time was imprisonment.

Bookmakers themselves, although decried by critics and moralists as "illiterate crooks" and "parasites of society", have been and always will be a very important part of racing culture. A bookmaker's reputation, also his turnover, was based on his honesty and fair play, as there was no profit without honour. Bookmaking morality may stoop as low as to stopping a horse, but it generally draws the line at refusing to pay a client. Clients who won too frequently were no problem; their accounts were simply closed. Far more of a worry was the danger of being caught with too much to pay out. This was more of a risk facing the street or office bookmaker, for on-course bets could be laid off further along the rails.

By the late 1870's there were now regular reports on horse racing in newspapers, the main ones being Bell's Life and the Sporting Life. There was one very neat coup carried out in the later part of the nineteenth cen-tury, when a small band of men, obviously one of them a printer, sent three newspapers, a race programme, and later the results of an imaginary race meeting, at a place by the name of Todmore. Both Bell's Life and the Sporting Life took the bait and printed the meeting and the results. To this day no-one knows who they were, or how much it cost the bookmakers, but they got away with it. By the 1890's there were three daily papers and a dozen weekly ones, all devoted to horse racing, and at the turn of the century there were twenty-five sporting newspapers in London alone. In addition, there were a large number of tipsters, circulars and racing sheets available daily from 10am. This now introduced racing to the working man as well as its already wealthy audience of readers. By the end of the nineteenth century the Post Office had created a specialist corps of turf telegraphists, and at the 1901 meeting of the St Leger, eighty-two telegraphists despatched 184,000 words of racing news direct from the Doncaster course.

In 1902, the Sporting Life helped to found the National Sporting League to defend betting interests. The League soon became an association of off-course bookmakers, with a further objective of preventing fraud and malpractice, and also to check the credit rating of punters. Street bookies had no such organisation, their only protection was to refuse credit to anyone. The off-course bookmaker had two major problems. Firstly, most of his betting was at starting price odds, which were determined by the on-course betting, so a local favourite, if not also course favourite, could be a very expensive winner. Secondly, telegrammed bets could arrive at his office after the race had been run, yet the telegram was sent before the official time of the race. Here, he was at a loose end, and had no option but to accept the bet.

Mr George Drake, (who was himself a bookmaker) in the early part of the twentieth century, once exploited the system to the full. When his horse, George Crag, ran at Sandown Park he put £300 on, and his commissioners £50 each, with all of them making a big show while doing so. The horse came nowhere. When it ran next at Manchester, Mr Drake was present, but did not back it with the odds drifting out to 8 – 1. Meanwhile, a small army of men on bicycles were busy sending off about one hundred telegrams, all at the latest possible time to the off, so that the bookmakers receiving them would not have time to lay the bets off, and thus lower the starting price. Mr Drake collected £60,000 and he could not be prosecuted. This particular coup led to the bookmakers' ruling which limited the amount of money that could be staked on late arriving telegrams. At least if bets arrived just before the race was off, the bookmaker had a chance to lay them off. The opening of an account with a bookmaker needed a registered name and address and the name of your bank. You would then place money with the bookmaker so that you were in credit, be it £5 or £1,000. You could then telephone and bet to your agreed credit limit which could be well in excess of the amount deposited. If you were to bet by telegram, the limit was usually £5, unless you agreed a limit with the bookmaker himself, which most gamblers did. When telephoning or sending a telegram you would use your nom de plume. But if you wished to withdraw money from the bookmaker (if you were in credit of course), then he had your real name and address, and a cheque would be posted. Otherwise, the account was usually dealt with monthly. Ladbrokes, however, had brought out a system with a telegraphic code, a copy of which is shown here, 'Courtesy of Ladbrokes'. It was a very innovative idea and was very popular.

TELEGRAPHIC CODE

Clients telegraphing instructions may find the following Code useful, but it is entirely optional.

Investments

Code Word

		£ s d
RED.........................	....	0 10 0
BLUE.......................	....	1 0 0
GREY.......................	....	1 5 0
MAUVE....................	....	1 10 0
CHOCOLATE.............	....	1 15 0
PINK........................	....	2 0 0
VIOLET....................	....	2 10 0
WHITE.....................	....	3 0 0
YELLOW...................	....	4 0 0
GREEN.....................	....	5 0 0
ORANGE...................	....	6 0 0
LAVENDER...............	....	7 0 0
LILAC......................	....	8 0 0
SALMON...................	....	9 0 0
PURPLE....................	....	10 0 0
CERISE....................	....	15 0 0
PUCE.......................	....	20 0 0
CHROME..................	....	25 0 0
MARBLE...................	....	30 0 0
SLATE......................	....	40 0 0
BRONZE...................	....	50 0 0
GOLD.......................	....	100 0 0
PLATINUM................	....	200 0 0
HARBOUR.................	....	Win and 1-2-3 or 1-2
PORT.......................	....	Win and 1-2-3 only
BAY.........................	....	Place 1-2-3 or 1-2

In the early twentieth century, the telephone simplified the laying off of bets, and also kept the bookies in contact with the racecourse itself, thus establishing an S.P. in the bookie's office. The development of the London and Provincial Sporting News Agency, commonly known as the "blower system", provided direct communication with the racecourse. The Agency was started in 1921 by Mr F Trueman, with interests in course bookmaking, and A L Forster, a racing journalist. It became organised as a limited company in 1929, by which time it offered bookmakers not only laying off facilities, but also a complete racing information service. Certainly bookmakers would no longer be fooled by the punter. But there is an old saying, "Where there's a will, there's a way".

The Betting and Gambling Act of 1960 saw the legalisation of street betting in 1961, and bookies offices opened their doors to Joe Public and all and sundry. A bet was written out in the bookmaker's office along with your stake and 6d tax in the £1. Then the ticket was put through a timing clock that stamped the time the bet was laid. However, on Bank Holidays in the 1960's resort of Tenby, some local scoundrels (of whom one was the late Ivor John) decided to try their own betting scam. The little bookies office of J M Charles was packed with holiday makers on one Easter Monday and the blower system could only give so many results at a time, because it was already commentating on the races in hand. "There were about twenty or so meetings this day," said Ivor, "and one of the lads had a radio channel giving out sport results including racing; another of the lads was having a bet inside and when he came out heard the radio results, which weren't being given out on the blower; so between us, we worked out which race and meeting to back, which we already had the winner of. The bookie couldn't complain about the time clock, because the place was so packed that everybody was in a queue anyway, and everybody was betting five minutes late. We got away with it every Bank Holiday for years, until they updated the blower and clocking system; that was about the time I went self-employed" he said, as he looked at me laughing all over his face.

LOCKED TIMING BAGS

These were a small leather pouch-type bag, about six inches long, three inches wide and about one and a half inches round at the top, where there was an aluminium clock, and a place to put the money and the betting slip. The bookie's runner, or street runner, would collect his bag in the morning and would collect his bets from any number of places, such as butcher's shops, bakers, florists, pubs, but most of all, his big business was done between 1pm and 2pm at the factories, steelworks, car plants, cotton mills, docklands, anywhere that people who wanted a bet and could not normally have one because they could not afford to have an account with a book-maker; so in general, the everyday working man.

At 2pm he would lock his bag, and the clock would register that time. The bag could not be opened again until the bookmaker opened it, usually in the evening, or early the next day. Just after 2pm a representative of the bookmaker would arrive, usually by taxi and collect the full bag and re-place it with an empty one if it was a Saturday or Grand National or Derby

Day; but in most cases, 2pm would be the end of the day for the runner. He was on a commission of 10% of his take, and a lot of runners would back a non-runner themselves now and again, and take the commission on the bet. So if they backed a non-runner £5 to win, they would have their £5 back next morning along with all their commission and the other winnings, and would make 10 shillings commission on the non-runner; until they were caught, and then they would have a little difficulty in walking for a while. Bets were written on any piece of paper, with the amount, name of horse, time of race, and a nom-de-plume. When you collected your winnings next day from the runner he would ask you your nom-de-plume before he paid out. You would then be handed your money. If you were a regular backer and well known to the runner, you would only give the slip of paper to him and settle at the end of the week. But there was a limit to this.

My father told me a story many years ago when he used to kill his own pigs on the farm (in fact it was my uncle Jack who was the knife-man, but nevertheless), along with a friend of theirs they bought an old hearse for £5. I think it was a Daimler, with cut-glass side windows, and along with it came two suits, two pairs of shoes, shirts, ties and two silk top haps. There were also two coffins in the back, empty of course. My uncle would butcher the pigs, cut them into hams and flitches etc, then salt them, wrap them in muslin and pack them into the coffins. These were then screwed down and put in the hearse draped with velvet cloths. Fully clothed as undertakers, the two of them would set off at a reasonable pace for Cardiff, having sold the pork over the telephone to a Cardiff butcher. When they got to the butcher's they had to enter through a back yard entrance, through locked gates. The meat was then unloaded and weighed, and put into the freezer room. They were paid their cash and that was that. They were offered mugs of tea and were talking to a local man sitting near the freezer door, saying they were from Tenby and hoped to visit quite often, if all went well. The man asked if they had a bet on the horses, to which they replied, "Yes" and he said, "hang on a minute and I'll give you a winner." He then opened the deep freeze door and took out a bookies "clock-bag". He told us he was a runner and if you put the bag in a freezer for so long, it stopped the clock for ten minutes as it was frozen. So he waited for a phone call at five past two with the winner of the 2pm race, then wrote it on a slip with his money and put it in the bag; the horse had won at 6-1 so my father put £2 on for each of them. When the bag defrosted it was one minute to two and the runner locked the "clock-bag". My father arranged regular visits with the butcher and made sure the bookie's runner was there whenever they came. "It was money for old rope, and we got away with it for years" said my father, "until somebody noticed that there were too many stiffs leaving Tenby" as he laughed aloud, "and we even made a profit on the hearse when we sold it". Laughing and drinking his glass of whisky he said, "we got up to some tricks in those days".

CHAPTER SIX
POST WAR

1920

A report from the Tenby Observor, reporter unknown:

The Tenby Annual Steeple Chase Meeting held on the 14th and 15th January 1920, was the first meeting held since 1914, and all concerned should be congratulated in the promotion of the meeting, which went to show that this long established fixture, has lost none of its popularity with the residents of both town and country. The weather, which has always been an important factor on such occasions, was fine on both days, with the first day in fact being more like summer than winter. The course had been prepared by Mr Ben Hooper of Jeffreston, and it must have been very satisfactory to him to know that Inspector Bell, from the National Hunt Committee, expressed entire satisfaction with the fences. Some people were inclined to think that the fences were too big, but those experienced in such matters know that a fence fairly built is safer for horses than those smaller and not so well made. The stand, which had been built more than twenty five years previous, was also carefully inspected by Mr L R Wood, with a view to ensuring its safety, and under his supervision any repairs necessary were put right by local builder and businessman, Mr W H Phillips and his staff. The catering in the refreshment rooms was under the management of Mrs Priest, and gave general satisfaction.

The duties of Clerk of the Scales were carried out by Mr T H Wilton Pye, and his name is sufficient for everyone to know that the duties were carefully attended to. Everyone was pleased to see Mr George Chiles, one of the Hon Secretaries and stakeholder, fit and well at the weighing room, and that the only matter of regret was that his co-Hon Secretary, Mr C W R Stokes was not present at the races, although we are pleased to know that on both days, he was on the course during the morning, putting the finishing touches wherever they were required. His work, although not done in the public eye, was largely instrumental in ensuing the perfection of all details. We hope and trust that the Hon Secretaries for many years to come will be able to carry out their good work, which, as everyone is aware, is done by them in the interests of the town and its sport.

The first race was won by Bedplate, owned by Mr H T L Young, whose colours are not strange to the meeting, as at the last meeting before the war were in the winners enclosure. His horse was favourite and won after a good finish with Brunswick. The next race was a steeplechase and the popular colours of Mr David Harrison were carried by Shaccabar, a well-known winner under National Hunt Rules, but broke down in the race leaving Joyce's

The Grandstand at Tenby Races 1920
The little lad on the left rail is the late Bobby Weigh, with his father and mother (point-
ing). A few yards to the right in the dark raincoat is Jack Smith, The Green, further to the
right in flat caps are Tudor Griffiths, and Vincent, The Lodge Farm.
The imposing figure in the left foreground, wearing a dark bowler hat, is Lord Kylsant,
surrounded by his three daughters.

Choice an easy winner. In this event Mr Rimington, on Hillock, came a purler at the ditch, but pluckily remounted and completed the course. We should mention that this gentleman is ably assisted in the management of his stables by Mrs Rimington, who is herself an excellent rider, able to school horses, and we are inclined to prophecy, that as soon as the powers that be, see fit to allow ladies to ride horses which they own, train and school, then Mrs Rimington will be one of the first winning lady riders. We have no doubt that ladies will soon establish their right to compete in racing, the same as they have done in other spheres of life, which old-fashioned people thought must always be confined to men. The next two races gave as fine an exhibition of fencing and horsemanship as it would be possible to see anywhere, with W W beating Pencoed by two lengths, and Ballymendel beating Stick to It by three lengths, both winners were ridden by Mr J R Anthony.

We should mention the two other horses were ridden respectively by Mr F B Rees and Mr L B Rees, between whom as horsemen, comparison would be unfair. Mr and Mrs Brychan Rees must be very proud of their sons, but any-one who has seen Brychan Rees ride between the flags or at a point-to-point know why his boys are such fine horsemen. The last race of the day was one of the best at the meeting. A field of seven faced the starter and a successful day's racing was concluded in a great finish between the two Rees brothers, with L B on Little Milford, owned by Mr D H Thomas, beating "Bubbly*", ridden by F B, by three lengths.

    *   Bubbly is a name to watch seven years from now

The second day's racing was not so good as the first, which was only to be expected, as horses are not machines and owners are not inclined to run them two days in succession. However, the best race of the meeting was undoubt-edly that for the Beauchamp Challenge Cup with 40 sovereigns added. The cup was presented by Mr L B Beauchamp, M.F.H. just before the war, and has to be won three times before becoming the property of anyone; the holder up to this year, was the donor, who had entered Llanthony, but to everyone's regret, he was unable to run, no doubt for some good reason known only to his trainer, the well known Fred Hunt. There were five starters, and White Boy, owned by Sir Henry Webb, Bart., was a hot favourite, although Camelot, owned by Colonel D H Leslie (a staunch and liberal supporter of the meeting, and well known to everyone in Pembrokeshire, when stationed at Pembroke Dock with the K.S.L.L) was the chosen of many good judges of racing. The running was made by Le Connetable, trained by Berg, the well-known trainer of Epsom, and ridden by V Duller (the brother of George Duller – who was known as the 'Prince of Hurdles'). The pace set was a good one and at the second hurdle Darley, ridden by the Hon Peter Roberts, came down, the rider fortunately escaping injury beyond a bruised head (which his rude friends said, had nothing in it that would hurt), but we are glad to say that no serious consequences ensued, and it seemed to be taken as all in a day's work by this genuine sportsman and first class rider, whose services are eagerly sought, by many owners and trainers. At this time White Boy, ridden by L Rees and Camelot by Mr J R Anthony, White Boy took the lead and was challenged by Camelot and Le Connetable at the final flight, and were all neck and neck, with Le Connetable being first to cry enough was enough, and it was not until well within the distance that White Boy asserted his superiority and won a

An example of sea fog on the racecourse

well deserved and popular victory for his owner, Sir Henry Webb Bart, and trainer, Mr David Harrison, who were heartily cheered and congratulated.

The meeting wound up with another well-contested duel, between Ballymendel and Stick to It, the latter being this time ridden by L B Rees; the fencing of the former, was more finished than that of the latter, who is only a young horse, and told its inevitable tale when they landed over the last fence side by side, although Mr Jack Anthony had to sit down and ride in earnest to beat off the attentions of the other, finally winning by three lengths. This resume of the races should not be concluded without a word of thanks to Dr Charles Mathias, for the prompt treatment of Mr F Sergeant, the rider of Darley, who fell on the first day at the stand hurdles; the fall looked a nasty one, as several horses appeared to strike the fallen jockey, but thanks to Dr Mathias and a good constitution this jockey was walking about in the paddock the next day. The stewards whose names appeared on the card – except Viscount St Davids (represented by Major-General Sir Ivor Philipps), who was unavoidably prevented at the last moment from attending the meeting, much to the disappointment of the committee, but who had liberally contributed to the funds, and Mr L B Beauchamp, for whom Mr Montague-Leeds deputised, were all present, but we are glad to say their services were not required, the whole of the racing passing off without any objections or question of any kind. The duty of starter was ably performed by Mr George Phelps*, who saw to it that no liberties were taken by any eager rider at the starting point. The duties of judge were entrusted to Mr Vincent Thomas and were accurately attended to.

> * Mr George Phelps was Dick Francis's great uncle. He was also the starter on that unforgettable day in 1927.

David Harrison's string on Cornishdown gallops

We were glad to see in the paddock Mr Ivor Anthony who has nearly recovered from the bad fall he had at Gatwick, some two or three weeks ago, when he was knocked out for over an hour, and in course of conversation he said he expected to be riding at Newbury this week, and hoped it would be a winner. This news will be welcome to his many friends in these parts as although he has not, like his brother Jack, ridden a Grand National winner, there is no finer horseman and judge of pace amongst present day jockeys than "Ivor" whose seat in the saddle, we have heard described as that of a "centaur".

We must congratulate all concerned on the promotion of the meeting, which was undoubtedly a success, largely as a result of the liberal patronage in entries and subscriptions from Mr David Harrison and owners for whom he trains, and we feel sure that his stables only won three races at the meeting, he and they, like good sportsmen, were well pleased, as without the opposition from away there would not have been such good racing. We trust now that the meeting has been revived, it will continue to flourish in the future as in the past.

Dr Charles Mathias, whose surgery was based in Tenby, was a local family doctor and enjoyed making house calls, as well as attending the racecourse meetings in his official capacity as duty doctor. Always known as Dr Charlie, he made his calls with his two spaniels in tow. He was quite a character and being well over six feet tall, he carried it well. He was, however, a gruff man, who could be very rude, but he was devoted to his patients. He drove a blue car with the registration number DE 67. He never drank any water, other than that from the village pump in Penally where he lived. As well as all the marshland and Holloway, he had the land where Strawberry Gardens is now built on which he grew all his food and also kept horses. At Holloway Farm, there was a gateway into one of his fields that needed painting, and when asked by Councillor Howells what colour he intended to paint the gateway, Dr Charlie replied rudely, "monkey's arse blue". On another occasion when Dr Charlie was walking up School Lane, a Mr Ernie Griffiths* was repairing a roof. "None of your shoddy work now Griffiths, do you hear what I say?" called Dr Charlie. Ernie replied, "My shoddy work is up here for all to see, your shoddy work is all six feet under."
* Ernie Griffiths was the grandfather of the actor Kenneth Griffith.

First Day Results

THE LICENSED VICTUALLERS SELLING HANDICAP HURDLE RACE
Mr H T L Young's, Bedplate, 5 y.o., F B Rees, 1
Mr D Harrison's, Brunswick, Aged, Ivor Anthony, 2
Mrs M Rimington's, Willis, 4 y.o., Mr Rimington, 3

THE GROVE SELLING STEEPLE CHASE
Mr H C R Homfray's, Joyce's Choice, Aged, L B Rees, 1
Mr D Harrison's, Shaccabac, Aged, Ivor Anthony, 2
3Mrs M Rimington's, Hillock, Aged, Mr Rimington, 3

THE WROUGHTON NOVICE STEEPLE CHASE
Mr Guy Hargreaves, W.W., Aged, Mr J R Anthony, 1
Mr D Harrison's,Pencoed, 5 y.o., F B Rees, 2

TOWN OPTIONAL SELLING STEEPLE CHASE
Colonel D C Part's, Ballymendel, Aged, Mr J R Anthony, 1
Sir Henry Webb's, Stick to It, 6 y.o., L B Rees, 2

THE VICTORY HURDLE RACE
Mr D H Thomas's, Little Milford, 4 y.o., L B Rees, 1
Mr D Harrison's, Bubbly, 5 y.o., F B Rees, 2
Mr H J Brueton's, Northcote, 6 y.o., Mr J R Anthony, 3

L B REES. F B REES.

Second Day Results

KNIGHTON SELLING HURDLE RACE
Mr H D Dennis's, Croquet King, Aged, 11st 4, L Rees, 3-1, 1
Mr H Young's, Bedplate, 5 y.o., 11st 3, F B Rees, 2-1 on, 2
Mrs M Rimington's, Willo, Aged, 11st, Mr Rimington, 20-1, 3
Winner trained by D Harrison, Tenby
Winner sold to Mr H C R Homfray for £120

TENBY SELLING HANDICAP STEEPLE CHASE
Mr A Chamberlain's, Johnson, Aged, 11st, Saunders w.over, 1

THE BEAUCHAMP CHALLENGE CUP
Sir H Webb's, Whiteboy, Aged, 11st 12, LB Rees 9-4 on, 1
Col D H Leslie's, Camelot, Aged, 11st 12, Mr JR Anthony 4-1, 2
Mrs F Barries, Le Connetable, 6 y.o., 10st, V Duller 6-1. 3
Winner trained by D Harrison, Tenby

THE LAWRENNY NOVICE'S STEEPLE CHASE
Mr Hargreave's, W W, Aged, 12st, Mr JR Anthony w. over, 1
Winner trained by Hastings

THE DEER PARK OPEN STEEPLE CHASE – THREE MILES
Col D Part's, Ballymendel, Aged, 11st 6, Mr JR Anthony 3-1 on, 1
Sir H Webb's, Stick to It, 6 y.o., 11st, L B Rees
Winner trained by Hastings

This meeting, being the first meeting at Tenby since 1914, seems to be the opportunity that David Harrison has to have the licence transferred into his own name from that of his friend Robert Weaver Smith. Nothing was ever mentioned about this so I presume that it was just a formality. Bobby Smith stayed at the stable as Harrison's right hand man, right to the very end, so I do not think that there was any ill feeling of any kind!

****

POST WAR GRAND NATIONAL

The return of the Grand National to Aintree in 1919 was marked by the success of another lady owner, Mrs Hugh Peel, with Poethlyn repeating for her his victory the previous year at Gatwick. He carried the top weight of 12st 7lb and was 11-4 fav. and was ridden by Ernest Piggott, who had also ridden Jerry M. to victory in the 1912 Grand National. Poethlyn had been sold by his breeder Major H Peel to a Shrewsbury hotelier for £7. He was then a weak and sickly yearling and as a two year old he was bought back by Major Peel for £50 as a gift for his wife.

A veteran of the Grand National Algy Anthony, who rode Ambush to victory in 1900 trained by J Hunter (another regular at Tenby Races), was now in training at the Curragh, from where he brought over an entry for the 1920 Grand National. This was the seven year old brown gelding, Troytown who was just over 17 hands, with bone and muscle in proportion, a clean and bony head, fine shoulders, great depth of heart, a powerful back and loins and a kind eye. He carried 11st 9lb and with the consent of the owner, Major Gerrard, Anthony got his kinsman, Jack Anthony to ride him. The combination of a great horse and a jockey of such proved quality at Aintree carried the day, which, from the point of the weather, was a foul one. It didn't stop raining from the morning onwards and the going was as heavy as it could ever be. Even so, Poethlyn, with 12st 7lbs was 3-1 favourite, with Troytown 6-1, in a field of twenty-four. The plucky Mr Harry Brown, with his own self-trained horse, The Bore at 28-1, had an understanding with his horse, like that between Alexander the Great and Bucephalus who, when wounded in battle, brought his master to safety before dropping dead.

Poethlyn fell at the first fence, but due to the bad light and weather it went unnoticed for some time. Troytown had led all the way while others behind him fell and blundered, but he gave Jack Anthony a moment of suspense, when, at the furze fence before the last of all, he made an uncertain landing, and before Anthony had got him to full gallop again, Mr Brown on The Bore was upsides him, but The Bore had given his all, and Troytown jumped the

120

last fence and galloped strongly home, as if enlivened by the cheers. The Turk II, a complete outsider, trained by Hon Aubrey Hastings (another name seen at Tenby on many occasions) got up to steal second place from The Bore and Mr Brown, who with 10st 11lb was the most heavily weighted of those that finished after Troytown, who was the only horse from up the handicap to get the heavy course at all. Some said that Troytown was greater than even

TROYTOWN (RIDDEN BY MR. J. R. ANTHONY).
BY ZRIA — DIANE.
WINNER OF THE GRAND NATIONAL, 1920.

Cloister and Manifesto, but he was not to live to prove it. He was on his way from the Curragh to take part in the Grand Steeplechase de Paris, when he was held up at the North Wall, owing to a strike of Dublin dockers. He remained there from day to day while negotiations took place for a settlement. At last, the sporting instincts of the Irish dockers were successfully stirred, and they allowed him to be shipped on the cross-channel boat for Holyhead. But, he had nothing like the preparation time that he should have had in France to get him ready for the big race, and in the order of fencing which has puzzled many great horses who were not familiar with the course and he ran third. A few days later he ran again, but he fell and broke his back and was shot. He was buried in the Paris Cemetery of Dogs. A steeplechase is called after him at Lingfield Park.

The 1921 Grand National saw King George V, Queen Mary, The Prince of Wales, Princess Mary and Prince Henry, all in royal attendance. It was a day of strong winds and heavy going. The Bore was favourite from Mr Joe Widger's Eamon Beag, which would have been called "De Valera" but for the objection of the Irish racing authority at the time. At 100-9 were Turkey Buzzard, who carried most weight, Garryvoe and Shaun Spadah, which does not mean "Jack of Spades" as was stated at the time, but "John" who keeps up with the leader in a running race. That is the "Spadah" man, the competitor whom the leader cannot shake off. His sire, Easter Prize, was sold for a hundred and twenty guineas after Mr Atty Persse had come second with him at Leopardstown. Shaun Spadah was the third foal of Rusialka, whose dam Sylvia was eighteen years old at Rusialka's birth and was sent to Vienna at the age of twenty-three. Bred by Mr P McKenna at Streamstown, County Westmeath, Shaun Spadah was sold to the trainer Mr R G Cleary, who reserved him for chasing after one race as a three year old. Shortly before the Grand National, he had won from The Bore at Kempton Park. Mr T M AcAlpine, son of Sir Robert McAlpine, bought him from Mr M H Benson, the principal of the bookmaking firm of Douglas Stuart, and he was trained at Lewes by Mr Poole, (who was only thirteen when he rode his first winner at his native Chelmsford).

At the first fence seven horses fell, and when Any Time was knocked over, Frank Wootton, who had been flat racing's leading jockey when a boy from Australia, just managed to scramble out from the ruck and save himself from being jumped on. Disaster came heavily; Eamon Beag, for whom Coulthwaite was sanguine, went down with a crowd, and the only ones to complete the first round were All White, Turkey Buzzard, Shaun Spadah, The Bore and Glencorrig. Shaun Spadah pecked at the water jump, but recovered like a grand horse when he was on his head and knees. Glencorrig, who was also sent from Coulthwaite, refused. A load of newspapers had blown up against the rail-ditch, and although All White got over with a long leap, he threw Chadwick, but he somehow held onto the reins and got back into the saddle to pursue Turkey Buzzard, Shaun Spadah and The Bore. Turkey Buzzard fell at Becher's Brook and also at the next two fences, but Captain Bennett managed to get back into the saddle every time. Afterwards, he said that he recollected only one such fall. Shaun Spadah and The Bore, the only horses that had not fallen, went on side by side from Becher's Brook. Fred B Rees who was on Shaun Spadah, had relinquished his amateur status and was riding his first season as a professional; his father Brychan Rees, the Tenby Veterinary Surgeon was there to watch both his sons ride, the younger son L B Rees had already fallen with Prince Clifton. Two fences from home The Bore fell and Mr Brown broke his collarbone, but, remounted, and with the reins grasped in one hand, got his faithful horse over the last fence sideways and without a fall. Shaun Spadah, the only horse to get the full distance without a fall, came in as easily as in an old fashioned walk-over. Mr Brown cantered in second in a condition which was more urgent for him to see the doctor than the clerk of the scales, while All White and Turkey Buzzard came in third and fourth respectively.

"Shaun Spadah."

Brychan Rees must have been a proud man that day, with F B having won the Grand National in his first season as a professional. The whole of Tenby would have surely been in fine voice and rich in pocket that night, I'm sure.

Cliftonhall, the sire of Music Hall, winner of the 1922 Grand National, stood at a fee of £5 at the New Abbey Stud, Kilcullen, County Kildare. Mrs Blacker (wife of Colonel Blacker, the old cross country rider and cricketer, who once said, "I sold a horse for thousands and he was killed first time out, I sold one for hundreds and he won the Grand National") had a mare Molly, who had several foals, one of which was Music Hall, at Kinneagh, Newbridge, near the Curragh. A Manchester cotton factory owner, Mr Hugh Kershaw, bought Music Hall from a Mrs F Stokes (who had had considerable success with him on the flat) for 3000 guineas. Owen Anthony had started his training career with Music Hall and two other horses belonging to Mr Kershaw. Molly and Cliftonhall had done well, as Music Hall had proved to be a bold chaser with a fine turn of speed, and he won a newly instituted Grand National trial steeplechase over four miles at Hurst Park. When he turned out at

Music Hall ridden by L B Rees

Aintree he was to be ridden by Brychan Rees's younger son Lewis Bilbee, carrying 11st 8lb and at 100-9 in the betting behind Southampton and Clashing Arms.

"The favourite's down!…and at the first fence too", was the cry. Mr Brown was the last to be thrown the previous year, and now his was the first calamity, a companion in earliest adversity being F B Rees with Shaun Spadah. Nevertheless, it was to be a Rees day and he was in time to get across to the winning post and watch his younger brother's triumph from the rails. Sergeant Murphy was making the running on the first circuit, when he slipped into the ditch at the canal turn, and in an awkward mix-up, All White, Norton, and General Saxham came down. Awbeg fell and broke his neck at Becher's Brook, and at the previous fence The Inca II broke a leg when another horse jumped on him as he lay on the ground. Clashing Arms ridden for Colonel W S Anthony by his brother Jack slipped on landing and fell. Hawkins managed to get Sergeant Murphy into action again, with much ground to make up. Music Hall was first at the water-jump with A Double Escape, Arravale and Drifter close at hoof, with Taffytus the last survivor, a distance behind. Arravale was frightened by Grey Dawn V lying in a ditch and when he saw the unconscious The Inca II, he swerved in flight against Music Hall, who kept his feet with remarkable ingenuity. A Double Escape and Drifter had come up alongside Music Hall at Valentine's Brook where, in a scramble, L B Rees lost control of a stirrup but managed to get his foot back in after he had taken the next fence. At the next fence A Double Escape fell and Captain Bennett remounted after chasing after his mount. Drifter had cut the coronet of his hoof so badly at Valentine's Brook that part of the hoof was hanging loose, and he raced from there, virtually on three legs. Music Hall nearly came down at the last fence, and those who saw him draw away from Drifter, to win by twelve lengths thought Mr Joe Widger's horse to be slow, but the owner and his trainer, Tom Coulthwaite, believed that with a sound fourth leg he would have won. Taffytus came in third, ridden by nineteen-year-old Ted Leader, who was riding in one of his first steeplechases. Sergeant Murphy came in fourth, with A Double Escape fifth. Young Ted Leader had to wait until 1927 when he won on Sprig, trained by his father, which was the first Grand National to be broadcast.

This victory brought a great double for the Rees brothers, winning in consecutive years. Tenby backers could surely not believe their luck, especially at 100-9, and I've no doubt that many hangovers were carried around the town for a day or two, and many overdrafts turned into credit.

* * * * * * * * * * *

1921

This is a story written by Mr R Ward-Davies of a Trip to the Races at Tenby in 1921, travelling by lorry:

"AN IMPRESSION"

"It was a mud plugging expedition, but none the less enjoyable. This is to say that the powerful lorry did the mud plugging business, and in it were gathered together a nice little crowd. They were all sports, and were bound for the outskirts of Tenby, where the races were held. The day was Wednesday. The lorry was shod with solid tyres and we had a real treat in the way of doing the seat-bouncing business. The dreadful condition of the roads was thus forced to the notice of every passenger, and between gasps, when a wicked stretch was reached, what was said was enough to make the phlegmatic authorities blink. But the lorry serenely trundled on. It is a very Nelson of vehicles, and nobly did its duty.

The day was cold, but the Clerk of the Weather had turned the tap off. Well it was so. Milton was reached with the cargo's livers well shaken up, and a move was made to interview mine host – and to pick more passengers up! The latter part of the job was the least important. The stop was not long. It's wonderful what can be done in a short time. Soon the concern was underway again. The driver saw to that, and he can drive. He handled the lorry in the manner born.

Overhead the sky was sullen. The wind whistled through the dripping trees. The saddened road loomed up brown and foreboding in the distance. The fields were gloriously green, and from the high point of vantage, a lovely landscape faded away into a horizon which met the leaden clouds. The pant of the engine sent the birds scudding for dear life into fields further away, but a sea gull kept us company, as we ploughed merrily on. But the bird soon got tired. Through winding lanes the vehicle trundled with the surface scarcely wide enough for its passage. Yet in good time the course hove in view, and we were there.

The officials at the gate, though busy were courteous, and in a trice we were inside. But the "motor track" the special motor track to the course! It was a beauty. Big cars stuck with their rear wheels, whirling round, and Lord Tom Noddy and party had to call for assistance, and do a bit of pushing! And it was pushing – in a sea of mud. In sooth, pride cometh before a fall, and in this case pride cameth before an elegant stick!

It was not nice on the course. Not at all nice. The wind played havoc with your ribs, and made you mourn for the summer long since gone. And the mud! It was a matter of squelching through it wherever you turned. It was of the good old fashioned sort, of the consistency of treacle. The very dainty shoes of the ladies, and their silk stockings soon presented a sorry spectacle. What fools some people are! They never garb themselves in attire suitable for mud, on such an occasion.

The paddock was a scene of animation. Many notable people were present, watching the horses as they were led round. The nags, one and all, looked in splendid condition, and they had to be, in order to complete the course, which was heavy enough going for anything. The racing was good. There is no doubt about that, though those who followed the favourites came unholy croppers. Big fields rewarded those who had braved the elements, and made their way to the scene of action. The jumping was poor. In one race there were four horses that absolutely failed to negotiate a small jump. So they were out of it – and so were their backers! I felt sad as I beheld the favourite in one race stumble and fall in the second lap. This is to say it came down on the corner of the course, and lay down with the wind up or its wind gone. That was all the run I had for my money. The last race was a beauty. A big field faced the starter and they nearly all completed the course.

Tenby races were a success. I am very glad. I have never seen better racing in Wales. Shades of Alleston! It was a great deal better than any I have seen there.

With the races over, we boarded the lorry, and bumped home in state. There was singing and music on the way. A few had heavy pockets, but mine were as light as my heart."

What a great little story!

The Tenby Observor reported:

The two day meeting of January 1921 recorded 155 entries which was ranked as amongst the most numerous to date, while the stake money offered totalled more than £500. Well known owners and trainers from Wales, England and Ireland were represented on both days. (*The weather can be described as accurate to Mr R Ward-Davies's story*). The arrangements showed a marked improvement, with the "new motor track" which gave easy access right onto the course being much appreciated. (*I believe Mr R Ward-Davies*). The grandstand was very well attended and was practically full of all the prominent sporting people of the Principality. Officials were: Hon Secs C W R Stokes and G Lort Stokes, Clerk of the course George Chiles; Mr Vincent Thomas, judge; Mr T H Wilton Pye (Worcester) Clerk of the Scales; Mr Rowland Leigh, handicapper; Mr George Phelps (Cresselly) starter; Dr Charles Mathias, Hon Surgeon; and Mr Brychan Rees, Hon Vet Surgeon. Of the bookmaking fraternity there was a large gathering, with well known commission agents from Swansea, Cardiff, Bristol and the West of England.

First Day

WROUGHTON NOVICE STEEPLE CHASE
50 sovs Two miles
Mr W Bankier's, Fiddle Bridge, Mr B Roberts, 1
Mr J Widger's (IRE), Drifter, Mr O'Connor*[1] (ref 1926), 2

LICENSED VICTUALLERS SELLING HANDICAP HURDLE
50 sovs Two miles
Mr C Williams, Yellow Girl, M Hehir, 1
Mr T Longworth's, Dee Boa, M Smith, 2
Mr M Rimington's, Gold Sand, Owner, 3

GROVE SELLING STEEPLE CHASE
50 sovs Two miles
Mr W Mille's, Rigicles, S Jones, 1
Mr J Bowden's, Dairymaid II, J Rennison, 2

TOWN OPTIONAL SELLING STEEPLE CHASE
50 sovs Three miles
Miss A Wright's, Lochar, L Bunn w over, 1

THE VICTORY HURDLE RACE
50 sovs Two miles
Mr E Trow's, Princess Miriam*[2], B Bullock, 1
Miss A Wright's, Rampage, L Bunn, 2
Mr R Watson's, John, H Walsh, 3

*[1] 1926 Mr O'Connor was about to become David Harrison's vet.
*[2] ref Ashley Colley's story about his younger brother Don

Second Day
In the Lawrenny Chase, Fiddle Bridge fell at the last while well clear, and out of the six starters Wreckage finished alone. In The Knightston Hurdle, Camel Lad fell and broke his neck and was shot. Pencoed won easily in the Deer Park Chase, for the Lawrenny owner Mr J F Lort Phillips.

KNIGHTSTON SELLING HURDLE RACE
50 sovs Two miles
Mr D Thomas's, Little Milford, J Mahoney (Sen), 1
Mr C Williams's, Yellow Girl, Mr Hehir, 2
Sir H Webb's, Stick to It, Mr P Roberts, 3

TENBY SELLING HANDICAP STEEPLE CHASE
40 sovs Two miles
Mr W Brocklehurst's, The Doctor V, H Whiteman, 1

Miss G Tredwell's, Seventy Five, M Hehir, 2
Mr M Walsh's, Little Slave, J Gill, 3

THE BEAUCHAMP CHALLENGE CUP
A gold cup value 50 guineas, with 40 sovs added Two miles
Col D Leslie's, Camelot, Mr P Roberts, 1
Mr H Dennis's, Sontley, Mr Dennis, 2
Capt C Whitaker's, Ballymacsea, Mr Rennison, 3

THE LAWRENNY NOVICE STEEPLE CHASE
50 sovs Two miles
Mr C Williams's, Wreckage, M Hehir, 1
Finished alone.

THE DEER PARK OPEN STEEPLE CHASE
50 sovs Two miles
Lieut-Col J F Lort Phillips's, Pencoed, J Mahoney, 1
Mr T Longworth's, White Cockade, M Smith, 2

THE UNITED COUNTIES HURDLE RACE
30 sovs Two miles
Mr Tudor Griffiths's, Little Violet, Owner, 1
Mr G Thomas's, Dewi Sant, Mr W Thomas, 2
Mr T Ormond's, The Barb, Mr G Ormond, 3

The winner Little Violet was owned and ridden by Mr Tudor Griffiths of the Lodge Farm, New Hedges, whose victory was enormously popular with the crowd. He was presented with the prize by Lieut-Col J F Lort Phillips, that fine Pembrokeshire sportsman.

****

1922

1922 was advertised as the biggest and most important meeting to date. A Tenby Observor report:

TENBY RACES
(Steeplechases & Hurdles).

January 25th & 26th, 1922.

198 ENTRIES
From leading Owners and Trainers in the
United Kingdom and Ireland.

The Leading Jockeys under N.H. Rules
will be riding at the Meeting,
including amongst others:-
Messrs. JACK ANTHONY, the rider of three
Grand National Winners; DICK REES, the
head of the list of Winning Jockeys for 1921,
and rider of the Grand National Winner,
SHAUN SPADAH; FRANK WOOTTON, of
Flat and Steeplechase fame; IVOR ANTHONY,
BILBEE REES, F. DAINTY, GEORGE
DULLER, the Crack Hurdle Race Jockey; F.
MASON, JOE CANTY, the Crack Irish Jockey, etc., etc.

An exceptional opportunity is given
to the locality of witnessing First-
Class Racing and Riding.

The Motor Track to the Course has been
greatly improved to ensure this year
easy access to the Winning Field.

SPECIAL RAILWAY FACILITIES
Train leaves Swansea, 9.5; Llanelly, 9.20;
Carmarthen, 10.3; Whitland, 10.40; Haver-
fordwest, 11.20. Special train from Pembroke
Dock, 12.30 each day. – See Railway Bills.

1st Race, First Day, 2 p.m. Second Day 1.20 p.m.

Overnight the course at Tenby was hard through frost and it was doubtful if racing would be possible today. During the night there was a fall of snow, but rain this morning helped to soften up the ground and delaying the start of the first race by half an hour.

2 p.m THE WROUGHTON CHASE
50 sovs Two miles
Mr T Edge's, Top Hole, F B Rees, 1
Winner trained by G Poole, Lewes

2-30 THE LICENSED VICTUALLERS' SELLING HURDLE HANDICAP
50 sovs Two miles
Mr J Rank's, Boyne Water, 6 y.o., 10st.6lb, L B Rees, 3-1, 1
Mr G Hande's, Lady Flare, 5 y.o., 11st 9lb, A Smith, 2-1, 2
Mr T Baker's, Ambridge, 5 y.o., 10st 2lb, S Jones, 100-8, 3
Mr F C Twine's, Decibel, 6 y.o., 12st 8lb, A Yates
Sir H Webb's, The Wish, 6 y.o., 11st 8lb, F B Rees 4-5F
Mr Ted Arnold's* J.C.B., 6 y.o., 10st 5lb, J Arnold
Mr H Young's, Exe, 4 y.o., 10st 2lb, Sergeant
Mr O Flaming's, Marriage Contract, 4y.o., 10st 2lb, J Payne
Winner trained by Poole, Lewes
Won by distance
* Edward (Ted) Arnold, the Worcester and England cricketer, soon to become a great
friend of Ben Warner, the Newbury professional gambler.

3-0 THE TENBY SELLING HANDICAP CHASE
60 sovs Two miles
Mr D Faher's, Northbrook, Aged, 11st 1lb, L B Rees, 4-5F, 1
Mr G W Hande's, The Savage, Aged, 11st 5lb, Willmott 2-1, 2
Mr Rimington's Breakaway, Aged, 10st 4lb, Owner 10-1, 3
Winner trained by Hatt, Wroughton

3-30 THE RUISLIP CHASE
55 sovs Three miles
Mr W Banking's, Superman, Aged, 11st 13lb, J Anthony, 6-4, 1
Mr T Baker's, Athos III, Aged 11st, Mahoney, 10-1, 2
Mr G Hande's, Any Time, Aged 12st 4lb, Mr O'Connor , 6-1
Mr J Moore's, Pacifist, Aged, 11st, J Canty 4-5F
Mr H D Dean's, Strauss, Aged 11st 13lb Mr P Dennis 10-1
Winner trained by A Hastings, Wroughton
Won by twenty lengths, only two finished

4-0 THE BEAUCHAMP CHALLENGE CUP
A gold cup value 50 guineas with 50 sovereigns added. Two miles
Sir Harry Webb's, Bubbly, Aged , 10st 11lb, LB Rees 5-1, 1
Sir Harry Webb's, Mr Madcap 5 y.o., 11st 2lb, J Anthony, 2-1 F, 2
Sir Harry Webb's, Whiteboy , Aged, 10st 5lb, F B Rees, 6-1, 3
Mr Livingstone, Learmouth's Havoc, Aged 11st 2lb, A Yates 6-1

Mr M Rimington's, Coaxer, Aged, 10st 6lb, Owner
Mr G Fleming's, Bessie Belle, Aged, 10st 6lb, Owner
Mr D Harrison's, Palm Sunday, 5 y.o.10st 5lb, J Mahoney
Winner trained by D Harrison, Tenby
Won by 2 lengths

Bubbly being led in after the 4pm race

Second Day

1-30 THE LLWYNARTHAN STEEPLE CHASE
60 sovs Two miles
Mr Bankier's, Fiddle Bridge, Aged, 11st 8lb, J Anthony, 4-1 on, 1
Mr T Baker's, Athos III, Aged, 11st 8lb, J Mahoney, 2
Winner trained by A Hastings, Wroughton
Won by 25 lengths

2-0 THE KNIGHTSTON SELLING HURDLE RACE
50 sovs Two miles
Mr D Learmouth's, Hasso, Aged 12st , A Yates, 5-2, 1

132

Mr P Sheehan's (IRE), Olivenna, Aged, 10st 9lb, L B Rees 6-4, 2
Mr M Rimington's, Coaxer , Aged, 11st 2lb, Owner, 10-1, 3
Mr G Hande's, Lady Flazo, 5 y.o. 11st, Mr O'Connor
Winner trained by A Yates
Won by 3 lengths

2-30 THE LAWRENNY FARMERS HURDLE
30 sovs Two miles
Mr W G Thomas's, Sunbank, 5 y.o., 11st 10lb, Mr W Thomas 2-1, 1
Mr Tudor Griffiths's, Cashbox, Aged, 12st, Mr P Roberts 6-1, 2
Mr J Anthony's, Salisbury Arms Aged, 12st, Mr G Anthony 7-4F, 3
Mr W Evans's, Ocean Pride, Aged, 12st, Mr G Evans
Mr S T Jones's, Songster II, Aged, 12st, Mr J Hull
Mr T O Ormond's, The Barb, 5 y.o., 11st 10lb, Mr G Ormond
Mr H H Gibbons's, Vaynor, 5 y.o., 11st 10lb, Mr H Collins
Mr G S Williams's, Just There, 5 y.o., 11st 10lb, Owner
Winner privately trained

3-0 THE VICTORY HURDLE RACE
50 sovs Two miles
Mr J Moore's, Pacifist, Aged, 12st, J Canty, 5-4, 1
Mr T Baker's, Ambridge, 5 y.o., 10st 12lb, Yates 10-1, 2
Mr A J Smith's, Playing Field, Aged, 11st 2lb, A Smith, Ev F, 3
Sir Harry Webb's, Reparation, 6 y.o., 10st 12lb, L B Rees
Mr D Harrison's, Mrs Tuck, 5 y.o., 10st 12lb, Mr P Roberts
Sir Marteine Lloyd's, Little Haven, 4 y.o. 10st 2lb, F B Rees
Mr D Harrison's, Palm Sunday, 5 y.o., 11st 2lb, J Mahoney
Mrs E McHenry's, St May, 6 y.o., 10st 12lb, Witchell
Mrs Basil Mundy's, One Sir, 4 y.o., 10st 2lb, Mr P Dennis
Winner trained by Barthropp, Tarporley
Won by 2 lengths

4-0 DEER PARK OPEN THREE MILE CHASE
50 sovs
Mr T Edge's, Top Hole, Aged, 10st, F B Rees, 7-2 on, 1
Mr G W Hande's, Any Time, Aged, 12st 4lb, Willmott, 2
Mr Henry Dyke Dennis's, Struan, Aged, 11st 13lb, L B Rees, 3
Won by distance

1923
January

<h2 style="text-align:center">"TENBY RACES"</h2>

There seemed a possibility overnight of the Tenby Meeting being spoilt by rain for the weather was boisterous, but a dull morning gave way to sunshine, and though a high wind prevailed during the afternoon the conditions were not bad. The feature of the day's sport was the double brought off for Mr George Lort Stokes, the popular Hon Secretary of the meeting. He took the first event with Roisel, and created great surprise when the friendless Great Western annexed the honours in the Deer Park Open Steeplechase. In the Knightston Hurdle, D Sweeney, the rider of Rosherville, earned the displeasure of the Stewards, who, after his explanation of the running of the animal, fined him £5 and administered a severe caution. This happening left the way clear for Life Buoy to give Mr David Harrison his only winner of the day, whereas he had been expected to win several events. The Grove Steeplechase produced a field of five, the biggest of the day, and Locator won well from The Nib, with Warebeam failing for second place, after a desperate effort, by a head. Then came the big surprise of the afternoon. Four animals faced the starter for the Deer Park Open Steeplechase, and the friendless one among them, Great Western, came out with a dash in the last four furlongs to win from the well-backed Gristle by a length and a half, after the latter and Martes had made practically all the running. Lady Webb was expected to emulate her husband's performance of last year by winning the Beauchamp Cup, but once again the odds were upset. Temeside winning a desperate race by two lengths.

The results were as follows:

THE WROUGHTON HANDICAP STEEPLE CHASE

50 sovs Two miles

Mr G Stokes's, Roisel, J Mahoney (Sen), 1

Mr S Stewart's, Equancourt, Owner, 2

Mr Laye's, Cage, T J Pagington, 3

THE KNIGHTSTON SELLING HURDLE RACE

50 sovs Winner to be sold for 100 sovs Two miles

Mr E Arnold's, Life Buoy, L B Rees, 1

Mr W Bankier's, Glandura, J Anthony, 2

THE GROVE SELLING STEEPLE CHASE

50 sovs Winner to be sold for 100 sovs Two miles

Mr V Scull's, Locator, G Wall

Mr W Pocock's, The Nib, A Yates

Mr V Hunt's, Wavebeam, R Trudgill

THE DEER PARK OPEN THREE MILES STEEPLE CHASE
50 sovs Three miles
Mr G Stokes's, Great Western, J Mahoney (Sen)
Mr F Phillip's, Gristle, F B Rees
Capt Powell's, Martes, G Wall

BEAUCHAMP CHALLENGE CUP VALUE
50 gns with 50 sovs added Two miles
Mr T L Walker's, Temeside, J Anthony, 1
Lady Webb's, Joseph The First, L Rees, 2
Mr W A Wallis's, Louvima, F B Rees, 3

Second Day N/A (Lost)

The meeting at Tenby on January 10th and 11th 1923, leaves Tenby as the only fixture left in West Wales, and, if anything is now stronger than it has ever been, with its theatricals, hunt-balls and meets of the hounds. Tenby is fortunate in having such gentlemen, who take a keen interest in the sport, such as: Mr C W R Stokes, Mr G L Stokes and the genial head of affairs, Mr George Chiles. Tenby has always been the home of the training of steeple-chasers.

In the late Mr Fred Bower's time, he had a large string of horses of his own with Mr R L Thomas and others in training. Since the advent of Mr David Harrison, it has attained marked success, attracting influential patrons, among them Lord St Davids, Sir Marteine Lloyd, Sir Henry Webb, the Hon Mrs Mundy, Mr W V H Thomas, and Mr D H Thomas (Carmarthen), in addition to his own privately owned horses. There was also Mr C C Bill Williams of Llanrumney Hall, Cardiff, a superior horseman and gentleman, also High Sheriff of Monmouthshire in 1925, and had been awarded the Military Cross in World War I. The best of his horses in training at Tenby were Ganzey, Attempt and Caldey Light, and he usually retained Willy Stott or Willy Speck as his jockeys. The Hon Mrs Mundy had many horses with David Harrison at this time. She was a sister to Lord Tredegar, whose father took part in, and survived the Charge of the Light Brigade at Balaclava. Lord Tredegar kept a fine stud of quality stallions and mares, but unlike his sister, Mrs Mundy, he was not a great lover of racing itself but loved to hunt with the hounds. The family wealth was drawn from "The Golden Mile", a stretch of railway that ran through Tredegar Park with the toll of one penny per ton of coal hauled, which yielded a very considerable income. However, the jockeys such as Ivor Owen, Jack Anthony, Fred B Rees and Lewis B Rees all owe their initial success to Mr David Harrison.

Another successful Tenby jockey was the late Arthur Smith; he was a fine horseman. One of his many successes was in the Grand National Hunt Steeplechase at Cheltenham, over four miles. Although he was short-sighted, he had such good hands that there was perfect sympathy between rider and horse; they seldom made mistakes or came to grief with Arthur in the seat. He was, however, killed in World War I.

****

Almost all Tenby residents were strongly influenced with the prowess of the local stable of Mr Harrison, with each claiming the horses as their very own, especially as the previous two Grand Nationals had been won by their very own Rees brothers. Also in 1923, Lieut-Col Lort Phillips of Lawrenny ran Pencoed in the 1923 Grand National without success, the race being won by Sergeant Murphy, the first American owned winner. He also ran Pencoed again in the Welsh Grand National a few weeks later, again finishing down the field. In 1923, F B Rees was champion jockey with 64 winner, but second in the table with 62 winners was top amateur Capt Bennett, having ridden Sergeant Murphy to victory. Capt Bennett was a qualified veterinary surgeon. However, at Wolverhampton on 27th December, he fell from a horse called Ardeen and was badly kicked by a following horse, smashing his skull. He died seventeen days later without regaining consciousness. It was his untimely death that led to the introduction of the compulsory wearing of *crash helmets. He was twenty-nine years old.

* The crash helmets to be worn were made from cork.

JANUARY 18th 1923
'ECHO OF THE TENBY RACES'
BOOKMAKER'S CLERK CHARGED WITH COAT LIFTING
ALLEGATIONS OF "WELCHING"

At a special meeting of the Tenby Police Court last Friday afternoon, before Messrs Henry Williams (Chairman), Benjamin Beynon, Charles Farley and Bennett Roberts, a bookmaker's clerk, Albert Edward Williams, whose address was given as 59 Western Street, Swansea, was brought up in custody and charged with stealing a gentleman's overcoat, value £4; one pair of kid gloves, value 5s, and a silk pocket handkerchief, value 2s; the property of Mr Eric Foster, a jockey (who rode at the Tenby Races) of Paddingham, Wolverhampton. The theft took place at the Royal Gate House Hotel on the evening of January 11th, and the prisoner was arrested shortly after seven o'clock the same night.

Eric Foster, prosecuting for himself and giving evidence, said he was a jockey, and had been staying at the Royal Gate House Hotel over the Tenby Races. On the previous night (Thursday) he went down to the railway station, and returned to his hotel about seven o'clock. As he went in he hung his overcoat and hat on a rack outside the dining room door, and then went in and sat down to dinner. He sat just inside the dining room door. Whilst he was having dinner he saw the prisoner pass the dining room and afterwards talking to one of the waitresses. Mr Foster then said to a friend with whom he was dining, "Who is that man? Is he after another coat?" When he said this he referred to another coat which had been stolen from the same place the night before. Continuing his evidence, the prosecutor said he saw the same man come back with a coat under his arm, though he did not know then that it was his own coat. Mr Foster then said he went out and proceeded down Frog Street. In front of him he saw the prisoner walking with his coat. He followed him down the street, and when five or ten yards from the prisoner met a policeman with another in private clothes, and told them that the prisoner had stolen his coat from the hotel. The prisoner was then taken back to the Royal Gate House Hotel, when he (prosecutor) identified the coat as his property. The coat, gloves and silk pocket handkerchief (produced) he valued at £4 7s the lot.

When asked if he had any questions to ask the prosecutor, Williams said, "I plead guilty". The clerk said he could do that later on. Meantime he could put any questions he wished to the prosecutor.

Prisoner – When I came back to the hotel did I ask you if there was another coat on top of yours?

Prosecutor – Yes, but you took that coat off the top of mine, and took mine away.

Police Constable James Griffiths (52) stationed at Carew, then gave evidence. He said that about ten minutes past seven on the previous night he was in Upper Frog Street, accompanied by Police Constable Stephenson (44) Penally, when he met the last witness, Eric Foster, who complained of a man having stolen his overcoat from the Royal Gate House Hotel. At the same time he pointed down the street and said, "There's the man standing in the dark." The witness then went up to the man standing in the dark and found he was carrying the overcoat in question over his left arm. He asked him his name, which he gave as Albert Edward Williams, of 59 Western Street, Swansea. He then questioned him as to where he got the coat from and he replied that he was staying at the Royal Gate House Hotel, and was going to dinner, and he took the coat, which was his own property. Police Constables Stephenson, Adams and himself (witness) then brought the prisoner into the

137

hotel, and from enquiries made there ascertained that he was neither staying there nor had booked a bedroom, and that he had no coat. Prisoner was then taken into custody and locked up. When charged he said "There is a mistake in the coat." He was then placed in a cell, and upon being searched a sum of £4 0s 2d was found on him.

In reply to Police Sergeant Warlow, the witness corroborated that they went together to Cambrian House, where the prisoner was lodging with Mrs Rogers, who handed them the coat now produced, stating that it was the prisoner's, but when the latter was shown it he denied that it belonged to him. That morning, however, he admitted that it was his coat, and wished to plead guilty.

Prisoner (to witness) – I told you it was a mistake in the coat?

Witness – Yes.

Prisoner – Did I tell you anything about a man "welching" me of £16 yesterday?

Witness – No.

Prisoner said he pleaded guilty to taking the coat, and wished to be dealt with summarily by that Court. He got "welched" of £16 at the Tenby Races the previous day, the same as other people had. The previous night he got absolutely saddened in drink, and what he had done was really a drunken freak. He expressed his intention of compensating the prosecutor.

Prosecutor – Look at the inconvenience you have put me to! I should have been home by now. I have got a lot of work to do.

Sergeant Warlow informed the Bench that he had communicated with the Swansea police, who had replied that the man who lived at 59 Western Street, was called Tom Williams.

Prisoner – he only lodges there. I will compensate the prosecutor for the trouble I have put him to. It was only a drunken freak.

Sergeant Warlow said the name which the prisoner entered in the register at his lodgings was Bert Warren, Cardiff. The Bench inflicted a fine of £2, which was paid, and the prisoner was released from custody.

1924
10th January

TENBY RACES

Yesterday (Wednesday), the first day of the Tenby Race Meeting, opened with bright sunshine and a clear sky, with the result that a large crowd gathered on the Knightston Course. Splendid sport was witnessed, all the six races being run off in good style. Many of the best steeplechasers in the country had entered; and with this year's champion jockey (Mr F B Rees) his brother (L B Rees) and the brothers Anthony amongst the riders, the conditions were favourable for the sport produced. Things went with remarkable smoothness, this happy state being mainly due to the careful work of the Stewards – Viscount St David's, Lieutenant Colonel Lort Phillips, Captain Hugh Allen, (acting for Sir Henry Webb, Bart., MP), Major Sir David Hughes-Morgan, Mr W H Bankier, and Mr H Dyke Dennis. The judge was Mr Vincent H Thomas; Clerk of the Scales, Mr T H Wilton Pye; Handicapper, Colonel D H Leslie; Clerk of the Course, Alderman G Chiles; Hon Secretary, C W Rees Stokes, who, by the way, has acted in this capacity for nearly half-a-century. The excellence of the racing may be gauged from the fact that only F B Rees brought a winner home, whilst not a favourite came first past the judges box. Amongst the distinguished company present in the enclosures were the Viscountess St Davids, Lady Merthyr, Lord Kylsant, the Earl of Westmorland, the Hon Mrs Basil Mundy, the Hon Anne Lewis, the Hon George Coventry, General Sir Ivor Philipps, Major Sir David Hughes-Morgan and Lady Hughes-Morgan, the Hon William B C Lewis, Brigadier-General Sir Frederick Meyrick, Bart, Major Sir Hugh Thomas, the Mayor of Tenby (Councillor G H Sandercock), Colonel O F Lloyd, Hugh Allen, Brigadier-General C P Triscott, Colonel T Roch, Colonel C Spence Colby, Major J G Moore-Gwynne, Colonel C Norman, Colonel Francis E Trower, Major G Rogers-Turner, Lieutenant-Colonel F Lort Phillips, Colonel Newton Seymour Allen, Major J Loftus Adams, the Hon A Hastings, Colonel T P Jones, Colonel W J Evans, Commander F O Plumber, Mr and Mrs and Guy Bancroft, Major Anthony Stokes, the Hon and Mrs Brooke, Major W Saurin, Captain J Howells, Mr and Mrs George Lort Stokes, Tenby, Mr and Mrs Meyrick Price, Captain A C Lancaster, Mr and Mrs T D S Cunninghame, Mr George Ace, Mr T P Hughes, Mr R H Farley, the Hon Mrs Coventrey, Mrs Newton Allen, Mr Protheroe Beynon, etc, etc.

In the evening, at the Royal Gate House Hotel, there was a convivial gathering of owners, trainers and jockeys. Major Sir D Hughes-Morgan presided and during the evening presented the Beauchamp Cup, won by Sir Henry Webb, MP, with Mr Madcap for the third time. In handing the Cup to the trainer (Mr David Harrison) the chairman said he hoped Sir Henry would present another trophy for competition. Mr David Harrison, acknowledging the Cup, said Sir Henry Webb regretted his inability to be present, but he felt certain he would give another Cup to take the place of that now won.

The following are the details of yesterday's racing:

THE GROVE OPTIONAL SELLING STEEPLE CHASE
50 sovs Winner to be sold for 100 sovs Two miles
Captain J M Kinsgote's, Cage, Mr P Roberts, 1
Mr F Fear's, Ramble, A Yates, 2
Mr Burroughs's, Flying Winkfield, G Wall, 3

THE KNIGHTSTON SELLING HURDLE RACE
50 sovs Winner to be sold for 50 sovs Two miles
Mr D J Power's, Doctor's Call, A Smith, 1
Mr W O Driscoll's, Earn's Glen, Corbett, 2
Mr E Arnold's, Honeysuckle, G Wall, 3

THE BEAUCHAMP CHALLENGE CUP
(presented by Mr L B Beauchamp, M H)
a gold cup, value 50gs, with 40 sov added Two miles
Sir H Webb's, Mr Madcap, F B Rees, 1
Mr W A Bankier's, Glad Joycie, J Anthony, 2
Mr J Holmes's, Barcedo, A Smith, 3

THE LAWRENNY OPEN THREE MILES STEEPLE CHASE
50 sovs Three miles
Lieut-Col F Lort Phillips's, Great Western, Mr D Thomas, 1
Col J H Starkey's, Northbrook, G Calder, 2

THE WROUGHTON NATIONAL HUNT FLAT RACE
40 sovs Two miles
Mr R Read's, Cash Box, Mr R Read, 1
Sir H Webb's, Bubbly, Mr P Dennis, 2
Miss Dyke Dennis's, Bed Rock, Mr V Dennis, 3

THE UNITED COUNTIES' STEEPLE CHASE
30 sovs Two miles
Mr T John's, Jumper, Mr D Steward, 1
Mr T R Morgan's, The Moy II, Mr T Griffith, 2
Mr G H Evans's, Biddy IV, Owner, 3

SECOND DAY'S RACING POSTPONED TILL TOMORROW
Owing to the very unfavourable weather conditions – a thick layer of snow covering the course – today's racing has been postponed until tomorrow (Friday). First Race at half-past one. Racing was abandoned.

REPORTS OF "WELCHING"

The fall of snow on Wednesday night which was as unexpected as it was rare at Tenby, had the effect of holding up the second day of the Race Meeting, the course at Knightston, in its exposed position, being rendered quite unsuitable for racing. As a consequence of this the meeting suffered to some extent, several of the horses entered for Thursday's events leaving for Lingfield and engagements elsewhere; whilst many racegoers, who did not bargain for a set back of twenty-four hours, returned home. Naturally, the attendance on the course on Friday was a comparative sparse one, the cruel conditions of the ground, combined with the bleak and piercing wind and the mud-churned snow, making racing something of an ordeal for all concerned. Even the most ardent and hardened followers of the Turf, found matters almost too trying before the last race was run off. Having regard to the very unfavourable conditions which prevailed, there were very few spills. In connection with this year's meeting there were many complaints about "welching", which appeared more prevalent than usual. There were many defaulters when the time came to pay over the successful backers, and several well-known local people were victimised, in one or two cases for substantial amounts. One correspondent, who has expressed his views on this matter, suggests that the Stewards ought to exercise a more vigilant supervision in the case of bookmakers who apply for "stands", and, if necessary, require a deposit from them before commencing business. If this were done it would very quickly eliminate the undesirables, and afford punters that measure of security which under existing conditions is lacking.

****

Let us see if the fashion has changed over the last thirty years. These are how the ladies dresses are described at the Race-Ball of 1924:

SOME OF THE DRESSES DESCRIBED

MRS DAVIES (Tenby) wore a gown of petunia with lace overskirt to tone and floral girdle.

MRS BIRT (Milford Haven) – a gown of peacock blue satin, with side panels and flounces of black and gold lace.

MRS CREER (Aberystwyth) – gown of black chiffon velvet with jet trimmings and purple flowers at corsage.

MRS SPENCE COLBY – a gown of ivory marocaine handsomely embossed with cape effect at the back.

MRS SEYMOUR ALLEN – gown of mist blue georgette, beautifully beaded silver, all over design.

LADY MERTHYR – gown of delicate blue, with an overdress of moonlight blue sequins, beautifully draped.

MRS BROOKE – a sheath gown of cloth of silver, with side panels of royal blue tulle.

MISS MEYRICK – gown of flesh coloured marocaine with gold lace.

MRS CURTIS – gown of deep blue velvet with side train and diamente shoulder straps.

MRS ROBERTSON – gown of cyclamen marocaine beautifully beaded in silver.

MRS YORKE – gown of black georgette gracefully draped with side train and gold lace at the corsage.

MISS DOWDESWELL – gown of gold tissue and lace with inset bands of gold tissue in overskirt.

MISS COOKE – a boussant gown of blue marocaine with inset bands.

LADY HUGHES MORGAN – gown of ivory, charmeuse with handsome design in silver, cut steel, with side draperies, train of beaded charmeuse and jade, silver head-dress.

MISS IRIS HUGHES MORGAN – a gown of silver mail with front panel effect; silver ribbon at waist and hem.

MRS MOORE GWYNNE – gown of flesh pink marocaine, with beaded floral trimming.

LADY LOVEDEN PRYSE – gown of sweet pea mauve shade, with beautiful diamante sunray embroidery; hip ornaments.

MRS LLOYD – a gown of black marocaine, with artistic lace draperies.

MISS MARJORIE PHILLIPS (Castleton) – gown of black, with alternating stripes of gold, with train of the same material.

MISS LLOYD – gown of blue sequins, with side draperies.

MISS PARKER (Tenby) – gown of blue georgette, with side draperies and ribbons at waist.

MISS DILLWYN – gown of ivory georgette, trimmed with pearls.

MRS EVAN JONES – gown of pale pink georgette, beautifully draped.

MRS SAURIN – gown of flesh pink georgette and a striking overdress of mist grey, silver and gold, with floral waist band.

MISS EILEEN BOWEN (Tenby) – cyclamen georgette, with deep hem of shaded ostrich feathers.

THE HON MRS COVENTRY – scarlet georgette, classically draped, with a sash tied on one side, and huge flowers at the waist.

MISS CUNNINGHAME – a gown of black Chantilly lace with touches of powder blue and silver.

MRS COPELAND (Saundersfoot) – gown of eau de nil and gold, with lace overskirt.

MRS FORBES – gown of deep blue, embroidered with sprays of natural coloured flowers.

MISS FORBES – a bouffant frock of cyclamen satin, with gauged hip line.

MRS GARNET (Pembroke) – gown of midnight blue georgette and gold lace, with side draperies.

MRS HALL (Tenby) – gown of black sequins, with side panels of fuchsia silver shot ribbon.

THE HON ANNE LEWIS – draped gown of flesh pink georgette and exquisite trimmings.

MRS O S LLOYDS (Sunnymead) – draped gown of pale primrose moiré silk.

MRS BRIAN LEWIN – dress of powder blue marocaine with crossed over bodice and diamante trimming.

MRS PRYSE – draped frock of silver grey brocade with fine point lace corsage.

LADY HUGH THOMAS (Milford Haven) – gown of gold tissue with overskirt of gold lace, beautifully draped.

LADY MEYRICK – cross-over gown of flesh pink charmeuse with silver sequin and silver lace corsage with side draperies and hip ornaments, the train being held up by a jewelled shoulder strap.

MRS WILLIAM HOWARD – black charmeuse gown draped with a jewelled hip ornament confining the side drapery.

MRS HUGH ALLEN – gown of black georgette, the skirt handsomely trimmed with jet and having a jewelled hip ornament.

MISS PILKINGTON – gown of ivory charmeuse with border of fur.

MRS LLOYD – gown of silver tissue over which was worn a green lace dress.

MRS JONES WILLIAMS – a gown of flesh pink georgette with silver bead embroidery.

MRS B ROBERTS – gown of silver charmeuse beautifully draped.

MISS WOODHOUSE – Ivory moiré silk gown with cross-over bodice and side train.

THE HON OLWEN PHILLIPS – a boussant frock of ivory moiré silk with silver beaded flowers.

* * * * * * * * * * *

Later in 1924 Ivor Anthony had a very bad fall at Ludlow Chases and through his injuries he was forced into retirement from the saddle.

At Cheltenham, the Gold Cup was run for the first time and was won by Red Splash, trained by F E Withington and ridden by Frederick Brychan Rees. The Gold Cup was intended to replace the National Hunt Chase, which had been run at twenty-five different venues, since it was first run in 1860. In 1889 it was run at Cardiff. However, since 1911 it has settled at Cheltenham. When the Gold Cup was instituted in 1924, it was worth £685 to the winner, whereas the National Hunt Chase at £1285 was the third most valuable race in the calendar.

At this time, Bobby Smith's daughter Violet, was in her mid twenties, and these are a few stories that she told me when I visited her in the 1980's, and early 90's.

Bobby (R W) Smith's daughter Violet Pritchard (nee Smith) was well into her late eighties when she told me how she would earn the odd penny or two as a young lady by collecting bets around the town for Oliver Thomas the bookie, as although they liked to bet, the public could not be seen going to Mr Thomas's to place a bet themselves. "I only carried sixpenny or one shilling bets" Violet said, "mostly if people had heard a whisper from the stables or maybe the Derby or Grand National."

"I could buy a new dress or blouse, if I had a couple of good days," she said. "Some days my father would collect the bets from the lads and the jockeys, only small ones you understand, and he would secretly give them to me to take to Oliver Thomas, saying that I must not tell anyone. I think you're the first one that I've told, after all these years, isn't it amazing," she said.

She also told me that when she was twenty-one that she was allowed to go to the dances in the town, with all the boys sitting on one side of the dance floor and all the girls sitting on the other side. "The boys were ever so shy in those days, but once one or two made a move, the others would generally follow quite quickly. The best dances of the year were always the ones held during the race week in January; because the bookies and their associates were never allowed to the race balls, they were frowned upon by all the owners and trainers. I felt sorry for them really, but they always came to the town dances and they were so much fun, having travelled from all parts of the country and with loads of money in their pockets, the girls had a whale of a time, and some even got into trouble, if you know what I mean? Oh! They were such marvellous dances," she said. Looking at her, I could picture her as a twenty-one year old; she must have been a real stunner.

"Also, one time I had been to the stables to see my father and when I came out I heard these two men talking in the street. It was race week and one man

said my father's name, so I listened, it was real Tenby dialect" she recalls, as one said to the other, "I tell ye bae, Bobby Smith told me 'imself, the 'orse is a good 'un, and *Dickie Rees 'imself rides 'im: That ort to satisfy ye."
* Frederick Brychan (F B was sometimes called Dickie, especially in Tenby.)

"MASTER ROBERT"
WINNER OF THE GRAND NATIONAL, 1924.
Ridden by R. Trudgill.   Trained by the Hon. A. Hastings.
From a picture by T. F. Earl.

Your Bob Trudgill

THE 1924 GRAND NATIONAL OF MASTER ROBERT AND BOB TRUDGILL

Bob Trudgill, who was a great friend of F.B. Rees, rode many times at Tenby Races and his partnership with Master Robert in the 1924 Grand National is a fairytale in itself. Master Robert was bred in Co. Donegal, Ireland, by Mr McKinlay. In a career plagued by navicular and thick-windedness, he also spent some time as a harnessed plough-horse. Originally trained by Algy Anthony on the Curragh he accompanied Troytown in his workouts but was only thought to be moderate. He was later brought to England by Harry Fordham as a potential point-to-pointer, and he won a race at the Hertfordshire point-to-point by the length of the proverbial street. His thick-windedness was still a problem though and he was sold to Lord Airlie and Major Green for Lord Airlie to ride in the Scottish Military Chase at Perth. He accomplished this carrying 13st 13lb, including a remarkable 37lb overweight. He then went to Aubrey Hastings at Wroughton and won some good chases, but he was increasingly troubled by navicular and only constant poulticing enabled him to be trained at all, and despite this he was intermittently lame. Aubrey Hastings entered him for the 1924 Grand National and the ride was offered to Bob Trudgill after Peter Roberts rejected it. Bob was a West Country jockey with iron nerves, would ride anything and consequently had some really terrible falls, including one the day before the Grand National for which he needed extensive stitching to his leg. With his leg heavily bandaged he rode like a demon bringing Master Robert home to a fine victory, but in doing so he burst all the stitches in his leg wound and collapsed upon dismounting. The joint owners gave him £2000 as a gift, and Aubrey Hastings said later "No other jockey but Trudgill would have won on Master Robert". Master Robert was not asked to race again. There is an hotel named after him near Heathrow Airport.

1925
FIRST DAY

TENBY RACES 9th JANUARY 1925
LOCAL SUCCESSES

Interest was purely local at the Wednesday meeting of Tenby Races. Each of the five races was won by a favourite, and only one of them – Irish Prince – started at odds against. F B Rees had two rides and won two races. L B Rees was also successful, which would please all local people, as the Rees's were born in Tenby, which is still their home. D Harrison, the local trainer, saddled three winners.

THE GROVE OPTIONAL SELLING STEEPLE CHASE
65 sovs Two miles
Major D Campbell's, Greenogue, F B Rees, 1
Mr S Ryland's, Sorrel Hill, F Mason, 2
Mrs B Mundy's, Harry Hart, Mr Dennis, 3
Mrs W Allen's, Gondolier, J Dillon
(Winner trained by Westmorland)
Betting – Evens Greenogue, 2 to 1 agst. Harry Hart, 6 to 1 agst. Gondolier,
and 10 to 1 agst. Sorrel Hill
Won by ten lengths; a bad third. Harry Hart fell at the last jump, but was re-mounted and
finished third. Greenogue was bought in for 145 gns.

THE KNIGHTSTON SELLING HURDLE
50 sovs Two miles

146

Lt-Col Lort Phillips's, Irish Prince, Mr D Thomas, 1
Mr J Smyth's, Roman Hackle, J Anthony, 2
Mr Baker's, Orlando Dando, Mr R Trudgill, 3
Mr H D Dennis's, Combination, Mr P Dennis, 4
Mr W Hall's, Glan Alpha, Mr West, 5
(Winner trained by D Harrison, Tenby)
Betting – 6-4 agst. Irish Prince and Roman Hackle, 4 to 1 agst Glen Alpha, 6-1 agst.
Combination, and 10 to 1 agst Orlando Dando. Won by ten lengths; a bad third. Glen
Alpha fell; Combination was pulled up.

THE LLWYNARTHAN CHALLENGE CUP
Value 50 guineas, with 40 sovs added Two miles
Mr J Holmes's, False Report, F B Rees, 1
Miss G Yates's, Smerdis, A Yates, 2
Mr W Bankier's, Marston Moor, J Anthony, 3
Col W Williams's, St Madoc, L Rees, 4
Mr M Lewis's, Clyno, R Trudgill
(Winner trained by D Harrison, Tenby)
Betting – 2 to 1 on False Report, 3 to 1 agst. St Madoc, 6 to 1 agst. Marston Moor, and 10
to 1 each agst. Smerdis and Clyno. Won by five lengths; a head between second and third.
Clyno was pulled up.

THE LAWRENNY OPEN STEEPLE CHASE
60 sovs Three miles
Mr H D Dennis's, Rousham, L Rees, 1
Capt R Stanyforth's, Condor, Owner, 2
Mr V Dennis's, Noble Guard, Owner, 3
(Winner trained by D Harrison, Tenby)
Betting – 6 to 4 on Rousham, 7 to 4 agst. Condor and 10 to 1 agst Noble Guard.
Won by five lengths; a bad third.

THE WROUGHTON NATIONAL HUNT FLAT RACE
40 sovs Two miles
Mr R McAlpine's, White Ronald, Mr Ridley, 1
Mrs W Allden's, Gondolier, Mr D Thomas, 2
Mr J Holmes's, Bubbly*, Mr P Dennis, 3
(Winner trained b Geo. Poole, Lewes)
Betting – 7 to 4 on White Ronald, 7 to 4 agst. Bubbly, and 10 to 1 agst Gondolier.
Won by five lengths; ten lengths between the second and third.
* Bubbly has now been bought by Mr J Holmes.

SECOND DAY
THURSDAY'S MEETING
There was again a large crowd present on Thursday, when some exciting sport was
witnessed.

PARK HOUSE HANDICAP STEEPLE CHASE
£75 Two miles

Mr D Harrison's, Equancourt, D Behan, 1
Mr Smith-Ryland's, Sorrel Hill, F Mason*
Mrs W Allden's, Gondolier, R Trudgill
(Winner trained by D Harrison, Tenby)
Betting – Evens Equancourt, 7 to 4 agst. Gondolier, 6 to 1 Sorrel Hill finished alone:
Gondolier and Sorrel Hill fell.
* F (Tich) Mason was still riding 25 years after he first became Champion Jockey

TOWN HANDICAP STEEPLE CHASE
£60 Three miles
Capt R T Stanyforth's, Condor, Owner, 1
Mrs B Mundy's, Harry Hart, Mr P Dennis, 2
Mrs F A Spencer's, Hopeful, J McDermott, 3
Mr V Dennis's, Guard, R Trudgill, 4
(Winner trained by Woodland, Chalderton)
Betting – 5 to 4 on Condor, 2 to 1 agst. Hopeful, 5 to 1 Harry Hart, 10 to 1 Noble Guard.
Won by a head; two lengths divided second and third.

LICENSED VICTUALLERS' SELLING HANDICAP HURDLE RACE
£50 Two miles
Mrs G M Yates's, Smerdis, A Yates, 1
Mr D H Thomas's, Little Milford, L B Rees, 2
Mr S B Peek's, Colcannon, P Allden, 3
Mrs Barthropp's, Carantuohil, J Anthony
(Winner trained by Yates)
Betting – 6 to 4 agst. Little Milford, 7 to 4 Smerdis, 3 to 1 Carantuohil, 100 to 8
Colcannon. Won by half a length; a bad third. Carantuohil fell.

VICTORY HURDLE RACE
£50 Two miles
Mr V H Jones's, Tretes, A Yates, 1
Lt-Col F Lort Phillips's, Pencoed, Mr D Thomas, 2
Mrs Hobart's, Drinkmore, J Anthony, 3
Mr D D Stewart's, Some Dance, Owner, 4
Mr H D Dennis's, Park House, D Behan, 5
Sir John Grey's, Pretext, L Rees
Mr Mansel-Lewis's, Clyno, R Trudgill
Miss A Paull's, BV, Doyle
Mr S Peek's, Psycho, P Allden
(Winner trained by Yates)
Betting – 2 to 1 agst. Some Dance, 5 to 2 Drinkmore, 4 to 1 Tretes, 6 to 1 BV, 7 to 1
Pretext, 10 to 1 Pencoed, 100 to 8 others. Won by a neck; a head divided second and
third.

UNITED COUNTIES FARMERS AND TRADESMEN'S HURDLE RACE
£26 Two miles

Mr W Evans's, Mill Lad, Tudor Griffiths, 1
Mr T G Phelps's, Sorrel, Mr P Dennis, 2
Mr T John's, Jumper, Mr D Steward, 3
Mr H Gibbon's, Peggy VII, Mr Williams, 4
Mr W James's, Mayflower II, Mr W James, 5
Mr T G Phelps's, Lady C, Mr V Dennis
Mr R Gibby's, Natal Day, Mr G Williams
Mr J Morris's, Causeway II, Mr D Thomas

(Winner trained privately)Betting – 5 to 4 agst. Sorrel, 2 to 1 Mill Lad, 9 to 2 Natal Day, 10 to 1 others.Won by a neck; six lengths divided second and third.

Silvo ridden by F B Rees, winner of the Grand Steeplechase de Paris 1925

1926

The meeting of 1926 was held on January 13th and 14th and the attendance was the largest by far since records began. The big attraction was a match between the country's top two jockeys, F B Rees and George Duller, with Rees being the "king of fencing" and Duller the "Prince of Hurdles".

The GWR put on special rates for rail travel over the two days:

G.W.R.
TENBY RACES
1926
WEDNESDAY & THURSDAY, JAN. 13 & 14

CHEAP TRIPS to TENBY,-Leave Carmarthen 9.40 a.m. (3/10), Sarnau 9.50 (3/2), St. Clears 10.0 (2/8), Haverfordwest 8.20, 9.55 (4/2), Fishguard Harbour 8.15 (5/5), Fishguard and Goodwick 8.19 (5/5), Mathry Road 8.35 (4/10), Clarbeston Road 8.49, 10.7 (3/7), Clynderwen 9.0, 10.18 (2/9), Whitland 9.20, 10.32 (2/-), Narberth 9.31, 10.44 (1/4), Templeton 9.40, 10.54 (1/-), Kilgetty 9.46, 11.0 (8d.), Saundersfoot 9.50, 11.5 (6d), Pembroke Dock 10.49, 11.18, 12.38 (1/3), Lamphey 10.53, 11.22, 1242 (1/-), Manorbier 11.1, 11.32 a.m., 12.50 p.m. (7d.).

TENBY RACES.
JANUARY 13TH & 14TH -1926
RECORD ENTRIES.
Special Race:
DICK REES
V.
GEO. DULLER
IN A MATCH FOR £100.
Two Miles over Hurdles on Horses belonging To Mr. G. C. Poole and Mr. G. N. Bennett.
A Special Motor Track has been laid on to the Course.

F. B. REES

There had been heavy ante-post betting on this match, and the betting was more for the jockey than for the horse, with Rees carrying a substantial amount of local money; but there was something about this race that does not ring true. I have studied it many times and on every occasion the only conclusion that I can come to is that it was a fix of some kind.

GEORGE DULLER.

150

This was one report from the Tenby Observor:

ANIMATED SCENE ON THE COURSE.

REES' SUCCESSES

FAMOUS JOCKEYS IN OPPOSITION.

Tenby Races have never presented so animated a picture as they did on Wednesday of last week, under a sun of remarkable brilliance. But there was a "catch" in that sunshine, for with it there was a wind out of the south-east that searched everywhere with icy fingers. Everybody had to keep briskly on the move to keep the circulation up, and it was this need to keep moving to get warm that gave an air of sprightliness to the biggest crowd that the Tenby Course has ever housed, as it moved in quick vigour about the paddock and course.

It was a sporting crowd, full of the love of steeplechasing, and with that touch of local enthusiasm that produced remarkable ovations for Mr. F. B. Rees, that famous Tenby jockey, as he steered two of the winners past the judges' box. The brilliant sun did not make for the best of racing conditions, but the turf was in excellent condition, and when the fields were representative the racing was keen enough to be exciting, though the "failure" of the "match" arranged between the mounts for Rees and Duller, the two well-known steeplechasers, left an awkward gap in the middle of the programme, and the last two events were spoiled from the spectacular point of view by the fact that, in each case, only two competitors turned out. There is something dreary about a race that is simply a struggle between two animals.

All the well-known lovers of the turf, for a long radius around South Pembrokeshire were to be seen in the paddock during the day, though two figures that are almost inseparable from Tenby were missed, in the persons of Sir David Hughes-Morgan, Bart., and Viscount St. Davids. There was a hearty welcome during the afternoon for the veteran master of the Hounds, Mr. H. Seymour Allen, who braved the cutting wind and took a keen interest in the afternoon's events. Viscountess St. Davids was also an interested spectator, and Lord Kylsant, C.M.G., M.F.H., was also in early attendance.

LLWYNARTHAN CUP WON BY FALSE REPORT

The going was perfect, and, as usual, favourites were to the fore. The local successes of Mr David Harrison, the popular Welsh trainer, F B Rees, and Jack Anthony were loudly acclaimed. Rees landed a useful double when riding Cool Warrior and False Report to victory. The latter's win in the Llwynarthan Cup was the second in succession for this valuable trophy, and incidentally, increased the Welsh jockey's record of victories in this class of event to five. He won the Beauchamp Cup three years in succession on horses belonging to Sir Henry Webb, Bart. On the cup having been thus won outright, Sir Henry Webb very graciously put up the Llwynarthan Challenge Cup under identical conditions. False Report is owned and trained by Mr David Harrison, who now has but to register one more victory to make the trophy his property. Eight animals competed for this year's event, and, in addition to the favourite, Miss G M Yates' Indelible was much fancied. There was also good money for Cocker, and an Irish importation in Larry the Flail.

IRISH PACE-MAKER

The last-named cut out the work at a surprisingly fast pace, and kept it up until reaching the bend for home. Larry was then done with. This left the favourite at the head of affairs, in company with Cocker. Coming from the last hurdle False Report drew away to gain a popular victory by four lengths, with Col. Lort Phillips' Pencoed two lengths away. Indelible gave a disappointing display, running his race in snatches, and could only finish fifth.

The opening event, the Grove Optional Selling Plate, attracted six moderate animals, of which Bodyguard and Rock Meadow were about the best of the bunch. The latter ultimately wound up favourite. The second fence proved too big an obstacle for two of the competitors, Wanderlust and Troublesome, who both came to grief. P. Mullen, the rider of Troublesome, was a little shaken as the result of the spill, but otherwise both riders and horses escaped injury. Going away on the far side the second time round Bodyguard and Rock Meadow were in the lead, but Bodyguard came down at a plain fence, leaving Rock Meadow to go on from Gondolier and John M C. The last-named was pulled up at the next fence, and although Gondolier challenged the favourite after negotiating the last fence Mr D Stewart came away to win comfortably by a length and a half and was well deserved having travelled all the way from Ayr in Scotland.

GONDOLIER'S RECORD

It is interesting to note that Gondolier has to date won twenty-nine races, and victory here would have meant his equalling the record of that popular old 'chaser' Tim. There was some brisk wagering in connection with the Knightston Selling Hurdle, but Mr Dollar's Mr Black, a winner at Leicester, quickly became a warm favourite, George Duller having the mount. The horse was looked upon as a real good thing, but he failed badly. Cleverly ridden by F B Rees, Cool Warrior always had the measure of the favourite, and disposing of a challenge from Minerva in the straight Rees won by half-a-length, with Mr Black two lengths away third.

Only two animals faced the starter for the Lawrenny Three Mile Steeple-chase, namely, Mr W A Bankier's Super Man, the mount of Jack Anthony, and Mask On, who was ridden by his owner, Mr M E Dennis.

A FOREGONE CONCLUSION

Super Man, with the advantage of 18lb in weight, was instantly a very warm favourite, and the odds were never in doubt. The Welsh jockey indulged his rival with the lead until about half a mile from home, when he went to the front to win with comparative ease by four lengths.

The concluding event: the Wroughton National Hunt Flat Race, cut up badly, for only the top weights, Old Times and Charlie Wise, in receipt of 17lb, turned out. Ridden by Mr H Davies, the latter was always superior to his rival, and ultimately won by a distance.

First Day's Results

First Race

THE GROVE OPTIONAL SELLING STEEPLE CHASE
65 sovs Two miles
Mr D Steward's, Rockmeadow, Owner, 1
Mrs S Allden's, Gondolier, P Mullen, 2
Mr C Clarke's, Bodyguard, Burford
Mr W Hall's, Wander Lust, Mr W West
(Winner trained by R Thomson, Ayr)

Betting – 11 to 10 agst. Rockmeadow, 2 to 1 agst. Bodyguard, 8 to 1 each agst. Gondolier and Troublesome, and 10 to 1 agst any other. Won by a length and a half, only two finished. Troublesome, Bodyguard, and Wander Lust fell.

Second Race

THE KNIGHTSTON SELLING HURDLE RACE
50 sovs, winner to be sold for 100 sovs Two miles
Mr P Sheenan's (IRE), Cool Warrior, F B Rees, 1
Mr Heneage's, Miniver, Mr W West, 2
Mr Dollar's, Mister Black, G Duller, 3
Mrs Hanby's, Stream, Mr Thomas, 4
Miss G Yates's, Tosari, A Yates, 5
Mrs W Allden's, Harewick, J Dillon, 6
Mrs M Hyslop's, Kroon Belle, T Wilmot, 7
Mr J Settle's, Fellowship, M Phelan, 8
(Winner trained by Roberts, Kinnersley)

Betting – Evens Mister Black, 4 to 1 agst. Cool Warrior, 5 to 1 agst Kroon Belle 7 to 1 agst Fellowship, and 10 to 1 each agst Miniver and any other. Won by half a length; two lengths between second and third.

Third Race

THE LLWYNARTHAN CHALLENGE CUP
Value 50 guineas, with 40 sovs added Two miles
Mr D Harrison's, False Report, F B Rees, 1
Mr G Whitelaw's, Cocker, T Morgan, 2
Lieut-Col L Phillips's, Pencoed, Mr D Thomas, 3
Mr W Allden's, Our Bill, J Reardon, 4
Mr Henry Dyke Dennis's, Park House, Mr P Dennis, 5
Mr C M Lewis's, Manister Flier, T Gaynor, 6
Mr R Power's, Larry the Flail, F Brookes, 7
Miss G Yates's, Indelible, F Foster, 8
(Winner trained by D Harrison, Tenby)

Betting - 5 to 4 agst. False Report, 2 to 1 agst. Cocker, 5 to 1 agst. Indelible, 8 to 1 agst. Pencoed, and 100 to 8 agst. any other. Won by four lengths; two lengths between second and third.

Fourth Race A MATCH
50 sovs Two miles over hurdles
"Declared void".

Fifth Race

THE LAWRENNY OPEN THREE MILES STEEPLE CHASE
60 sovs Three miles
Mr W Bankier's, Super Man, J Anthony, 1
Capt M Dennis's, Mask-On, Owner
(Winner trained by Hastings, Wroughton)
Betting – 2 to 1 on Super Man. Won by four lengths.

Sixth Race

THE WROUGHTON NATIONAL HUNT FLAT RACE
40 sovs Two miles
Mr G Whitelaw's, Charlie Wise, Mr C Davies, 1
Mr Filmer-Sankey's, Old Times, Major Cavanagh
(Winner trained by Whitelaw, Wantage)
Betting – 5 to 4 on Charlie Wise. Won by a distance.

Second Day's Results

First Race

THE PARK HOUSE HANDICAP STEEPLE CHASE
75 sovs Two miles
Mr E Stanley's, His Luck, J Anthony, 1
Col M Lindsay's, Relay, Mr D Thomas, 2
Mrs S Allden's, Gondolier, J Reardon, 3
Mr G Whitelaw's, Hackdaile, G Green
Mr W Hall's, Wanderlust
Mr W West, Mrs G Harrison's, Equancourt
T Duggan Winner trained by Hastings, Wroughton
Betting – 5 to 4 on His Luck, 4 to 1 each agst Hackdaile and Relay, and 10 to 1 each agst
Gondolier and any other. Won by two lengths; ten lengths between the second and third.

Second Race

THE TOWN HANDICAP STEEPLE CHASE OF 60 SOVS THREE MILES
Mr H Dennis's, Rousham, J Hogan, 1
Mrs N Roberts's, Sir Eyre, Mr D Stewart, 2
Col Lindsay's, P S, Mr D Thomas, 3
Mr C Clarke's, Bodyguard, J Anthony
Winner trained by D Harrison, Tenby
Betting – 2 to 1 on Rousham, 9 to 4 agst Bodyguard, and 10 to 1 agst Sir Eyre and PS.
Won by five lengths; a bad third. Bodyguard ran out.

Third Race

A MATCH 25 sovs aside. * Two miles over hurdles

Mrs W Allden's, Harewick, G Dulle, 1

Miss G Yates's, Tosari, F B Rees, 2

(Winner trained by Allden, Epsom)

Betting – 2 to 1 on Tosari. Won by ten lengths.*Shown here is the result: 25 sovs aside not the £100 match prize originally advertised. Also in the main poster advertising the match it says that the horses belong to Mr G C Poole and Mr G N Bennett but this report states otherwise. I can find no evidence why this is.

Fourth Race

THE LICENSED VICTUALLERS' SELLING HANDICAP HURDLE RACE

50 sovs Two miles

Mr G Parry's, Regicles, H Graves, 1

Mr P Sheehan's(IRE), Cool Warrior, F B Rees, 2

Mr E Merrell's, Gramophone, A Ansell, 3

Mrs M Hyslop's, Toc, T Willmot

Mr R Lawrence's, Suffolk Dumpling, D Davies

Mr B Coulson's, Tretes, A Yates

Mr D Harrison's, Little Milford, T Duggan

Mr V Pollard's, Ulidia, A Smyth

(Winner trained by Bullock, Pattingham)

Betting – 5 to 4 on Regicles, 3 to 1 agst. Cool Warrior, 6 to 1 each agst. Gramophone and any other. Won by five lengths; four lengths between the second and third. Tretes was pulled up.

Fifth Race

THE VICTORY HURDLE RACE

50 sovs Two miles

Mr D Heneage's, Miniver, Mr W West, 1

Mr R Power's, Larry the Flail, J Hogan, 2

Mr W Thomas's, Green Wheat, Mr D Thomas, 3

Mr W Allden's, Our Bill, J Reardon

Maj Barrett's, Troublesome, P Mullen

Mr G Jackson's, Astonishment, M Phelan

Mr C M-Lewis's, Manister Flier, G Gaynor

Mr H D Dennis's, Enfield Lad, Mr P Dennis

Mr G P Rice's, Folly Bird, Owner

Mr D Stewart's, Attempt, Owner

Mrs C Williams's, Brockton, T Duggan

Miss G Yates's, Tosari, F Foster

(Winner trained by Read)

Betting – 2 to 1 each agst. Miniver and Our Bill, 4 to 1 agst. Engield Lad, and 10 to 1 each agst. Larry the Flail, Green Wheat, and any other. Won by eight lengths; four lengths between the second and third. Troublesome, Astonishment, Folly Bird and Tosari, were pulled up.

Sixth Race
THE UNITED COUNTIES FARMERS' & TRADESMEN'S HURDLE RACE
26 sovs Two miles
Mr H Gibbon's, Nishpin, Mr D Williams
Mr T Phelps's, Temptation II, Mr P Dennis
Mr W George's, Camrose Boy, Mr Higgon4
Mr J Morris's, Bridegroom, Mr R Read
(Winner trained privately)
Betting – 2 to 1 on Temptation III., 4 to 1 agst. Bridegroom, 7 to 1 agst. Nishpin, and 10 to 1 agst. Camrose Boy. Won by eight lengths; a bad third.

NB Tosari ran again in the 5th race, The Victory Hurdle Race, being pulled up. Something is not quite right somewhere. The horse obviously not running on its merit, running twice within one hour.

The late Ashley Colley, who was stocktaker and book-keeper at the Royal Gate House, told me some years ago that there was a terrible disturbance and row that evening. There were many of the racing fraternity drinking in the bar including David Harrison and Brychan Rees, and it seemed to me that there was something afoot as there was much shouting and arguing amongst the main group of people that were there. "As it turned out," he said, "Rees and Duller had swapped horses on the toss of a coin, but I was there all the time, and I didn't see any coin being tossed," said Ashley. I later found this report.

AFTER RACE REPORT
On the second day, additional interest was lent to the events by the inclusion of the match between Fred Rees and George Duller. Tenby hoped for a chance to cheer their local hero on to victory in this test between Britain's two "cracks" but they were to be disappointed. Rees was quite ready to oblige but his mount was unwilling. And it was the toss of a coin which meant this. Originally, the Tenby born jockey was to have had the mount on Harewick, the ultimate winner, but discussion having ensued late on Wednesday night, it was decided that the jockeys should toss a coin for their mounts. Rees lost and therefore had to give his mount to Duller, which was Harewick, with Rees riding Tosari. Backers were soon aware of this and had wondered what was happening; however, they now changed their allegiance from Harewick, to Tosari, Rees's new mount, backing it into 2-1 on. Tosari seemed a very tired animal after half the distance had been covered, and it was no surprise to me, and in fact most of the people on the course, when even though Tosari jumped alongside Harewick at the last and when called upon for a final effort by Rees the tank was empty, with Harewick stretching out to win by a very comfortable ten lengths.

I cannot find any information of any enquiry having taken place over this incident, not even with the change of match prize money from the original match, which should have taken place the day before. Why was Tosari also entered in the second race before the match on the first day, and ran in fifth at 10 to 1? Where were the stewards? Something like this cannot go unnoticed. It is impossible! Pockets are being lined somewhere, but where?

THE RACES DESCRIBED

Followers of favourites must have enjoyed a profitable time these last couple of days, for, excluding the match, they scored eight successes in the ten events, which is a record seldom attaining to the sport. On Wednesday local owners, trainers, and jockeys took the majority of the honours, and on Thursday they added to their successes.

To begin with, the Park House Handicap saw Jack Anthony steer His Luck to victory. He had quite an easy ride on an animal which found favour with backers and which carried quite a lot of money, and though he made a slight blunder three fences from home to lose a couple of lengths, he made up the leeway before the last jump was reached, to then come out from Colonel Lindsay's Relay and win by a couple of lengths. Early on Hackdaile led from Relay, His Luck, and Gondolier, and this order was maintained for a mile. At the water Equancourt fell, the rest hereabouts being bunched, with Hackdaile still with a slight lead. In the dip Relay and His Luck went out with a six lengths lead. Three fences from home His Luck blundered, but Anthony, getting his mount quickly balanced again, made up the couple of lengths lost and the pair named took the last fence together. Up the straight Relay could make no impression on the favourite, which came out to win comfortably by two lengths, with Gondolier third ten lengths away. Wanderlust was fourth and Hackdaile last.

Town Handicap Steeplechase – Here again a favourite scored, though it was buying money to bet, for the bookmakers were always asking for odds. Rousham won somewhat easily, to gain a popular victory for Mr Dyke Dennis, of Ruabon, and add to Mr David Harrison's total of winners from his stable. Bodyguard was second in demand and seemed to have a reasonable chance, but for the second successive day disappointed by running out at the fence in the dip. Rousham was left to make the running from Sir Eyre and P.S., and though Sir Eyre once did go in front for a short distance, but Rousham came away and won by five lengths. It is interesting to note that Mr D Steward who rode Sir Eyre for the first time, was unable to claim his amateur allowance of 5lbs having ridden Rockmeadow to victory on the previous day, making it his tenth winner, and so lost his allowance.

Eight started for the Licensed Victuallers' Selling Hurdle, in which Regicles was odds on favourite. Toc cut out the running from Tretes, Ulidia, and Gramophone for half the distance, when Tretes broke down. At this distance Toc was still in the lead, but Regicles coming along with wet sails to the last hurdle, came out to win by five lengths from Cool Warrior, a strongly fancied second favourite, Gramophone being third four lengths away, with Toc fourth, Ulidia fifth, and Little Milford, who was badly tailed off, last.

The Victory Hurdle provided the biggest field of the meeting, twelve runners being under the starter. Here there were joint favourites in Miniver and Old Bill, the former, despite his additional burden, obviously coming into favour through his narrow defeat of half a length by Cool Warrior on the opening day. Confidence reposed in him was not misplaced, for no fewer than eight lengths separated him and Larry the Flail at the finish. The latter cut out the work at the start, but once really settled down Brockton made the running from Larry the Flail, Manister Flier, Enfield Lad, Miniver and Old Bill. A mile from home Larry the Flail again assumed command, but could not hold his position in a fast run finish, Miniver winning comfortably.

The United Counties Farmers' and Tradesmen's Hurdle Race attracted only four runners, but more than ordinary interest was attached to the event by reason of the fact that all the animals are locally owned. The result was a victory for Nishpin which, ridden by the popular Carmarthen rider Mr D D Williams, won easily from the odds-on favourite Temptation III.

* * * * * * * * * * *

Later in 1926, saw the death of Major Sir Basil Mundy, the husband of Hon Mrs Mundy. He had never really recovered from his wounds from the Boer War, and was a sad loss for Mrs Mundy, especially having lost her son in World War I.

TENBY RACE STEWARDS' DINNER

STRIKING TRIBUTE TO THE CHAMPION JOCKEY

On Wednesday evening the Annual Race Stewards' dinner to owners, trainers, and jockeys was held at the "Royal Lion Hotel", when Colonel F Lort Phillips presided. A notable company included: F B Rees, the year's champion over the sticks and his brother L B Rees, both Tenby boys; those other famous Kidwelly jockeys, the brothers Ivor and Jack Anthony, Sir David Hughes-Morgan, Mr H Dyke Dennis, Mr Brychan Rees, Mr E P Barthropp, Sir John Grey, Mr Ben Warner[1], Major D Campbell, Mr Ted Arnold[2], Mr T Wilton Pye, Mr Hancock and Mr Hugh Peel.

In proposing the loyal toast, Lieut-Col. Lort Phillips described the Prince of Wales as the best sportsman in Europe. Sir David Hughes-Morgan, in presenting the Llwynnarthan Cup to Mr D Harrison who had won it for his patron (Mr J Holmes), pointed out that in previous years the famous Tenby trainer had personally won outright the Beauchamp Cup and had followed it this year by winning the new cup presented by Sir Harry Webb for one of his patrons, who, although new to racing was a sportsman of first water. He (Sir David) asked them to drink the health of Mr Holmes, the winner of the Llwynnarthan Cup, and to couple with it the name of a famous trainer, Mr David Harrison. The toast was musically honoured. Mr Harrison, in a happy little speech, responded.

[1] Ben Warner, the Newbury based professional gambler.

[2] Ted Arnold, the Worcester cricketer and big gambler.

FOSTERING THE BEST SPORT

Col. Hughes-Morgan, in proposing the "Stewards of the National Hunt Cup," said that was a much criticised body in some sections of the press, but they were men who honestly did their best for the sport of the country. He thanked the National Hunt Stewards for their interest in the Tenby meeting which was the only steeplechase meeting in the west. At the same time he hoped the National Hunt stewards would encourage the course that was being constructed at Chepstow. The course and stands were being laid out more or less on the lines of those at Newbury. A feature of the stands would be that there was to be a balcony to enable the patrons to see the whole of the paddock without going down to the ring. The jockeys would be able to follow races from their dressing rooms.

Lieut. Col. Lort Phillips, responding, said the National Hunt Stewards did their utmost in as disinterested a way as possible to help sport in every way and to lift it to the highest plane. Mr Dyke Denis proposed "The Trainers", to which Mr Owen Anthony and Mr Percy Alden responded. The Chairman, proposing the toast of "F B Rees", said that nothing that he could say would add lustre to the splendid things the press had said about Dick Rees. Dick Rees not only came from Tenby, but his grandfather had been a tenant of his (the speaker) and would have shared his pride as a Pembrokeshire man in the wonderful performance of their champion jockey. For a steeplechase jockey to beat a flat race jockey with about half the number of mounts the other had was an achievement of which every lover of the sport of kings ought to be proud. The demonstration which marked the honouring of the toast was a striking tribute to the crack jockey.

****

On May 15th 1926, there was a death that was to sadden the whole of the Principality and the hunting and racing fraternity in general. Lieut-Col John Frederick Lort Phillips was probably one of the last horse-back squires. He looked after his many tenant farmers and his large staff of servants in a way that was much appreciated by one and all, and in return they showed him the respect that he greatly deserved. He would love to see them win at Tenby Races whilst backing one of his horses, and I am sure that on many occasions he purposely entered two or more horses in a race so that he would have to "declare to win". This gave a great thrill to his followers, as they all knew that they would be on to a good thing, which they inevitably were.

Lieut-Col J F Lort Phillips
BIG ESTATE OF WELSH SPORTSMAN.
BAN ON CATHOLICS.
HIS THOROUGHBREDS TO BE DISPOSED OF.

Lieut-Col John Frederick Lort Phillips, JP, of Lawrenny, Kilgetty Pembrokeshire, one of the oldest stewards and a former chairman of the National Hunt Committee, a well known breeder of racehorses and steeplechasers, a former high sheriff of Pembrokeshire, a director of the Neyland Steam Trawling and Fishing Company (Limited), who died on May 15th, aged 72 years, left unsettled property of the gross value of £190,945, with net personally £83,623. Probate of his will, dated August 14, 1925, has been granted to his widow the Hon. Maud Lort Phillips, of the same address, Mr George Lort Stokes, solicitor, of Wonford Lodge, Tenby, Col Henry Everard Du Cane Norris, of Pennygarth, Crickhowell, Brecon, and Mr George Moreton Buckston, of Sutton on the Hill, Derbyshire. He left to his wife certain household effects absolutely, and whilst she shall reside at Lawrenny the use of the balance of his effects at Lawrenny (with remainder to devolve as heirlooms) and an annuity of £3,000 free of tax, income-tax, or super-tax, and should she reside elsewhere a similar annuity of £1,000, and on removal a legacy of £500. He left annuities of £50 each to Geraldine and Norah, daughters of his half sister Adelphine Newsom, an annuity of £25 to Mrs Martha Shanklin, annuities of £20 each to his stud groom George Legge and his woodman Tom Bowen, if respectively still in his service. And he directed that these several annuities should cease if 'the intended beneficiary should "be or become a Roman Catholic or bankrupt."

Testator further left:

> £200 each to his former agent, Mr Charles William Rees Stokes, and his solicitor, Mr George Lort Stokes, both of Tenby.
>
> £50 to C Absolam if still in his service.

£25 each similarly to Jimmy Rogers, his cook Mary Jackson, his gardener George Jenkins, and his butler William Edmonson.

£15 similarly to his blacksmith William Thomas.

£10 to each other servant or labourer in his service at his decease if of fifteen years' service.

£25 to Thomas Williams, schoolmaster, of Lawrenny.

£200 each to his nieces Florence and Ethel Gillet, his property Currane, Ooughterard, Co. Galway, and his effect there to his brother Ethelbert Edward Lort Phillips for life, with remainder to his great nephew Richard Ynyr Burgess absolutely.

All other his property he settled upon his great-nephew Patrick Herbert Shoubridge (eldest son of the late Gen. Thomas Herbert Shoubridge) and his heirs in tail, whom failing to his grand-niece Margaret Eldrydd Shoubridge and her heirs similarly, whom failing to his great-nephew.

CHAPTER 7
THE OYSTER MAID SCANDAL AND AN IRISH AFFAIR

The betting coup of 1927 was initially intended to help Ivor Anthony, who had a serious riding accident at Ludlow Chases in 1924. His injuries were serious enough to end his riding career and as there was no insurance for jockeys in those days, David Harrison thought that he would do something to help Ivor Anthony financially, especially as he had been with David Harrison from the opening of the Tenby Stable.

Harrison had to be very careful, he was now a leading trainer and well respected by his contemporaries. His plan would have to be 100% foolproof. He spoke to his closest and oldest friend, George Stokes, and Stokes being heavily in debt through his gambling addiction was in full agreement. In fact, they had discussed it the previous year. At this stage they spoke of it to no-one and were to wait for the opportunity to test the water with some of the other owners and big gamblers.

In the early spring of 1926, Brychan Rees approached David Harrison concerning his workload as the veterinary surgeon. There were now over forty horses in the Tenby Stable and Brychan Rees, the gentleman that he was, told David Harrison that he needed help, and there were also owners that he disliked and did not wish to be associated with, apart from being almost sixty years old. David Harrison agreed and advertised for a vet: there were many applications, but one that he immediately took to was an Irishman named John O'Connor. Harrison knew of him as an amateur jockey riding at Tenby Races some years earlier, yet had not formally met him. He was forty years old and he was single with no family ties. He could start work during the early summer months and this suited both Brychan Rees and David Harrison. His references were excellent from trainers in Southern Ireland, whose names were known to David Harrison. He was employed by the stable and was to rent a cottage in the town. He arrived in May to take up his post and soon became a popular member of the establishment with a typical Irish wit, lots of enthusiasm and above all he was a very good vet and hard worker.

AN IRISH AFFAIR

About a month later it was reported to David Harrison that O'Connor had been seen in hotel bars with a beautiful woman near to his own age; this caused Harrison a little concern as no-one recognised her as being from the locality. David Harrison approached O'Connor as to who this mystery woman was, as he had been given the job under the assumption that he had no family ties. O'Connor said that he did not understand what all the fuss was about and that it was only his sister who had come to visit him for a while, as she had not been to the U.K. before. He had written to her, telling her what a lovely place Tenby was and all about his new job. Harrison was very apologetic, saying that it had come to his notice via members of the staff and he just wanted to know so that he could put the record straight. O'Connor was in no way offended, saying that they were probably jealous, thinking it was his wife or girlfriend and insisted on David Harrison meeting her. They agreed to meet for a drink the following evening in the Royal Gate House Hotel.

The reports that David Harrison had heard were all true, "she was beautiful with long red hair" (Quote A.C.)* and Harrison turned on his charm. He was besotted with her, but asked O'Connor to keep her away from the stables (for what reason I wonder?). David Harrison began to meet O'Connor's sister at very quiet locations, and an affair was inevitable. John O'Connor now became a close friend as he acted as go-between twixt Harrison and his sister, Patricia. O'Connor knew that Harrison was married, yet his sister was single and at thirty years old she was old enough to know what she was doing. Anyway, it made his job much easier if she was sweet with Harrison, and O'Connor was not short in telling his sister so. She was happy with the situation. Where would she find a man of Harrison's wealth and charm willing to bestow his favour upon her? Harrison kept her out of the public eye and their meetings were well organised by O'Connor, and all was kept quiet. It was Harrison's Irish affair that was to later play an important role in the Oyster Maid scandal.

*A.C. Ashley Colley

The 1926 season was now almost under way, and he had big plans for the future of his stable. He arranged a private meeting with George Stokes concerning their previous discussion over money for Ivor Anthony. Anthony was soon to be invited to join the stables of the Hon Aubrey Hastings as assistant trainer, at the Wroughton Stable, and they decided that a coup could be set up with the help of certain owners and close friends. But they had to be certain that those approached would immediately say yes, otherwise word would get out and all would have to be denied. This was why each person was spoken to in the privacy of a solicitor's office with only David Harrison and George Stokes present. Those that were invited, accepted and were sworn to secrecy, except one, Lord Kylsant, who invited Harrison and Stokes to his family home. A private car was sent to Tenby for Stokes and Harrison and they were taken to Lord Kylsant's home. Although they were very good friends, Lord Kylsant could not be seen visiting a solicitor in Tenby, tongues would wag and this was what they did not want. No-one should have cause to be suspicious of anything untoward taking place.

Those that were in the coup were: David Harrison, George Stokes, Lord Kylsant, Ben Warner (professional gambler and owner of Oyster Maid), Edward (Ted) Arnold (heavy gambler and owner of Bubbly), and the very trustworthy landlord of the Sun Inn, Mr Cecil Gwyther. It was all agreed that the coup would take place in January at the Tenby Races, but they would not know which race until the New Year. No more was said.

David Harrison was now travelling all over the U.K. to race meetings where horses from his stable were running, and to a certain degree with a good success rate. However, he had not told anyone that his mistress, Patricia O'Connor had been travelling separately, and meeting him secretly at hotels all over the country. Her brother the vet knew but he was not a threat. Harrison now approached George Stokes with an idea. He told Stokes that his mistress had been meeting him, travelling separately and staying with him in hotels, and no-one knew or suspected anything. Harrison suggested renting a house in Manchester for six months under a false name, the house was to have an upmarket address and a telephone line. This could then lead to opening a bank account in Manchester, with a High Street Bank, and also would give credibility as to opening accounts with top bookmakers. Stokes thought the idea to be excellent, but what about the woman? They had said that they all agreed no-one else was to know, but Harrison said he trusted her, and that she was a good Catholic. Stokes went mad shouting at Harrison, saying that he only had one thing on his mind, and it wasn't the betting coup! They argued intensely and then they cooled down. George Stokes then said that if she was a good Catholic she should go to the R.C. priest and be sworn to secrecy in front of them both. If this was done then he would agree and no-one else should know. The event took place, and they went ahead with their plan. George Stokes arranged a marriage certificate for Mr & Mrs Deer, backdated some five years, and along with a receipt of payment in advance rental for a house in Manchester. They opened a joint bank account, then with these papers accounts were opened with large bookmakers who would take telephone and telegram bets in the name of Mr Deer at the Manchester address and phone number. Harrison made sure his account with the bank and his bookmaker were always well in credit, betting most days, some winners but mostly always big losers. All this aroused no suspicion at all. Even the electric, heating, phone and council rate bills were paid in advance. Everything was organised to precision.

Harrison now arranged with Grace that he should take her to London to go shopping for three of four days. Leaving the stables with Bobby Smith

165

was no problem; he was more than capable of running the establishment, as he had for years anyway. There is no doubt that Harrison was in love with Grace, and she in love with him. He treated her like a queen and she was not one for complaining anyway; they would usually go shopping about this time of year for a new dress for her to wear at the Race Ball in January; but there was a special reason for going to London. Harrison was a big gambler and when he bet it was usually on the course and he would take a board price. He now wanted to see how the working man in a place like London would bet. Grace went about her shopping while he checked out the gambling dens. He visited a lot of pubs and bars and soon found out that the majority of the men gambled via the clock-bag system. He put this into practice by ensuring himself a number of winners (by making a few phone calls) with different street runners in different areas, returning the next day to collect his winnings. No questions were asked, apart from giving the correct nom-de-plume. He was also told of the factories and large work places where the bags were locked at 2pm. This was the answer, this was the ideal way to bet, this was his plan. On returning to Tenby he met with George Stokes and explained what he had done; as Stokes only backed with bookmakers on account, he was surprised yet excited at what he had heard.

It was early December and George Stokes arranged for all six of them in the coup to meet at a Hotel that was unknown to any of them, a long way from Tenby. Some had met for the first time, and in some cases, the last time in person. The one common denominator amongst them all was that they would all be present on the racecourse at Tenby when the coup was pulled off, and none of them were to back the horse in question that day on the course themselves. Someone else would be nominated to do this. They would not know the name of the horse until a few days before the meeting.

What they had to do now was to arrange between them which areas each onc would cover. They would also need half a dozen men each that they could trust with their own money. This was the problem of the individual involved, as it was their own money that they were staking. It was not a pool of money to be staked and it was not to be a pool of money that would be divided equally after the coup. What was agreed was that a reasonable percentage was to be given to Mr George Stokes, so that he could make a charitable payment to Ivor Anthony on behalf of the Tenby Stable. Ivor Anthony was to be no wiser than that this was a one-off payment collected from owners and jockeys for his allegiance and long service to the Stable at Tenby. They were all told by Harrison of the clock-bag system (of which some knew anyway) that should be used by placing the bets before 2 o'clock. The earlier this was done the better, because the clock-bags were not collected until just after 2pm and this could then be forgotten about, as these bets could not be laid off as the bags were not opened until that evening. Concentration could then be aimed at sending telegrams to their account bookmakers. The telegrams were to be sent ten minutes before the horse was due to run, giving the bookmakers very little time to lay the bets off and with the telegrams arriving on time there would be no limit to the amount staked. Also, private telephone account bets were to be left as late as possible. They could also give £500 each, no more, to a personal friend for a last minute bet on the course. These six men with the £500 each were to be in the secretary's office to wait for a last minute call to get the money on with different course bookies; this money they would keep until they were contacted by their mutual friend the next day.

The plan was perfect. They were to pull off a 9-4, 2-1 or perhaps even money coup. There would be no suspicion as the money was to be spread all over the country and at this price it would probably go unnoticed, apart from the course bet, which would not be unusual as the horse would be the likely favourite at this late stage anyway, and the bookmakers could easily lay that amount off in seconds further along the rails. They were told that they would have to bet big money, well spread and if they all followed the plan in their own way they would at least double their money. The horse would be guaranteed to win, the owners and jockeys would be well chosen, as would the race itself. This was all down to David Harrison to organise. They now only had to agree upon which areas of the U.K. they would each control.

1   Lord Kylsant would choose London, having an address there and being an M.P. he would be above suspicion by his visits to the capital in order to make his arrangements.

2   Ben Warner already had a reputation of being a professional gambler and would bet within his own area of Newbury and parts of London that he knew, or generally use his usual bookmakers or gambling partners.

3   Edward Arnold, who was also a cricketer for Worcester and England, would concentrate on Worcester, Birmingham and Leicester areas.

4   Mr Gwyther, the landlord of the Sun Inn was from Cardiff and would also cover Swansea and the valleys.

5   George Stokes had very good friends countrywide. Due to his profession and his money his bets would be well spread.

6   David Harrison would cover Manchester.

That was all they had to know for the time being. All they had to do was wait for the name of the horse and the time it was to run at Tenby. They would be told in plenty of time and it was now up to each individual to organise his own event. If there was a leak, Harrison would call the whole thing off. This was serious business and his future and reputation as a good trainer were at stake.

Patricia O'Connor went home to Ireland for Xmas to stay with her parents and family. When she returned to stay with her brother in Tenby early in the New Year, she met up with David Harrison for an evening to discuss what they had planned previously; she was to talk to her father in private, to organise six men who her father could swear to secrecy, to cover the Manchester bets. She told him that her father was to come himself, and those men that he brought with him would not breathe a word of it. Harrison had trusted her to her word so far and she was in love with him. He agreed, on one condition, which was that they would not know the name of the horse until the morning of the race. Her father agreed, and they were to stay with Patricia at the Manchester address, two days before the race, when Harrison would come to Manchester to meet them. He told them that Patricia was in charge, she had the money and that she knew all the moves and what time to make them. They would be well paid as long as they followed his orders. Under no circumstances were they to visit pubs and get drunk. They were here to do a job, and they could go back to Ireland well paid for keeping quiet and doing what Patricia told them.

The race was to be the 2pm on Thursday, January 13th 1927:

The Licensed Victuallers' Selling Handicap Hurdle Race

'50 sovereigns'. Winner to be sold for '100 sovereigns'.

Over Two miles.

The horse that was going to win was Oyster Maid, owned by well-known professional gambler and racecourse character Ben Warner and ridden by Billy Stott and trained by David Harrison. Billy Stott was to be the champion jockey in 1927 and was to remain so for the next five years. The favourite was Ted Arnold's 'Bubbly' ridden by F B Rees and trained by David Harrison. The other horse trained by David Harrison was Fairy Light, which was also owned by him, and ridden by one of his stable jockeys, Tommy Duggan. Fairy Light was the horse that did all the damage physically and it certainly had the right man in the seat. Tommy Duggan rode all David Harrison's rogue horses, or as some said, "his not so good 'uns". If the money was right Tommy Duggan would see to it. Fairy Light was renowned for lashing out with his hind legs and just before the off Paddy Milestone was very badly kicked and later needed veterinary surgery. It also disrupted the start. Tommy Duggan and Fairy Light were there to ride out the jockeys and horses that were not in on the coup. This was to be done in the blind spot, before coming up the hill for home.

However, on the day of the race everything had so far gone to plan. The starter was George Phelps (Dick Francis's great-uncle) and there was a very large crowd with good entries. There was a dampness in the air, and nearing the start of the first race a sea-fog began to come in from the south-west, but did not hinder the racing. However, at about twenty minutes to two a snow storm started to blow up out of nowhere. This was soon followed by a howling wind and sleet and rain. People ran for the cover of the stand and the sheltered area of the paddock, in fact anywhere they could find shelter. The horses had gone to start and those in the coup knew that their bets were safely placed. The nearest telephone was at Brynhir Mansion, about three quarters of a mile away, three hundred feet above sea level as was the grandstand, and on a normal day the tic-tac men at the balcony of Brynhir could easily send semaphore to the men on the grandstand as the bets were telephoned in to keep the bookies informed as to any movement of money on a certain horse. But the telephone was red hot at Brynhir with bookies having received late telegrams and account bets on Oyster Maid, and of course the bookies had no idea of what was about to happen.

My grandfather was a steward on the course that day as usual, and he was at the gate with a police sergeant from Haverfordwest. This was to stop anyone coming in ten minutes before or after the race, as they would have to cross the course to get to the enclosure and it was a racecourse rule that this was not allowed. A man on a motorbike raced up to the gates, leaping off it and shouting at the police sergeant that he had come from Brynhir and had to get to the bookies with vital information, shouting the word Oyster Maid over and over again. The policeman, having no idea what was going on, handcuffed the man to the gates until the race was over, "for his own safety", he said, telling the man to keep quiet! It was about three minutes to three and the six men with £500 each in their pockets to back Oyster Maid were in the secretary's office. Ashley Colley was the treasurer that day and he told me, "I was in the office with George Stokes the secretary, and these men had been standing in there for about ten minutes. George Stokes didn't say anything so I took no notice, I just thought that they were sheltering from the storm and I couldn't blame them for that. Anyway, it was nothing to do with me; when all of a sudden this man rushed in, and I recognised him as Lord Kylsant's chauffeur, he just said, "The bet is off, his Lordship says do not bet, the bet is off". With that they left and George Stokes got up and said "I'm going to watch the race Ashley, will you hold the fort?" I told him that I wasn't going out in that weather anyway; and when he came back he got a bottle of scotch out of the drawer in his desk along with a few glasses, and said, "God, it's cold out there, have a drink Ashley! Have a drink!" His mood had suddenly gone from one of silence to that of 'the cat that got the cream', and it wasn't until that evening that I realised what had happened, and during the weeks that followed it was the talk of the whole racing world."

With Oyster Maid at 100/6 at the off, they were actually three minutes late starting at 2-03, so had that man got past the policeman it would have been another story. Also, if those six men had put their £500 each on, it would have changed things dramatically, but it was that last minute move by Lord Kylsant to call off the bet that saw Oyster Maid win at 100/6, with Bubbly second at 5-2 on, and Orange Plume third at 6-1. Orange Plume was in fact trained by Ted Gwilt, who was later to train some of Ben Warner's horses in the 1930's.

The jockeys involved in the coup were paid £500 each, and were told that the race was fixed to raise money for Ivor Anthony, which was quite true. There is another fact which somewhat sickens and distresses me and that is that Bubbly was walked to the course that day by one of the stable lads and was only shod one hour before the race by Henry Nash in New Hedges village, which was about 300 yards from the course, and the lad told Henry Nash that Harrison had said to 'stick one in the frog'* or he would take his business elsewhere, leaving Henry Nash no option. Bubbly was then walked the rest of the way to the course along the grass verge, and the shoes were taken off immediately after the race by David Harrison, as this would stop any further swelling (This fact is to be noted for a later date).
* The sensitive frog is the very soft inner part of the hoof, and it would literally be like a human running with a thorn in their foot, probably worse.

The bookies had been stuffed, there was nothing they could do but pay up. Oyster Maid won by 5 lengths, with two lengths between second and third. I have tried many times to work out an estimated sum of how much was won and each time I arrive at an amount, through various permutations, it begs belief. The main fact is that they were betting big money for an even money coup and some of those in the coup would have been able to afford more than others.

Ashley Colley was an accountant/ bookkeeper/ stocktaker at the time, and had many businesses on his books, mostly licensed premises. One of which was the Sun Inn, and he told me that Mr Gwyther alone won £50,000. Mr Gwyther would have been the one person with the least amount of money to bet with; so £3000 on a 100/6 would bring exactly £50,000. The others would have backed about £10,000 each to win £10,000 at evens. But £10,000 at $16^2/_3 - 1$ works out at £166,000 approximately. Now multiply this by five, and the amount is astronomical especially for 1927, £830,000 and Mr Gwyther's

£50,000 = £880,000. Even if Harrison, Stokes and Ted Arnold did not put this amount on, then Lord Kylsant and Ben Warner would certainly have, if not more, especially Ben Warner, who was forever a thorn in the flesh of any bookmaker.

There is yet another twist in the tail, and that is there is no newspaper report of that day locally that exists or has existed during my research, which has covered the last twenty plus years. There is not even a paper in the National Library of Wales in Aberystwyth or Cardiff Library. The only reports in Wales were in the Western Mail.

Reports are shown by kind permission of The Western Mail & Echo Ltd.
    Wednesday 12th January – Race Report Western Mail.
    The brothers Rees rode the first two winners today at Tenby for David Harrison's local stable, which was the extent of that trainer's successes. He may supplement the number of winners tomorrow. Mr Harry Brown had no difficulty in winning the Challenge Cup for Lord Londesborough on his versatile performer Dudley. The last two races were won by horses belonging to Lady Lindsay, which had made the long journey from Fife, in Scotland. Capt. Fielden was the successful jockey on each occasion, and in the case of his win on Always Ready that was the only instance of failure on the part of an odds on favourite. The one to break the sequence was Hornet's Pride, ridden

by Bob Gordon. The "Star" selection for the meeting is 'Bubbly' tomorrow, and the "Star" Double, is 'Bubbly' and 'Amorite'.

First day, first race.

1-30 LAWRENNY STEEPLE CHASE
60 sovs Three miles
Mr D Harrison's, Harry Hart, Aged 11st 13lb, L B Rees, 6-4 on, 1
Capt H Holt's, Fairy Priestess, Aged 10st, J Gorst 100/8, 2
Mr J Morris's, Causeway II, Aged 10st, Mr D Steward 100/8, 3
Winner trained by D Harrison, Tenby. Won by 8 lengths.

2-05 KNIGHTSTON SELLING HURDLE
50 sovs Two miles
Mr C Williams's, False Report, Aged 11st 9lb, F B Rees, 6-4 on, 1
Mrs Barthropp's, Bachelor's Secret, Aged 10st 11lb, Mr Sutton, 4-1, 2
Lt Col S Green's, Clean Report, 5 y.o.11st 4lb, D Williams, 100/8, 3
Winner trained by D Harrison, Tenby. Won by 5 lengths.

2-40 THE LLWYNARTHAN CHALLENGE CUP
Two miles Value 50 guineas with 50 sovs added
Lord Londesborough's, Dudley, Aged, 11st 2lb, Mr H Brown, 3-1 on, 1
Mrs N Roberts's, Marmot, 5 y.o., 10st 5 lb, J Middleton, 10-1, 2
Mr R de Reuter's, Killucan, Aged, 10st 11lb, W Stott, 100/7, 3
Winner trained by H A Brow, Atherstone. Won by 3 lengths.

3-15 THE GROVE OPTIONAL SELLING HURDLE
95 sovs Two miles
Lady Lindsay's, Always Ready, Aged, 11st 10lb, Capt Fielden 9-2, 1
Mr D Stewart's, Attempt, 6y.o., 11st, Owner, 2
Lord Allendale's, Hornet's Pride, Aged, 11st 10lb, R Gordon 2-1 on, 3
Winner trained privately at Fife. Won by 8 lengths.

3-45 THE WROUGHTON NATIONAL HUNT FLAT RACE
50 sovs Two miles
Lady Lindsay's, Dunzar, Aged, 11st 10lb, Capt Fielden 7-4on, 1
Mr C Williams's, Ganzey, Aged, 11st, Owner 4-1, 2
Major S Montefiore's, Voice Control, Aged, 11st, Major Cavenagh 10-1, 3
Winner trained privately at Fife. Won by 6 lengths.

Second Day

Attendance excellent. In attendance were:

Sir David Hughes-Morgan, Bart and Lady Hughes-Morgan, Mr and Mrs Hughes-Morgan, Mr Jim Hughes-Morgan, Capt and Mrs Brian Lowin, Mr Cyril Brickhill (Eastbourne), Mr and Mrs Haddon Howard, Mr and Mrs C C Llewellyn Williams (Llanrumney Hall) Lord and Lady Kylsant. Capt and Mrs N Seymour Allen, Capt Hugh Allen, Miss Vera Curzon, Mrs Roger Lloyd, Miss de Burge, Mr and Mrs G Lort* Stokes, Miss E Herlot, Mr H A Brown, Mr and Mrs Nax Harthropp. The Hon Miss Coventry, the Hon George Coventry, Capt F Howell, M F H, Capt B A M Hall, Mr Lithgow, the Hon Anne Lewis, Col M J Evans, D S O, Mrs Evans, Miss Edmunds, Col W J Holmes, D S O, Mahor C S Hamilton, Capt and Mrs Harold Johnson, Capt G W Burdon, Lieut Thatcher, Lieut K G Richmond, Lieut Drury, Lieut Hewatt. Mr and Mrs H Dyke Dennis, Mrs George Ace, Capt Graham Ace, Mrs Graham Ace, Miss Wing, Col and Mrs Jennings (Gellideg), Col Rogers, Miss Rogers. General Sir Frederick Meyrick, Bart, Col and Mrs Delme Davies-Evans, Baron de Rutzon, Mr Hoskyns, Mr David Evans, Miss Atkinson Clark, Mr Banfield, Mr Cattley, Mr W G Thomas, Mr and Mrs H M Taylor, Mrs Murphy, Miss Harvey Bathurst, Capt and Mrs George Pryse, Mr and Mrs Phelps. Capt and Mrs Travers, Capt A J C Pollock, Capt Goldrey Grey, Capt and Mrs Eaton Travers, Spencer Lewis, Miss Bowen Summers, Capt George C Rees Mr Oliver Anthony, Miss Nesta Lindsay, Col Morgan Lindsay. Mr and Mrs David Harrison, Capt and Mrs Collins, Major Morgan Jones, Capt Rogers, Mrs Armstrong, Mr and Mrs W H Roche, Mr W F Rees, Mr and Miss Miles, Mr Protheroe Beynon, Mr Oakshott, Mrs Ashton (Wellston Court). Major Latham (Springfield), Mr T P Hughes, Mr Percy Howells, Miss Evelyn Lewes, Mr Archibald Taylor, Miss Balfour, Mr Julian Spicer, Mr and Mrs R H Farley (Tenby), Mr and Mrs Hodges, Miss Thompson (Wofferton Grange), Mrs Stella Moore, and Mr John Phillips.

* George Stoke's father (C.W.R. Stokes) was the land agent for Mr J F Lort Phillips, and as Mr Lort Phillips was George's god-father he was given the name 'Lort' at birth. He was born in 1875, and given a private baptism as he was not expected to survive.

Second day Thursday January 13th

1-20 VICTORY HURDLE RACE
50 sovs Two miles
Mrs N Roberts's, Marmot, 5y.o., 11st 4lb, Mr P Dennis 20-1, 1
Miss N Paull's, Kilgubbin, Aged , 10st 13lb, J Delaney 5-4, 2
Mrs D Harrison's, Equancourt, Aged, 10st, T Duggan 6-1, 3
Winner trained by Mitchell, South Yelverton
Won by 3 lengths

2 pm off 2-03 LICENSED VICTUALLERS' SELLING HANDICAP HURDLE

50 sovs Two miles. Winner to be sold for 100 sovs

Mr Ben Warner's, Oyster Maid, 4 y.o., 10st 7lb, W Stott, 100/6, 1

Mr E Arnold's, Bubbly, 12 y.o., 10st 13lb, F B Rees, 2-5, 2

Mr H Dennis's, Orange Plume, 5 y.o., 10st 7lb, Mr P Dennis, 6-1, 3

Mr D Harrison's*, Fairy Light, 4 y.o., 10st 5lb, T Duggan, 4

Mr W Robinson's, Cheekily, 5 y.o., 11st 2lb, Mr R Gubbins, 8-1, 5

Sir John Grey's, Any Excuse, Aged, 10st 13lb, W Mahoney, 100/6, 6

Miss G Yates's, Paddy Milestone, Aged, 10st, J Hamey, 6-1, 7

Mr C Turpin's, Baalbek, Aged, 11st 2lb, J Reardon, 10-1, 8

Winner trained by D Harrison, Tenby

Won by 5 lengths and two lengths

* With the position of 4th place, the reader can see how well Tommy Duggan had done his job, especially if you read the positioning of Fairy Light in the following report.

2-30

Mr D Harrison's, Harry Hart, Aged 12st, L B Rees, Evens, 1

Mr D Thomas's, Miss Balscadde, Aged, 11st 9lb, Owner 6-4, 2

Mr W Greenwood's Pumpkin Pie, Aged, 10st, W Stot, 100/8, 3

Winner trained by D Harrison, Tenby.

Won by 8 lengths

3-10 THE UNITED COUNTIES FARMERS AND TRADESMEN'S HURDLE RACE

50 sovs: for horses bred by farmers in the counties of Pembroke, Carmarthen or Cardigan, bona fide the property on and since Nov 1st 1926, of farmers or tradesmen in the said counties that have not won a race under N.H. Rules.

Run over two miles.

Mr J Morris's, Mayboy III, Aged, 12st 7lb, Mr C Evans, 6-4, 1

Mr G Williams's, Skipper V, Aged, 12st 7l, Mr J Ward, 5-1, 2

Mr J Richard's, Eastbourne Lad, 5 y.o., 11st 13lb, Mr A Griffiths, 5-1, 3

Winner trained privately

It is perhaps ironic that the name Fairy Light should appear on this day, especially in the coup, because if you refer to the 1901 meeting, Fairy Light was Mr Deer's (late Mr Harrison's) first winner for the Tenby Stable. It is also the first time since 1909 that the name Mr Deer is mentioned, this time in the opening of bookmaker and bank accounts in Manchester, for the purpose of the coup.

The night before the race, Miss Hopkins, who was the head receptionist (and a girlfriend of one of the local jockeys) was asked by a gentleman who was signing the hotel register if she had any tips for tomorrow. She was heard to whisper, "Oyster Maid won't get beaten", by one of the stable lads who informed Harrison. Miss Hopkins was told in no uncertain terms that if she ever repeated what she had just said, she would lose her job forthwith. (Quote V.P.)*

*V.P. Violet Pritchard.

A photograph taken shortly before the Oyster Maid race

Both the following reports are taken from the Western Mail:

"A Great Surprise at Tenby"

Three of the eight runners in the Licensed Victuallers' Selling Hurdle came from David Harrison's Tenby Stable, and the public quickly fixed upon 'Bubbly' as the 'good thing'. He soon became an odds on favourite, but some of the shrewd judges preferred his stable companion Oyster Maid and took 10-1 on her chance. (Whoever they were, they could not have laid much money, as the price went out to 100/6.) After an "interesting" race, Oyster Maid scored from Bubbly. Any Excuse made the running from Fairy Light, Oyster Maid and Paddy Milestone, with Orange Plume last. Later, Bubbly and Oyster Maid went to the front and were together entering the straight. At the final flight however, Oyster Maid drew away to win by five lengths.

"Hot Favourite beaten by Stable Companion"

The racing at Tenby today furnished one great surprise in the defeat of Bubbly, who started 5-2 on in the Licensed Victuallers' Hurdle. The surprise was all the more confounding to the majority of people in as much as Bubbly was beaten by a stable companion Oyster Maid, whose S.P. was 100/6 against. Paddy Milestone was very badly kicked and it may be some time before he will be able to race again.

****

David Harrison contacted Patricia O'Connor in Manchester and after she told him that all had gone to plan, he told her to tell her father to stay until the clock-bag money was all collected and banked in Manchester. He said that he would contact all the bookmakers Mr Deer had opened accounts with and that settlement cheques were to be sent to the Manchester address and as soon as she received these, they were also to be banked. He said that he would come to Manchester in a few week's time, as he had horses running there and would stay for a few days to discuss the future.

Things in Tenby were fairly hot as to rumours of how much had been won, and Mr Gwyther forked out a considerable amount of money on a top of the range coach built "Talbot 18/55", which cost well over £1,000, from George Ace (Tenby car sales), whereas an "Austin 7" was £120. This fuelled the rumours, but there was no connection proven with the stable or with Harrison, as Mr Gwyther was a heavy gambler anyway and it was not long before Mr Gwyther sold his properties in Tenby, as he drove off into the sunset, as it were.

Harrison had now gone to Manchester where he stayed for a few days. He closed the bookmaker accounts and withdrew all the money from the bank, also closing that account. He then returned the keys of the rented property, as Mr Deer disappeared for the final time. Patricia went back to Ireland with a considerable amount of money. She had kept her word, and was to continue to visit her brother in Tenby and obviously to see David Harrison. Her absence had not been noticed at all in Tenby, with everyone thinking that she was at home in Ireland. She continued to visit Tenby on a regular basis for some time to come.

George Lort Stokes had paid off his gambling debts and had more money than he wanted. Somehow his father Mr C W R Stokes had heard a whisper or had noticed a change in his son's behaviour. George Stokes was an upstanding citizen in the town, he had been the Town Clerk for many years, and was trusted and respected by all and sundry. Stokes & Stokes were a big solicitors firm in the town, and George Stokes had a guilt complex about this coup. He had done nothing illegal, yet he felt guilty and it was as if people were pointing a finger at him; but it was all in his imagination. He took it

Particulars.

THE FREEHOLD PREMISES No. 28, HIGH STREET, TENBY

having frontages to High Street, Sun Lane and Crackwell Street, inter-communicating and comprising
THE FULLY LICENSED

SUN INN

containing—Bar, with Bottle and Jug Department, partitioned off ; Smoke Room ; Urinal ; and Cellar in basement.

THE SUN STORES having a Wine and Spirit Merchant's Licence, and consisting of modern shop and office.

Access through a passage from Crackwell Street is obtained to the upper portion.

First Floor—Lounge ; Dining Room ; Kitchen.

Second Floor—Three Bedrooms ; Bathroom ; W.C.

The whole premises are occupied by Mr. Cecil Gwyther, and will be sold with possession on completion.

The position for trading is perhaps the best in Tenby, and with its street frontages renders the property a very attractive site for other businesses than those carried on for so many years past.

LOT 2.

COMMODIOUS

FREEHOLD BOTTLING STORES

in UPPER FROG STREET, TENBY,

stone built and slated with good Yard backing on to the Town Wall, through which there is an access to South Parade.

The premises contain Three Rooms with Lofts and W.C.

Occupied by Mr. Cecil Gwyther, Wine and Spirit Merchant.

The premises are conveniently placed to Lot 1 and will be sold with possession on completion.

very badly and went into a deep depression and on November 22nd 1927 he took his own life, at the age of 52. This broke his father's heart and he died on January 5th 1929. There were no children and the Stokes & Stokes business folded. Between them they had been racecourse secretaries for well over fifty years. George Lort Stokes' obituary read 'he died suddenly from a short illness'.

David Harrison then took over as secretary; it might not be very unusual for the local race horse trainer to take on this responsibility, but Harrison may have had alternative motives for becoming the racecourse secretary. He may have been aware that George Stokes, his good friend, chose to omit things from the minutes of meetings, or that things could be added, as it was only the secretary that ever used or saw these minute ledgers. Harrison himself may have foreseen the benefits of being the minute taker. But this is purely speculation. However, the situation smacks of something mysterious, if not mischievous, as Harrison had never been on the committee before, he took over from one of his closest friends and a co-conspirator, and all of the records were destroyed (of which you will read later).

Nothing has ever been mentioned to me at all of Brychan Rees, Bobby Smith or John O'Connor having any knowledge of the betting coup. I cannot comment on this, other than to say I have found no evidence of it. Violet Pritchard was adamant that her father knew nothing of it, and even if he had he would have had nothing to do with it. I would say that it was highly likely that they knew of it, and that it was a small coup to help Ivor Anthony financially, but they were probably unaware of its scale. Both Brychan Rees and Bobby Smith were with David Harrison from day one, and they were also there to the very end, which is quite an allegiance.

N.B. The starting price coup was finally killed off in the nineteen thirties when Tattersall's Committee, who are the final authority in adjudicating on betting disputes, ruled that where it could be established that a batch of telegrams backing the same horse had been dispatched, a limit of 4-1 against the horse could be imposed.

CHAPTER 8
THE BIG GAMBLERS

BEN WARNER

Ben's father owned the bakery business in Woolhampton, near Newbury, and by the time Ben reached his mid teens he realised that as the seventh son there wasn't going to be a future for him in the bakery business, so he started working for a bookmaker in Newbury, and shortly afterwards he set up on his own. By the mid-twenties he was buying horses, and was soon to become a well-known professional gambler. The best known of Ben Warner's horses were Residue and Free Fare, trained by Owen Anthony and Ted Gwilt, respectively.

He went racing most days of the week, and his wife Margaret was told by many of Ben's friends that she should not worry when Ben was staying away overnight, because the only thing that would be in bed with him was his form book. He looked upon betting as a science and there was nothing that he relished more than to be faced with a huge field in a handicap, like the Lincoln or the Cesarewitch, and to sit down and work out every possible eventuality that could in any way have an effect on the result of the race. As his success grew, he thought that it was time for him to have a car and a chauffeur. His first chauffeur was called James Wells, whose wife Mary was the cook at his home, Rotherwood.

Many well-known racing figures would call in to visit, especially at the Newbury meeting, such as Reg and Bruce Hobbs, Sam and Millie Wragg, the Smythes, the Dicks, Tommy Westhead and Archie Hyams. Gerald and Lilian Dainty joined the Rotherwood staff in 1937. Gerald had a head start in his interview with Ben, having worked previously for Ted Gwilt and Harry Cottrill in Lambourn, so he spoke the right language. He became chauffeur and his wife worked in the house. All he had to do now was to learn to drive Ben's Rolls Royce.

It could be said that Ben Warner was lucky with horses that he owned, but the secret was that he could see the potential in a horse and he could place a horse in a certain race, knowing that it would be close to coming in the brackets. On the course he was a cheery, good-natured man, and one who was not afraid to lose. He would smile the same smile, win or lose. On one occasion, Billy Speck was riding his horse Free Fare in the Packington Chase at Bromford Bridge, Ben had a lot of money riding on Free Fare that day, and coming to the last he was six lengths clear from Gerry Wilson on General Crack. Then Speck under the impression that he was winning in a canter began to pull up his mount patting him on the neck. He little realised that Gerry Wilson had shaken up his horse General Crack and got up to win by a head. Billy Speck was sickened by his defeat, but Ben Warner patted him on the shoulder and said, "Don't worry about it".

(left to right) Ted Mason, Ben Warner and Tommy Westhead
"The men who beat the bookies"

His first win was at Windsor with The Saint, which went on to win sixteen more races for him. His next horse Preface won eight out of ten maiden chases, including the Novice Chase at Cheltenham. He won five good sprints with Monastery Garden, and then sold him to Mr James de Rothschild. Annam won a long list of races for him, while Zero which he purchased cheaply won eight races. At the sale of the late Lord Durham's string in training, he paid 1300 guineas for Residue. By the time Residue was eight years old, he had competed in 87 races of which he had won 28, including the Imperial Cup in 1931, ridden by George Pellerin and trained by Owen Anthony. One report read, "Mr Ben Warner is one of the most courageous backers of today and has brought off some useful financial hauls with his wonderful old horse, Residue; winning or losing he is just the cheery optimist who never fails to smile".

Another report read, "Ben Warner is one of the boldest and shrewdest professional backers in racing. He looks more like a prosperous farmer, big, burly,

red-faced, smokes a pipe, and thinks and bets in multiples of a thousand, never afraid to gamble high stakes."

Pictures
in
the Fire
By
"SABRETACHE"

[No, 1746, December 12, 1934]

"RESIDUE"

MR. "BEN" WARNER

A real live wire of the jumping world. He trains with Owen Anthony, and his wonderful money-spinner, "Residue," has probably won more races than any other horse now in training

One report read:

"Free Fare, a former champion hurdler and a winner over fences, won the last big race of the flat-racing season, when he carried off the November Handicap at Manchester yesterday by five lengths from Lord Derby's Thrapston, at 22-1. It was Ben Warner's third successive attempt to win this race with his horse. Two years ago, Free Fare swerved badly in the last few yards and allowed Jean's Dream to beat him. Last year he swerved again, and Pip Emma beat him, and cost his owner Ben Warner £60,000 in wagers. But yesterday, he ran straight and won in a canter. Mr Ben Warner said after the race, "I doubt if ever a steeplechaser has won the Manchester November Handicap before. I did not win anything like the amount that I would have done previously, when he lost through swerving. All the same, I have had a good bet at good odds." Lord Derby was one of the first to congratulate the successful owner."

Another report read, "Mr Ben Warner, the owner of Free Fare, is, of course, one of fortune's favourites in so far as the Turf is concerned. He bets big and frequently wins large sums of money. When he really fancied one of his horses, not many people would care to oppose him."

With his love for the West Country, Ben was easily persuaded to buy two hotels, The Gibbons and The Queens, overlooking the harbour in Torquay. He went down there quite frequently, where he entertained lavishly, especially when there was local racing. Ben Warner's presence on the racecourse was that of a genial one amongst his friends and other race-goers, but I cannot speak for the bookmakers as I am sure that it sent a shiver down the spine of many of them just to know that Ben would be there, and to some I am sure that he was a walking laxative.

His involvement in the Oyster Maid Coup was undoubtedly one of mammoth proportions. It suited him that it was organised by David Harrison, in that he could bet as he wished, and actually knowing that the horse was going to win was more than a bonus. As he was the owner of Oyster Maid he could have a good bet. How much he actually won or was won will never be known, and he said that he would take the truth with him to his grave, which he did. The diaries in which he kept record of his wins and losses are shown here.

I have read these diaries and some of the amounts of money that he laid are nothing short of frightening, even losing it did not seem to worry him as in the next week he would win double the amount that he lost the week previous. I am talking about serious five figure sums in the 1920's. There would be no gambler today on the racecourse circuit who would come anywhere near Ben Warner. He was betting the same amount of money in 1930 as betters are today in 2003. The man was a phenomenon. The only person that I would consider to be on the same or similar gambling par today would be Omar Shariff. A scientific gambling tactition (N.B. The entry for January 12th and 13th 1927 – "Tenby not included". I think that is magical! That's Ben Warner!)

(left to right) Mrs Warner, Ben Warner, George Pellerin and Molly Warner.
(Bens' daughter)
Ben and his wife, presented with the Imperial Cup by G Pellerin, the jockey, who won on Ben's horse, Residue in 1931, on their arrival home from holiday in South Africa, aboard the Balmoral Castle.

Party time with Ben Warner on board the Balmoral Castle

****

Taken from Wisden's 1992:

EDWARD (TED) G ARNOLD. Worcester and England.

He played first class cricket for Worcester from 1899-1913 inclusive. Until 1992 he held the following records in first class cricket:

1902	1067 runs and 113 wickets
1903	1157 runs and 143 wickets and 2 centuries
1904	1039 runs and 114 wickets and double century
1905	1148 runs and 115 wickets and 3 centuries

In 1903 he scored a century in both innings v Cambridge Univ. 101 runs in the 1st innings and 128 runs in the second innings.

In 1905 he took 9 wickets for 64 runs in one innings v Oxford Univ. He also holds the records for the two double centuries.

In 1909 200 runs v Warwickshire.

In 1910 215 runs v Oxford University.

In his first class career from 1899-1913 he scored 15,853 runs and he took 1069 wickets, which in itself is a first-class cricket record.

However, his other love was horse racing, and having owned horses in training with David Harrison, he met Ben Warner in 1924 and they became close friends. Ted Arnold* was already a compulsive gambler, but he was not in the same league as Ben Warner. In fact, it was said to me that Ted Arnold and Ben Warner were often seen together in the pubs and Hotel bars of Tenby, and that Ted Arnold would bet £100 even money with Ben Warner whether a man or a woman would be the next person to come into the room. That is what you call a compulsive gambler.

* I know little more than this of Ted Arnold, but his name always cropped up in my research of the Oyster Maid Scandal in which he was definitely involved. Also, being a close friend of Ben Warner speaks for itself.

****

LORD KYLSANT

'A Report from 1925'

Lord Kylsant is one of the most remarkable figures in London. He is the son of a clergyman, a descendant of a family which was famous in West Wales when William the Conqueror landed at Hastings, and as Owen Cosby Philipps he began his career on a clerk's stool in a Newcastle shipping office. From his boyhood days at Newton College, South Devon, he had a passion for engineering, for ships, and for the sea. Every step of his career was marked with ships and more ships. At last he controlled a great shipping combine with an aggregate capital of £200,000,000. His wealth increased with his commercial importance, and when he was raised to the peerage in 1923, he was regarded as one of the richest men in Great Britain. At his London home, Chelsea House, Cadogan-Square, S.W. he entertained lavishly.

Lord Kylsant was M.P. for Haverfordwest from 1906 to 1910. He was then a Liberal, but in 1916, he was elected for Chester as a Conservative. He married the daughter of the late Mr Thomas Morris of Coomb, near Carmarthen, thus uniting two of the oldest families in the West. He has no son. His three daughters married the Earl of Coventry, Lord Suffield, and Mr Alexander G Henderson, Lord Farringdon's heir.

OWEN
BARON KYLSANT
OF CARMARTHEN

'A Report of July 31st 1931'

Lord Kylsant was charged with having as a Director of the R.M.S.P. Company, in May 1927 and May 1928 made circulated, or published, or concurred in so doing, annual reports of the Directors of the company for the years 1926 and 1927 which he knew to be false in a material particular with intent to deceive the shareholders of the company. It was alleged that Mr Morland, auditor of the company, aided and abetted Lord Kylsant. It was on these charges that both Lord Kylsant and Mr Morland were found not guilty. The further indictment against Lord Kylsant of which he was found guilty, was of making, circulating, or publishing, or concurring in so doing, a prospectus which he knew to be false in a material particular with instant to induce persons to entrust or advance property to the company.

Mr Justice Wright in his summing up, which lasted four hours said, "This

is a trying case; it is also an important case, because it has involved the ventilation of many questions connected with the finance and the accounts of companies. Quite apart from any question of success or failure, I think that the prosecution in this case has been, and will be, of very great service to the commercial community. We have heard a great deal about the keeping of secret reserves and the commercial advantages which may flow from that practice. There may be very great evils with regard to those who control and manage companies for the benefit of shareholders if large portions of the company's assets are left in the secret disposition of the managing authority. Taking this case, you have heard of a large sum of money, the nature and use of which remained a secret from the shareholders. What happened as a result? There were balance sheets and profit and loss accounts published for seven years which did not disclose whether the company was earning any profit or not. During the seven years there was expended out of those items mainly connected with the war no 'less' than £5,000,000 not out of current earnings but out of those items which in the main arose out of the war. During all that period the shareholders were told nothing, and they drew their dividends presumably in the simple faith that all was well in the condition of the company. It may be said very well, they got their dividends. Times might have changed. When these items of income came to an end others might take their place and conditions might improve. But on the other hand, surely if the shareholders had been told that this company had no earnings – because earnings are the life blood of a company – they might have taken steps which has been done in other cases, and certainly they should have had the opportunity to take steps, for the reconstruction and rearrangement of the company's affairs, the cutting down of expenditure and reduction of services – all those things which have to be done when a company is not paying its way. The sooner that is done the better. It seems incredible that this should have gone on in a big company all those years, but so it was." The jury retired at 3.34 p.m. and returned their verdict at 6.30 p.m.

Lord Kylsant was sentenced to twelve months imprisonment in the second division. Accompanied by two wardens Lord Kylsant entered a taxi-cab behind the law courts and was driven to Wormwood Scrubs to serve his sentence, having appealed and lost. Lord Kylsant, as a prisoner in the second division will have meat only at the mid-day meal. Breakfast is tea, bread and margarine. He will occupy a cell with a small wooden table and stool – which he will scrub everyday – and a bed with two rough sheets and two blankets. His work for eight hours a day outside his cell may be making mailbags or mats or helping in the kitchen or carpenter's shop, but it will be governed by his age and physique. He may take books from the library and will receive exercise by walking behind other prisoners in the yard under supervision. Second division men receive no privileges except that they do not associate with hardened criminals and receive more letters and visitors. Otherwise their food, work, cell and discipline are the same as those of men sentenced to hard labour. By good conduct prisoners serving sentences longer than one month may earn remission of sentence not exceeding one month.

During the period that he has been on bail Lord Kylsant has made many improvements on his estate at Coomb near Carmarthen. A press correspondent says he gathers that Lord Kylsant will live entirely at Coomb in the future, and settle down as a farmer.

Lord Kylsant was Chairman of the Royal Mail Steam Packet Company. Mr Justice Avery said the prospectus was issued on June 29th 1928 and invited subscriptions for five per cent debentures. The issue was over subscribed. The material parts of the prospectus stated that dividends on the ordinary stock from 1911 to 1927 had varied from five to eight per cent. One of the purposes of the debentures was to pay off the bank overdraft of £500,000. The total cost of the trial and the appeal is believed to have cost Lord Kylsant about £40,000.

On his release, Lord Kylsant was met by Lady Kylsant at 7 a.m. on August 18th 1932. They were driven to their town house and then left for Coomb shortly before 9 o'clock. When Lord and Lady Kylsant reached Coomb late in the afternoon, they found a large crowd of Welsh tenants, tourists and hikers waiting outside the festooned main gates of the estate. During the night a triumphal arch of laurel and evergreen had been built over the gates and bore the inscription, 'Welcome Home'. The drive was bordered with flags. No sooner had the car reached the gateway than the crowd made its progress impossible. Long ropes were quickly fastened to the front of it and 40 men drew it at a running pace about a quarter of a mile to the entrance of the mansion. At the house there was a touching reunion between Lord Kylsant and his daughter the Hon Mrs Gavin Henderson. Lord Kylsant drew her affectionately towards him and kissed her on both cheeks. Then for the next ten minutes he shook hands with many of the old servants of the estate and with officials. Several of the estate workers wept as they grasped his hand, saying, "Welcome home, my Lord".

CHAPTER 9
THE BEGINNING OF THE END

In 1927 owners with David Harrison included:
Hon Mrs Basil Mundy, Viscount Lord St Davids, C C Williams (Llanrumney Hall), Sir David Hughes-Morgan, Edward Arnold, Ben Warner, Ivor Anthony, Mr Henry Dyke-Dennis, Sir Henry Webb, Mr J Holmes, G Lort Stokes, Mr G P Rise, and Sir Daniel Cooper. Fourteen owners with two or three horses each plus his own. That is a good stable! And having had good results why risk it all for a betting coup? There was surely another way to raise money for Ivor Anthony; they were all rich enough to dip into their own pockets. I have no answers for the questions concerning the motives underlying the coup. It's so sad, so sad. This is the beginning of the end of Tenby Races.

Ivor Anthony was invited to join Hon Aubrey Hastings as assistant trainer in the management of Wroughton Stable. It was very apt that he was to be

MR IVOR ANTHONY

involved in the training of the great 'Brown Jack', who defied the rules of racing by winning the Champion Hurdle in 1928 as a four year old ridden by Lewis Bilbee Rees before success on the flat. Steve Donoghue was with Hon A Hastings at Cheltenham and they watched the race together. After the race Mr Hastings asked Steve Donoghue if he thought Brown Jack would win on the flat? Donoghue replied, "Yes Sir! And I'll ride him for you." In 1929 Brown Jack won the Queen Alexandra Stakes at Ascot, and went on to win six years in succession from 1929-1934 inclusive, with Donoghue in the saddle, he was owned by Sir H Wernher. In May 1929, the Hon Aubrey Hastings collapsed and died suddenly after a game of polo. He was 51. The stable was taken over by Mrs

Hastings and Ivor Anthony. Ivor's successes as a trainer were as follows:
Welsh Grand National: Boomlet 1930; Pebble Ridge 1933; Sorley Boy 1936
Champion Hurdle: Chenango 1934 (bred by Lieut-Col J F Lort Phillips)
Imperial Cup: Flaming 1933
Scottish Grand National: Kellesboro Jack 1936-1938
Grand National: Royal Mail 1937
Gold Cup: Morse Code 1938; Poet Prince 1941
The Grand Military: Klaxton 1950-52
"Fifty years of success in the saddle and as the gov'nr, what a record!"

His younger brother John Randolph Anthony retired in 1927 and took out a license to train at Letcombe Regis on the Berkshire Downs. Among his owners was the American millionaire Mr "Jock" Hay Whitney for whom he trained Easter Hero to win the Cheltenham Gold Cup in 1929 and 1930. He also trained Thomond II, who was bred in Ireland, and had lost an eye from a shotgun blast caused by the 'Black and Tans'. Thomond II won 17 chases for Jack Anthony including the Becher Chase at Liverpool in 1932-34, he was owned by "Jock" Hay Whitney. It was, however, Thomond II that was responsible for the 'fiasco' in the 1935 Grand National. The decision to run Thomond II in the 1935 Gold Cup was a last minute one. It was assumed that he would by-pass Golden Miller and go for the two mile Coventry Cup, which was at his mercy. But with the arrival of his owner from America, Thomond II, who had beaten Golden Miller once and whom the hard ground suited much better than his heavier rival, was re-routed to the Gold Cup, and his challenge produced the most thrilling finish ever recorded in that race to date. The battle started three fences from home and it was not until 100 yards from the finish post that Golden Miller's superior strength asserted itself, as he inched ahead to win by three quarters of a length.

Both horses were due to run in the Grand National in 15 days time, and while the chances of neither had been improved by this titanic struggle, it was thought that Thomond II would suffer the worst. Golden Miller was 2-1 hot favourite and unseated Guy Wilson at the 11th fence, two after Valentine's. Thomond II, who was once described by an unkind racing correspondent as "looking no more than a ham sandwich", ran a heroic race and in fact landed just in front of Reynoldstown at the last, but weakened on the run-in to finish third, ridden as usual by Willy Speck. Jack Anthony also trained Brown Tony to win the 1930 Champion Hurdle ridden by Tommy Cullinan, who also rode Easter Hero. In 1930 Tommy Cullinan also rode Shaun Goilin to win the Grand National giving him a unique treble (NB At the outbreak of World War II, Tommy Cullinan joined an anti-aircraft unit, went into a deep bout of depression and shot himself). Jack Anthony, after a long career in the saddle without serious injury, permanently lamed himself getting off a hack while on holiday in the U.S.A. Afterwards, he permanently used a walking stick.

Billy Stott and Billy Speck were two of the top jockeys of this period, and at the Chepstow meeting of November 1927 they were in contention for the title which Stott held from the 1926-27 season until the close of the 1931-32 season, with Speck continually at his elbow. Close friends out of the saddle, Speck and Stott gave no quarter to anyone whilst in it, least of all to each other, and in the Penarth Selling Hurdle Race that day their leg-pulling comradeship turned into a bitter personal set-to as they jumped the last flight together. To see these two ride a finish was an experience at any time, but on this occasion they were welded together, brandishing their whips and giving each other as many cuts as they could muster in their battle royal to the post. Billy Stott got home by a head on Mr Claude Williams's False Report (trained by D Harrison), Billy Speck coming second on Bob Martyn, having to concede victory. A similar event happened about two weeks before at Worcester when they were hauled before the stewards and reprimanded, but at Chepstow the enjoyment of the spectacle had been so great that the authorities turned a blind eye.

Two of Pembrokeshire's best jump jockeys of the period were Tudor Griffiths of The Lodge Farm, New Hedges and Spencer Williams who owned Knightston Farm where the races were held. Both of them rode many times in the big Cheltenham Chases, especially the Foxhunter Chase. "They could be seen on the side of the road throughout the 1920's and 30's with their boots and saddles, hitching a lift to racecourses, and were always given a lift there and back somehow; in fact it was quite a talking point in Pembrokeshire at the time as to who was to be the one who picked them up this week," said Ashley Colley. "I gave them a lift dozens of times, and if one of them rode a winner or was paid a decent fee, they would stay the night and hitch back the next day." One day at Tenby Races he said that his younger brother Don who was only sixteen at that time in 1921, had wanted to come to the races with him. Ashley told Don that if he wanted him, he was to come to the secretary's room. Later in the day, Don came into the office saying that the bookies wouldn't take an even shilling. He gave him 10 shillings and told him to put it on the outsider in the last race, because there were only three runners. The favourite refused at the water jump in front of the stand after leading by a distance, the second horse refused three times at the same jump, two fences ahead of the outsider, which was 'Princess Miriam' who jumped the last to tumultuous applause at 10-1, after a police sergeant on a huge grey horse rode onto the field and when he saw Princess Miriam coming rode at the water jump and cleared it splendidly, finishing the race behind Princess Miriam, amidst cheers and bouts of laughter. Ashley said Don came running to the office shouting that he'd won at 10-1, saying, "What shall I do?" Ashley told him to go to the bookie with his ticket and ask for £5-10s, making sure to get the stake back. Ashley said, "I followed him discreetly and heard him say to the bookie, after being paid, "That'll bl—dy teach you not to take an even shilling, won't it?" as he ran away. "If the bookie had caught him, he'd have had a thick ear," said Ashley.

1928

The meeting of 1928 was held on January 11th and 12th. The first day was one of brilliant sunshine with good going, and there was a somewhat unusual event concerning Count de Bosdari, the owner of the much-fancied Blank Dawn in the Llwynarthen Challenge Cup, the principal race of the day. The horse lost, and just after the race, the Count left for London in his own aeroplane, taking off from a field far enough from the course to prevent interference, but near enough to give a thrill to the crowds as he made a perfect take-off. Shortly after a message came through that he had landed safely at Croydon (as there was now a telephone on the course).

The splendour and mildness of the day brought a visitor to the course who has not been on the ground for some years, the veteran Mr H Seymour Allen but he never left his closed car all day. Those present included Brigadier General Ronald Cheape, the Hon Mrs Basil Mundy, Lord and Lady Kylsant, Sir David and Lady Hughes-Morgan, Capt and Mrs Buckley, Dr C Mathias, Mr and Mrs David Harrison and David Harrison junior, Mr and Mrs J Bancroft, Mr and Mrs Meyrick Price, Mr and Mrs F B Rees, Mr R de G Hunter, Count A de Bosdari, Mr and Mrs G Ace, Mr F T B Summers (Chief Constable of Pembrokeshire).

Before the first race there was a one minute silence for the late Mr George Lort Stokes. All jockeys wore black armbands.

The results are sparse, I'm afraid.

First Day
1-0 THE LAWRENNY STEEPLE CHASE
60 sovs Three miles

Miss M F Cantrell-Hubbersty's, Firecracker, Jockeys, N/A, 7-4, 1
Mrs Darby Rogers, Express Forest, Jockeys, N/A , 2-1, 2
Also ran Holiday Hall, Causeway II, Active II Jockeys N/A
Winner trained by T Rayson
Express Forest trained in Ireland.

2-05 THE KNIGHTSTON SELLING HURDLE RACE
50 sovs Two miles

Mr W Pocock's, Ripley, Trudgill Jockeys, N/A, 20-1, 1
Mrs N Roberts's, Piping Rock, Roberts Jockeys, N/A, 8-1, 2
Mr R Lee's, Poobah Trudgill Jockeys N/A, 8-1, 3
Also ran: Arbilain, Joseph the First, Bubbly, Tudor, Palefroi, Extra Bold
Bubbly this year owned by Mr H Isaac, trained by Burroughs

After the second race the late Mr George Lort Stoke's horses were offered for sale without reserve:

MILBURN – B.G. aged, by Machakos ex Celia; own brother to Ballinode. A good jumper, maiden, under all rules. Likely to win a Hunt Steeplechase; to 14 stone.

GUSTY – Br. Mare, 6 years, by Earla Mor ex Bird of Bree. A good jumper. Has been placed over hurdles.

WHITE LIGHT – B.G. aged, by Morena or Lightsome, ex Foolish Maid. Up to14 stone. Winner of numerous Point to Points. A maiden under all rules. Likely to win a Hunt Steeplechase.

2-40 THE LLWYNARTHAN CHALLENGE CUP
Value 50 guineas presented by Sir Harry Webb, Bart 50 sovs Two miles
Trainer
Mr H B Brandt's, Right Ho, Private, Jockeys N/A, 5-1, 1
Lt Col S J Green's, Redmayne, A Hastings Jockeys N/A 100-8, 2
Mrs Ronald Cheape's, Dix-Sept, Hardcastle Jockeys N/A , 100-8, 3
Also ran: White Flag, Music Star, Black Dawn, Grand Mariner, Begin Well.

3-15 THE GROVE OPTIONAL SELLING STEEPLE CHASE
90 sovs Two miles
Trainer
Mr C C Williams's, Ganzey, D Harrison Jockeys N/A, 2-1 on, 1
Major H Lyon's, Holiday Hall, A Hastings Jockeys, N/A 5-1, 2
Squadron-leader C A Ridley's, Glenann, G Poole, Jockeys N/A, 7-1, 3
Also ran: True Knight.

3.45 THE WROUGHTON NATIONAL HUNT FLAT RACE
50 sovs Two miles
Trainer
Mrs C C Williams's, Attempt, D Harrison, Jockeys N/A, 4-1, 1
Strong One, Jockeys N/A 100-8, 2
Major J T North's, Bridge of Athlone, FA Bowen 5-2, 3
Also ran: Aubretia, Benjamin Cherry, Odin, Desert Lady.

Second Day
    Also in attendance were: Baron de Rutzen, Lady Bruce, Lieut-Col Morgan Lindsay, Mr H Dyke Dennis, Mr Pat Dennis, along with yesterday's attendance. Mrs George Ace celebrated her 67th birthday in the grandstand.

1-0 *Jockey*
Mrs Ronald Cheape's, Dix-Sept, Kettlewell, 4-1, 1
Mrs C C Williams's, Brockton, W Stott, Evens, 2
Mr R C Morel's, Begin Well, J Middleton, 5-1, 3
Also ran: Desert Lady, Charlock, Hapshill, Wicked Greek, Breconian.
Winner trained by Easterbee.

Mrs N Roberts's, Piping Rock, J Middleton, 2-1, 1
Mr F J Honour's, Achilles, W Parvin 6-4F, 2
Mr H Dyke Dennis's, Orange Plume, F Brookes, 2-1, 3
Also ran: Coxhill.
Winner trained by Roberts.

2-0
Mr D D Stewart's, Historical Gift, Mr D Steward, 100-8, 1
Mr R Lee's, Poobah, Trudgill, 8-1, 2
Mr D Harrison's, Hard Case, W Stott, 8-1, 3
Also ran: Boreas, Bubbly, Sweet Lady, Cabriolet (F), Baalbek, Arbilain, Magenta,
Sun Trap, Boyne Water, Flanigans Ghost.
Winner trained by Stewart.

2-30
Unknown, Nannie II, R Renton, 2-1, 1
Unknown, Brown Jap, Mr Eillio, 4-5 F, 2
Also ran: Miss Balscadden, Nannie II finished alone, but Brown Jap – who
fell – was remounted and placed second.
Winner trained by Thrale.

3-10
Mr Tudor Griffiths's, Lady C, Mr Tudor Griffiths, 4-5, 1
Unknown, Somerton Girl, Mr S Williams, 3-1, 2
Unknown, Splendid, Mr Hughes, 6-1, 3
Also ran: St Gowan, Pelcomb, Lady Grey.
Winner trained by D Harrison.

With the 'also rans' we should get the number of entries who actually ran
in 1928. With the runners who ran on both days, I make it sixty runners over
two days.

Ben Warner's Causeway II was an also-ran in the first race, his only
entry at the meeting. He and Ted Arnold still had horses with David
Harrison for the time being. But, Mr Henry Nash the blacksmith had
noticed that Bubbly was entered at the meeting and went to see the owner.
Mr Nash had felt very guilty of what he had done last year and when he
found Bubbly's owner, Mr Isaac, he told him that he wanted to see Ted
Arnold. Mr Nash told Ted Arnold what he had been forced to do last year
and how guilty he had felt about it ever since. He said that he had never
hurt a horse in his life and was ashamed, and it would not happen again
under any circumstances. He said he would rather go bankrupt. Ted
Arnold told him it was alright and thanked him for telling him so, and that
he knew nothing about it. Ted Arnold then told Ben Warner what Mr Nash
had said and Mr Warner was livid. It was not the way that he won races by

doing such a thing to a horse. That evening they confronted David Harrison and told him that they would be taking their horses from the stables next week, and that what he did was despicable. Ben Warner moved his horses to Owen Anthony and Ted Gwilt. I do not think that Ted Arnold bought another horse after that.

1929

Tenby – Tuesday night before the meeting

A Western Mail Report:

LEADING JOCKEYS TO RIDE.
FROM OUR RACING CORRESPONDENT

Once again owners and trainers have given clear evidence that they, at any rate, are anxious for the Tenby fixture to survive by supporting it in no half-hearted manner. For the two days there are no fewer than 216 entries, and of these a large proportion are certain runners. Already 64 horses are on the spot, and others are on their way to the meeting. It now only remains for the public to give the meeting a full measure of patronage to ensure the success of what is unquestionably one of the happiest, if not the most important, gatherings of the National Hunt season.

WELL-KNOWN OWNERS AND JOCKEYS

Among the well-known owners who are according the meeting their support are Sir David Llewellyn, Bart, Mr H Dyke Dennis, Mr C C Llewellyn Williams, Llanrumney Hall, Mr Claude Williams, Lord Londesborough, the Hon Mrs Basil Mundy, Sir Daniel Cooper, Lord Tredegar, Princess Wiasemsky, Mr Ralph Morel, Lord Allendale, Sir John Grey, and Mr D Heneage. It is also interesting to note that, with no opposition meeting, all the leading jockeys will be in attendance. These include W Stott, the popular Cheltenham rider who has the distinction of being the champion jockey of the season, and as such, will have the honour of replying to the toast of the "Knights of the Pigskin" at the annual dinner to owners, trainers, and jockeys tomorrow (Wednesday) evening; W Speck, F Sergeant, S Ingham, Monty Rayson, J Harvey, P Fitzgerald, G Pellerin, J Hogan, W Parvin, and T Chesman.

THE CHIEF EVENT

The principal event on tomorrows card is the Llwynarthan Challenge Cup for which there are likely to be fifteen runners. The versatile Dudley will share the honours of top weight with White Flag. Owing to Eastern Hero having been struck out, several of the candidates are much fancied, but in spite of his age Dudley may account for the opposition. The local trainer, David Harrison, will have about half a dozen runners tomorrow, and of these Ganzey is the most likely to prove successful.

The weather at the time of writing is mild, and there is no possible chance of the meeting being interfered with on account of frost. As a matter of fact, when I walked round the course this afternoon I found the going in excellent order. The jumps had been nicely built up, and given a continuance of the present weather conditions, the sport should be highly enjoyable.

SELECTIONS
Lawrenny Steeplechase – GANZEY; if absent, GILBERT'S SELECTED.
Knightston Selling Hurdle – STOW HILL.
Llwynarthan Challenge Cup – DUDLEY.
Grove Optional Selling Steeplechase – GANZEY; if absent, REDMAYNE.
Wroughton National Hunt Flat Race – GOLDEN ASHE (nap).

First Day
    The Tenby meeting of 1929 took place on Wednesday January 16th and Thursday January 17th.
First Race

1-30 THE LAWRENNY STEEPLE CHASE
70 sovs Three miles
Sir David Llewellyn's, Breconian, G Bowden, 6-4 on, 1
Mr J Balding's, Drinmond, J Mahoney, 4-1, 2
Mr P Sheehan's (IRE), Dove's Pride, Mr T Sheehan, 3-1, 3
Winner trained by Lindsay, Ystrad Mynach
Won by 6 lengths.

2-05 KNIGHTSTON SELLING HURDLE
50 guineas With 50 sovereigns added Two miles
Mr C Williams's, Attempt, W Speck, 5-4 on Fav, 1
Mr D Heneage's, Irish Cheddar, Gerry Wilson , 5-1, 2
Mr Gosden's, Polish King, H Reed, 4-1, 3
Winner trained by D Harrison, Tenby
Won by 5 lengths

2-40 THE LLWYNARTHAN CHALLENGE CUP
50 guineas With 50 sovereigns added Two miles
Mrs Mundy's, White Flag, W Speck, 6-4, 1
Miss O Jones's, Stow Hill, W Stott, 2-1, 2
Mrs L Drago's, Borjom, D Dick, 8-1, 3
Lord Tredegar's, Taradiddle, M Thomas
Winner trained by D Harrison, Tenby
Won by 5 lengths

3-15 THE GROVE OPTIONAL SELLING STEEPLE CHASE
50 sovs Two miles
Mr C Williams's, Ganzey, W Speck, 1
Mr A Villar's, Italian Summer, Parvin, 2
Mrs C Jones's, Pongo, J Hamey, 3
Winner trained by D Harrison, Tenby

3-45 THE WROUGHTON NATIONAL HUNT FLAT RACE
50 sovs Two miles

Mrs R Huggett's, Golden Ash, Capt Webber, 1
Sir Daniel Cooper's, Wild Duke, Mr C C Ll Williams, 2
Lord Allendale's, Some Toft, 3
Winner trained by Owen Anthony
Won by 4 lengths

Second Day

1-0pm THE GATE HOUSE HURDLE RACE
50 sovs Two miles
Mrs Mundy's, Lough Mor, W Speck, 6-1, 1
Mr G P-Rise's, Yarlington, Tommy Duggan, 4-1, 2
Princess Wiasemsky's, Borealis, Parvis, 4-1, 3
Winner trained by D Harrison, Tenby.

1-30 THE PARK HOUSE SELLING HANDICAP STEEPLE CHASE
80 sovs Two miles
Mr D Heneage's, White Cargo, Gerry Wilson, 2-1, 1
Mr J Lombard's, Buffoon, J McCarthy, 10-1, 2
Miss G Yates's, Bay Rock, Foster, 3-1, 3
Winner trained by Hall.

2-0 THE LICENSED VICTUALLERS' SELLING HANDICAP HURDLE
50 sovs Two miles
Mr J Gosden's, Polish King, F Brookes, 8-1, 1
Mr C Williams's, False Report, W Speck, 5-4 on F, 2
Mr D Heneage's, Irish Cheddar, Gerry Wilson, 6-1, 3
Winner trained by J Gosden
Won by neck.

2-30 THE TOWN HANDICAP STEEPLE CHASE
70 sovs Three miles
Mr C Neville's, Sturton, R Lyall , 5-4, 1
Mr H Dyke Dennis's, Fairfield, Tommy Duggan, 3-1, 2
Sir David Llewellyn's, Miss Ballscadden, G Bowden, 3-1, 3
Winner trained by Gale, Waltham

3-10 THE UNITED COUNTIES FARMERS' AND TRADESMENS' HURDLE
45 sovs Two miles
Mr W Roch's, Splendid, Mr H Hughes, 7-2, 1
Mr T Morris's, Little Whyna, Mr R Reid, 7-2, 2
Mr T Phelps's, Steeple Jack III, Mr J Castle, 7-1, 3
Mr Tudor Griffiths's, Lady C, Owner, 5-4 on Fav, 4
Winner trained by W Roch
Won by 10 lengths.

LOCAL TRAINER
SADDLES THREE OF THE WINNERS
BY OUR RACING CORRESPONDENT

TENBY, Wednesday.

Conditions for racing could not have been more ideal than they were here today. The weather was bright, the going perfect, and fields, in the main, of quite satisfactory dimensions. Welsh owners were well to the fore, the outstanding feature being the treble scored by the Tenby stable, over which Mr David Harrison is the presiding genius. His success was shared by W Speck, who, in steering the three horses Attempt, White Flag, and Ganzey to victory, completed the "hat-trick". These were the popular little jockey's only mounts during the afternoon, and he received hearty congratulations for his achievement. Attempt and Ganzey are owned by Mr C C Ll Williams, the Squire of Llanrumney, who thus landed a useful double.

The Hon Mrs Basil Mundy was present to see her good horse, White Flag, carry off the Llwynarthan Challenge Cup, and made no attempt to conceal her delight at the horse's success, while Sir D R Llewellyn, Bart, also shared in the spoils of victory, his consistent horse Breconian crediting him with the Lawrenny Steeplechase. Favourites were well to the fore, so that backers must have had much the better of the duel with their friendly rivals the bookmakers.

A FEW FALLS

There were a few falls during the afternoon, but, fortunately, unaccompanied by injuries to either horse or rider.

It was not surprising to find Breconian much in demand for the opening event, for he had won his last three races in fluent style. There was just the point that he had not been over the three mile course before, but evidently the layers had little doubt about his ability to get the distance, as they were asking for substantial odds right from the outset. The public, too, showed their confidence by supporting the horse for some substantial amounts.

The race proved an interesting one, the horses keeping well together for most of the journey. On the back stretch the last time round, Mr T P Sheehan, who rode Dove's Pride, sent his mount to the front, but four fences from home the horse pecked on landing and came to grief. He left Drinmond in front and the favourite, but after negotiating the final obstacle Bowden brought Breconian along with a good burst of speed to win comfortably by six lengths. It is possible, however, that had Dove's Pride stood up he would have been a great danger to the winner as he was going particularly well when the mishap occurred.

SPECK'S "HAT-TRICK"

Backers again showed their judgment when they selected Attempt for the Knightston Selling Hurdle, as though Irish Cheddar, Polish King, and Nice One were somewhat fancied, by their connections, neither had much chance when it came to racing. Speck waited on his rivals until reaching the straight, when he came on the favourite, Attempt, to win by five lengths from Irish Cheddar, with Polish King two lengths away third. Nice One was fourth, Trim Gate fifth and Diatonic last. Friponne fell, and Laurence was pulled up. The winner was bought in for 140gns.

With Easter Hero and Dudley absent from the Llwynarthan Cup, Mrs Basil Mundy's White Flag was quietly installed favourite and won easily, ridden by Billy Speck.

GOOD FIELDS ON SECOND DAY
SPLENDID REPORT
ANOTHER WINNER FOR MR HARRISON
FROM OUR RACING CORRESPONDENT

TENBY, Thursday.

Favourites did not do quite so well here today as on Wednesday, but still, backers went away fully satisfied with the sport provided. It seems a big thing to say, but it is a fact that this is the first occasion in the last sixteen meetings that two fine days have been enjoyed for the racing.

The opening event – the Gate House Hurdle – provided the Harrison-Speck combination with the opportunity to get their fourth success of the meeting. The "nap hand" according to the book, should have been gained in the Licensed Victuallers' Hurdle, but here False Report was beaten into second place by the friendless Polish King.

OPEN MARKET ON FIRST RACE

The Gate House Hurdle attracted eleven runners, and backers were hard to satisfy. This left the market quite an open one, with the result that Yarlington and Borealis were joint favourites at 4's. The running provided a different story. Yarlington led for the first half from Borealis with Balmynach tailed off, but, coming to the distance, Lough Mor, which had all the while been laying handy, moved up, and at the last obstacle came away to win by three-quarters of a length from its stable companion, Yarlington, Borealis being third eight lengths away.

The Park House Selling Steeplechase provided a fair amount of wagering, four of the six runners coming in for support. White Cargo was generally most in favour, and wound up at the head of the market. Making the whole of the running, Mr D Heneage's horse won, pulling up, by twenty lengths from Buffoon, with Bay Rock four lengths away third. Polynia and Guitar fell at the water the first time round.

BIGGEST FIELD OF MEETING

The biggest field of the meeting – thirteen runners – faced the starter in the Licensed Victuallers' Hurdle. It was expected that Mr David Harrison would complete his "nap hand" by the aid of False Report, who was, consequently, heavily backed from the outset. Weight, however, told against Mr Claude Williams' candidate, who, though making a plucky effort, was beaten a neck by Polish King, with Irish Cheddar third. Idolatry, who had made most of the running, but tired in the straight, was fourth.

The Manchester winner, Sturton, was so well handicapped in the Town Steeplechase that the race looked a real good thing for him. The connections of Fairfield, however, fancied their charge somewhat, and at one time he appeared likely to depose Sturton from favouritism. At the flag fall, however, the latter was firm at 5 to 4 against. The early running was made by Simon's Light, Miss Balscadden, Fairfield and Sturton. Passing the stands the second time, Sturton was lying second, and on the far side took up the running. Entering the straight, Fairfield joined issue, but after negotiating the last fence Sturton drew out to win cleverly by one and a half lengths, with Miss Balscadden six lengths further away third.

A GOOD RACE

As usual, much local interest was centred in the United Counties' Farmers' and Tradesmens' Hurdle. Lady C, who won the race last year, again found many friends, but some shrewd judges showed a decided preference for Mr W H Roch's Splendid.

OWNERS, TRAINERS, AND JOCKEYS
Guests Of Stewards At Dinner

The Mayor of Tenby (Alderman W H Thomas) presided at the annual dinner at which the stewards of the Tenby Steeplechases entertained the owners, trainers and jockeys attending the meeting at the Royal Gate House Hotel on Wednesday. The mayor was supported by Sir David Hughes-Morgan, Bart, Mr H Dyke Dennis, Mr C C Ll Williams, M F H, Col Morgan Lindsay, Mr A E Hancock, Capt Hugh Allen, M F H, and Mr David Harrison. In the company were many well-known figures, including W Stott, the champion jockey under National Hunt Rules, and W Speck, who rode three winners out of three mounts.

The Mayor proposed "Success to the Tenby Meeting", to which Sir David Hughes-Morgan responded. He commented upon the success of their Tenby trainer, Mr David Harrison, and said the meeting was going through hard times which were common throughout the country, but more intense in Wales, than anywhere else at the moment. Mr C C Llewellyn Williams responded for the owners.

Col Morgan Lindsay, proposing the health of the jockeys, said he had been told that he had been selected because it was said that he was up to all the tricks of jockeys. But there were no tricks known to jockeys. If they did not have jockeys there would be no racing. W Stott, the champion jockey under National Hunt Rules, whom the company insisted should respond from a chair, reminded the gathering that it was his third year in Tenby. Last year he had expressed the hope that he would succeed F B Rees and L B Rees to the championship, and he had succeeded earlier than he hoped. He trusted that he would hold it again this year. If not, he hoped he would be succeeded by his friend W Speck.

Several other jockeys described Tenby as the most sporting meeting in the kingdom, and expressed their ambition to ride winners at the meeting. Capt Hugh Allen, M F H, proposed "The Trainers".

****

'A Western Mail Report'

These are two interesting reports on the proposals of the TOTE, and its future on the betting scene. These appear in the 1929 press.

WHEN WILL THE "TOTE" APPEAR?
BOARD NOT YET COME TO A CONCLUSION.
FROM OUR SPECIAL CORRESPONDENT.
LONDON, Wednesday.

It appears that there was a meeting of the Betting Control Board in London earlier in the week, and a report of the recent work of this body was issued this afternoon. So far as can be learned from that report, very little that matters has been done. Certain people have been given jobs on the staff, but so far as I can find out none of them have ever had anything to do with "Totes" before, nor much with racing in any form whatsoever.

AN OFFICE AT LEEDS

It is interesting to learn that the board propose to have an office at Leeds, as well as in London, but what we racing people want to know is the deduc-

tion to be made from all bets, and also when the "Tote" in some form or other is going to appear on our racecourses.

It would seem that the board cannot make up its mind about a "Tote" and that it is rather more than flirting with the pari-mutuel form of betting, by which is meant the hand-worked machines which have been discarded in so many places in favour of the Julius machine, which, for some reason which I cannot make out, the board do not seem to have heard of at all.

As I have said before, the board seem to be a terribly long time in coming to a conclusion about many things which matter. The Bill was hurried through Parliament so that we could have the "Tote" this season, but very little has been done since last summer beyond ordinary arrangements, and, so far as I can see, we are no nearer the real mechanical "Tote" than we were a year ago.

NEW BETTING RULES
To Become Operative in February.

The *Western Mail & South Wales News* is informed that: "It having been brought to the notice of Tattersall's Committee that the new Rule 152 of the Rules of Racing – referred in Rule 5 of the new Rules on Betting which are dated February 1, 1929 – does not come into operation until March 1, 1929, Tattersall's Committee have decided that the new Rules on Betting shall be applicable as if the new Rule 152 of the Rules of Racing were in operation on February 1, 1929."

Rule 5 on betting has been altered to read as follows: "When the signal had been hoisted over the number board as provided for in Rule 152 of the Rules of Racing, the bets go to the horses as officially shown on the board, and no objection made subsequent to the hoisting of such signal shall disturb the destination of the bets." Under the former rule, if there was a disqualification as the result of an objection within seven days, exclusive of the day on which the race was run, then bets went with the stakes. The settling was not otherwise disturbed except in cases of fraud. The following addition has been made to Rule 7 on betting, which deals with dead-heats: "In the event of a dead-heat the bets go to the horses as officially shown on the number board as provided for in Rule 152 of the Rules of Racing. No subsequent decider shall disturb the destination of such bets. The decider shall constitute a separate race."

Tattersall's Committee has sole authority to settle all questions relating to bets with bookmakers, and the alterations have been made so that the last-named shall not be at any disadvantage with the totalisator when it is installed on the racecourses.

Also, I stumbled across this on a page of the January 1929 Western Mail, and may be of interest.

"PRESENTS" TO A JOCKEY.
DONOGHUE AND MR WHITE.
INCOME-TAX BLAMED FOR FAILURE.

Stephen Donoghue, the noted jockey, was publicly examined at the London Bankruptcy-court on Wednesday, and told the Official Receiver of his relations with the late Mr James White. Donoghue said that during his career he had made money, but had been too good to his friends. He was friendly with the late Mr James White, from whom he had a verbal retainer of £6,000 a year from about 1915 or 1916. Mr White had never, as had been suggested, given him a retainer of £11,000 a year, but he had told him that he would buy shares for him in the Beecham Trust. As a fact, Donoghue said, he received £3,000 in shares on which no dividends were paid by Mr White, from whom, however he got money from time to time. Before 1923 Mr White paid him various sums for bloodstock, not for presents, and made substantial sums by backing Donoghue's mounts. If Mr White made £20,000 out of backing a horse which he was riding White would not put any money on the horse for him but might make him a "present".

£21,000 PROMISSORY NOTE.

He had seen a statement of James White of all the money paid by White to him, and White wanted it paid back to him. He (Donoghue) was induced to sign a promissory note for £21,000. When Mr White died the question of the promissory note cropped up, and the result was that the solicitors for White's executors accepted £250 to settle the whole matter.

Four years ago, said Donoghue, he was sued by the Income-tax Commissioners for £8,000 owed for income-tax, and two years ago he paid that £8,000 for which he had to borrow from moneylenders. During the last two years he had had transactions with moneylenders, but the large amounts which he borrowed were used to pay income-tax. He signed a joint promissory note to a moneylender to assist a friend, and had to repay the whole amount himself. He was not then himself in want of money, and would not have gone to the moneylender if he had been.

CAUSES OF FAILURE.

Donoghue said that his failure and insolvency were due to his liability under guarantees and in promissory notes signed by him jointly with another person for advances of which only a portion was received by himself, to interest on borrowed money, and to having been assessed for income-tax on a larger amount than that eared by him. His accounts showed total liabilities of £33,265, of which £16,819 is expected to rank, and the assets estimated to produce £590 were absorbed by preferential claims. The examination was concluded.

****

1930

In 1930 the meeting was held on January 9th and 10th, Wednesday and Thursday.

First Day

The weather was cold and wet, but was no excuse for the dismal amount of entries; as you will see here.

1-30 THE LAWRENNY STEEPLE CHASE
70 sovs Three miles
Lord Allendale's, Heartburn, W Speck, 5-4 on Fav, 1
Mr E Hayne's, Golden Knott, E Foster
Winner trained by Gordon, Wroughton
2 ran. Heartburn finished alone. Golden Knott fell, was remounted, but later pulled up.

2-05 THE KNIGHTSTON SELLING HURDLE
50 sovs Two miles
Mr C Williams's, False Report, W Speck, 6-4, 1
Mr P Sheehan's (IRE), Polish King, Mr J Sheehan, 5-1, 2
Mr A Dorey's, Always Blue, C Rhodes, 6-1, 3
9 ran
Winner trained by D Harrison, Tenby

2-40 THE LLWYNARTHAN CHALLENGE CUP
Value 50 guineas With 50 sovereigns added Two miles
Mrs Mundy's, White Flag, W Speck, 11-4 on Fav, 1
Mr C P Rice's, Yarlington, J Hamey, 10-1, 2
Mr M Williams's, Tetripipe, Mr Raymond, 20-1, 3
6 ran
Winner trained by D Harrison, Tenby

3-15 THE GROVE OPTIONAL SELLING STEEPLE CHASE
80 sovs Two miles
Mr E G Hayes's, Golden Promise, E Foster, 4-1, 1
Mr C C Williams's, Attempt (Fell), J Hamey, 2-1 on Fav, 2
3 ran.
Winner trained privately

3-45 THE WROUGHTON NATIONAL HUNT FLAT RACE
Mr A Bostwick's, Strong One, Mr G Bostwick 7-4 on Fav, 1
Mrs Mundy's, The Danube, Mr A Cottrill
Mrs N Roberts's, O'Hara's Fancy, Mr Tudor Griffiths
4 ran
Winner trained by Ivor Anthony, Wroughton

Second Day

1-0 THE GATE HOUSE HURDLE RACE
50 sovs Two miles
Mr T Lant's, Marrifirth, W Speck, 1
Miss D Harris's, Bello, Sergeant, 2
Sir D Llewellyn's, Dracos, A Legge *, 3
11 ran
Winner trained by D Harrison, Tenby
* Probably the son of George Legge, who was one of Kirkland's grooms.

208

1930. **1930.**

❧ TENBY ❧
hunt Steeple=chases & hurdle Races
(Under National Hunt Rules).

FIRST DAY—WEDNESDAY, January 8, 1930.

Stewards.

Viscount ST. DAVIDS, Col. MORGAN LINDSAY, Sir D. HUGHES-MORGAN, Bart.,
H. DYKE DENNIS, Esq.

Officials.

Judge—Mr A. E. Hancock.
Clerk of the Scales—Mr T. H. Wilton Pye, Unicorn Chambers, Worcester.
Handicapper—Colonel D. H. Leslie.
Clerk of the Course and Stakeholder—Mr George Chiles, Clifton Rock, Tenby.
Starter—Mr George Phelps, Cresselly.
Auctioneer—Mr J. A. Roch, Pembroke.
Hon. Secretary—Mr David Harrison, The Grove, Tenby.
Assistant Hon. Secretaries—Mr J. H. Fitzgerald Burke, and Mr. Arthur Powell.
Auditor—Mr Fred J. Warren, F.S.A.A., Haverfordwest.
Hon. Surgeon—Dr. C. Mathias, Tenby. Hon. Vet. Surgeon—Mr B. J. Rees, Tenby.

NOTICES.

WEIGHTS.—In Weight-for-age Races the Weights on the Card are only published
for the convenience of the Public, and Owners of Horses engaged should
calculate for themselves. Any alteration will be exhibited on the board.

WEIGHED-IN.—When the Winner has passed the scales, " Weighed-In" will be
signalled.

OBJECTION.—When an Objection has been made notice will be signalled.
No Lists, Clogs, Stools, or Ready Money Betting allowed.

1-30 THE PARK HOUSE SELLING HANDICAP STEEPLE CHASE
80 sovs Two miles
1 Miss C Hubburty's, Kamandros, Escott, Walked over
Trained by Rayson, King's Worthy

2-0 THE LICENSED VICTUALLERS' SELLING HANDICAP HURDLE
50 sovs Two miles
Mr P Sheehan's (IRE), Polish King, Mr J Sheehan, 7-4, 1

Capt L Davies's, Formidable, J Hamey, Ev Fav, 2
Mr I Rickards's, B Jay, G Bowden, 3
5 ran
Winner trained in Ireland

2-30 TOWN STEEPLE CHASE
Mrs L Tate's, Biggin Hill, Foster7-2, 1
Mrs Mundy's, Dove's Pride, J Hamey Ev Fav, 2
Lt Col M Lindsay, Cairbre, Mr D Thomas, 3
3 ran
Winner trained by Tate
Won by neck

3-10 THE UNITED COUNTIES FARMERS' AND TRADESMENS' HURDLE
45 sovs Two miles
Mr W Roch's, Splendid, Mr Hughes, 2-1 on Fav, 1
Mr J Hodges's, Phoebe III, Owner, 20-1, 2
Mr J Morris's, Mayboy, Mr Vincent Griffiths, 5-1, 3
*Miss Bailey's, Lady C, Mr Tudor Griffiths, 7-1, 4
Mr M Lewis's, Early Dawn, Owner, 7-1, 5
5 ran
Winner trained privately

There were 49 runners over the two days.
* Miss Bailey was the proprietress of the Royal White Lion Hotel, Tenby.

"TENBY RACES EXCELLENT SPORT"
W SPECK PERFORMS THE "HAT TRICK".

Though fields in the main did not pan out quite as anticipated, patrons had ample compensation in the excellence of the sport. Except for the opening event, there was something of real interest in the racing the feature of which was the success of W Speck, who scored the coveted "hat-trick", by riding the first three winners. He opened with a victory on Lord Allendale's Heartburn, trained by R Gordon, and followed with Mr Claude Williams's False Report, and the Hon, Mrs Basil Mundy's White Flag.

The last named, as was expected, carried off, for the second year in succession, the principal race of the afternoon – the Llwynarthan Challenge Cup, presented by Sir Henry Webb, Bart – and thus completed a double for the stable presided over by Mr David Harrison.

BACKERS DO WELL

The going proved to be in tip-top condition and though there were a few falls, horses and riders fortunately escaped injury.

From a backer's point of view it was a real good day, four out of five favourites being successful, the only failure being Mr C C Ll Williams's Attempt, who destroyed his chance by a mistake at the water the second time round.

Only Heartburn and Golden Knott faced the starter for the opening event, and layers appeared rather generous in only asking for 9-4 about Lord Allendale's candidate. The apparent generosity may have been due to the fact that the horse had only recently been put to the bigger jumps, and, further, had never negotiated a three-mile course. Those who laid the odds, however, had little cause for anxiety as Golden Knott came down at the third fence, and although remounted, could never get on terms with Heartburn, who won comfortably.

A LOCAL WINNER

A good field turned out for the Knightston Selling Hurdle, in which the locally trained False Report was always best in demand, winding up a 6 - 4 favourite. Polish King, a winner over the course 12 months ago, found some friends, while Emphatic and Always Blue also came in for support. It was really the most interesting race of the afternoon, Assignee making the running from Boneblack, Abdulla, Set Fast, and Emphatic, with Always Blue last. Going away on the far side, Abdulla took up the running from Set Fast, Bronblack, False Report, with Rock Arrow bringing up the rear. Passing the stands the second time, Abdulla was still in the lead, followed by Always Blue, Set Fast, Boneblack, Emphatic, and False report. Entering the straight, Always Blue took up the running, but was promptly challenged by Polish King and False Report, the latter drawing away from the last flight to win by five lengths from Polish King, with Always Blue a similar distance away third. Assignee was fourth, Emphatic fifth, Boneblack sixth, Abdulla next, and Set Fast last. At the subsequent auction there was no bid for the winner.

WHITE FLAG'S DOUBLE

Only Sir David Llewellyn's Astir was backed with any confidence to beat the Hon Mrs Basil Mundy's White Flag for the Llwynarthan Challenge Cup, though there was some small money for Mr G C Pryse-Rice's Yarlington, trained in the same stable as the favourite. The backers of Astir had the mortification of seeing their mount come to grief at the flight approaching the stands, and in doing so he nearly brought down White Flag. Speck, however, managed to pull his mount together, and continued to lay handy behind Yarlington and Bedguard. These positions were maintained until going away on the far side a second time, when Speck took White Flag to the front, and making the remainder of the running won easily by ten lengths, with Tetripipe a bad third. Greenery fell early on and Bedguard was pulled up.

A THEORY JUSTIFIED

Those who favour the outsider-of-three theory had a pleasant surprise in the Grove Optional Selling Steeplechase. Backers pounced upon Mr C C Ll Williams's Attempt as the "good thing", and he quickly became a 2-1 on chance, with Expert the next best fancied, and Golden Promise, the outsider of the party. Those who declined to lay the odds on the favourite found it possible to trade at 10-1 about the outsider, and this price appealed so forcibly to some of the shrewd people that the price quickly fell to 4's. For half the journey it looked any odds on Attempt, especially when Expert came down, but backers of Golden Promise were able to smile when the favourite made a bad mistake at the water the second time round and his jockey parted company. Though quickly scrambling back into the saddle, the rider had no possible chance of making up the leeway, and Golden Promise went on to win, pulling up by a distance.

This was the first set-back that backers experienced, but they recovered themselves in the concluding event by supporting Mr A C Bostwick's Strong One, trained by the former Welsh jockey, Ivor Anthony. There was some support for The Danube, possibly by reason of the fact that Mr A Cottrill had the mount, but when it came to racing there was only one in it, Mr Bostwick bringing his mount through in the straight to win a clever race by four lengths from The Danube, with O'Hara's Fancy five lengths away third.

SECOND DAY

Rain completely spoiled what promised to be a good wind-up to the meeting on Thursday. It commenced to fall from an early hour, with the result that the course, which on the first day was perfect, became very holding, and this no doubt was responsible for the decision of some owners not to start their horses. In the Park House Selling Steeplechase, for instance, only Miss M F Cantrell-Hubbersly's Skamandros faced the starter, other entrants who were on the course, including Angelo II, declining the engagement after those connected with them had seen the state of the going.

THE BIGGEST FIELD

Consequently the sport was reduced to four races, of which the opening event – the Gate House Hurdle – proved the best. Eleven horses – the biggest field of the gathering – went to the post, and wagering was fairly brisk. Those coming in for best support were Swift News, Marrifirth, and O'Hara's Fancy, while Sir David Llewellyn's Craignure also found friends. The outsider, Greenery, destroyed whatever chance he might have had by swerving at the first fence and running out, and Dracos settled down in front of O'Hara's Fancy, Swift News and Marrifirth. Little change occurred until going away on the far side for the second time, when Bello joined the leaders. At the last fence O'Hara's Fancy fell and interfered with Swift News. This gave Bello the first run, but Speck brought Marrifirth along in the straight to win cleverly by two lengths, with Dracos six lengths away third. Caldey Light was fourth, Yarlington fifth, Swift News sixth, and Severn Slip last.

POLISH KING'S SUCCESS

Only five horses turned out for the Licensed Victuallers' Hurdle, and backers were divided between the Chepstow winner, Formidable, and Mr Paddy Sheehan's Polish King, a winner at the last meeting, and who also figured prominently on the first day. The odds fluctuated continually until just before the off, when Formidable became favourite at even money. These two, with B Jay, had the race to themselves from start to finish, Formidable setting the pace until reaching the straight, when young Mr J T Sheehan closed with the leader, B Jay, also lying handy. After negotiating the final flight Polish King drew out to win by a length from the favourite, with B Jay a length and half away third.

Conditions were even more atrocious by the time the Town Steeplechase was reached, and backers appeared somewhat chary about laying the odds on Mrs Basil Mundy's Dove's Pride to beat Cairbre and Biggin Hill. Many who had profited by the outsider-of-three theory went for the last-named instead of backing the favourite, and once again their judgement proved correct, Biggin Hill running Dove's Pride out of it in the straight to win cleverly by a neck. Cairbre fell early on, but Mr David Thomas pluckily re-mounted and completed the course.

The United Counties Farmers' and Tradesmens' Hurdles attracted five of the six entrants, these including last year's winner, Splendid, and a previous winner in Lady C. The bookmakers asked for odds about the former, who was reported to be in fine condition. There was some little support for Phoebe III and May Boy III, though Phoebe III might have made a better fight of it had her owner-rider, Mr J S Hodges, not had to put up with a lot of deadweight. In such going this was undoubtedly a big handicap.

Skamandros, who walked over in the Park House Selling Steeplechase came up for auction, but failed to raise a bid.

WHY NOT ALTER THE DATE?
BY "A SPORTSMAN"

This year's Tenby Race Meeting is over, and one is now free to sum up the situation. The first day was all that could be expected by the most captious sportsman – ideally fine weather, a fairly large crowd on the course, a good "field", and some tip-top racing. So far so good. But the gilt came off the gingerbread with a vengeance that next day! Wretched weather, small rain-bedraggled attendance, much abridged "field", and nothing very exciting about the running. Well, how could it be expected under such depressing conditions?

If expenses were cleared on Wednesday, and, taking a hopeful view, a little profit left over, the following day's fiasco was bound to have swallowed it. For some years now there have been intermittent suggestions that the holding of the local meeting during January is not, on the whole, a good arrangement, and that the event would be very much more successful and enjoyable if the date were fixed later in the year. The rejoinder to this has generally been that the difficulty is the finding of an open date. There may be something in this, but all the same I think it could be surmounted if a genuine attempt were made.

January is proverbially an unstable month as regards weather, and the course at Knightson is hardly a pleasant spot on which to spend a few hours when the elements are unkind. But people who are supposed to know, say that if the Tenby Hunt Week is deprived of the races it will collapse. With all due respect to this opinion I don't think such would be the case. For many years the Hunt Week was run without the races, and it was always a success. The races were held in a separate week, and they also proved successful.

Of course, if the question of expense does not enter into the matter then the promoters can please themselves, but all the same I strongly incline to the view that a change of date would be beneficial all round.

"WELCHING" AT TENBY RACES.
YOUNG BOOKMAKER WHO ABSCONDED.
SAUNDERSFOOT AND CRESSELLY MEN TRICKED.
SUPERINTENDENT'S SMART CAPTURE.

A twenty-one-year-old bookmaker, Arthur Green, alias Ted Evans, of 4, House Court, Dartmouth Street, Birmingham, was brought up in custody before the Narberth Magistrates on Thursday last, Captain Hugh Allen in the chair, with feloniously stealing 11s, monies belonging to Albert Beddoe, Railway Terrace, and Wm Fred Gunter, Hobb's Hill, Mountain, Saundersfoot, and Fred James Turner, of White Hall, Cresselly.

Supt T B James, who prosecuted, explained that the offence in question occurred at Tenby Races and was commonly know as "welching". It was a very mean and contemptible sort of theft, which had been carried on at the local races for many years. The police were determined to put a stop to it. They had one case last year and the accused got away this time, but they were able to trace him.

Albert Beddoe spoke to attending the races on the 9th inst. and when he had a bet on a horse named "Biggins Hill" with the accused. He speculated seven shillings on the horse, for which he was given a ticket (produced).

The Chairman: Are you in the habit of dealing with this bookmaker?

Witness: They are strangers to me.

Continuing, witness stated that prisoner gave bigger odds than the local bookmakers. The horse eventually won the race, but when he returned to claim his money, which was 28s, prisoner was not there. After having a look round he reported the matter to the police.

The Chairman: Did he leave his board behind?

Witness: Yes.

The Chairman: Was there another man with him?

Witness: There was a clerk with him, but neither were there when I returned.

In answer to another question by the Chairman, witness stated that the odds on this particular horse was three to one. Wm Frederick Gunter and Fred James Turner told the court that they put bets on 1s. and 2s respectively on the same horse, but on going to claim the money failed to find the prisoner.

PC Griffiths gave evidence of receiving accused into custody from the Birmingham City Police on the 22nd inst. When charged he replied, "My clerk made such a mess of the book that I could not stop to face the people." Witness conveyed accused to Narberth.

George Thomas, of North Street, Bufferland, Pembroke Dock, spoke to driving the Superintendent to the races on the 8th and 9th, and added that he saw the accused trading under the name of "Ted Evans". On instructions from the Superintendent he took the board, which he produced.

Prisoner, who pleaded guilty to the offence, elected to be dealt with summarily, and made a statement, in which he put the fault on his clerk as he made a £3 10s mistake the first day and £2 5s the second day. When they came to the fifth race on this particular day he made another mistake and the book was so upside down that he didn't know where he was.

The Chairman (Captain Hugh Allen): Is this clerk still with you?

Prisoner: Only twice I have employed him.

The Chairman: Did you have any trouble the first time?

Prisoner: Yes.

Replying to another question, Green stated his clerk had got them all wrong and had an indelible pencil. Asked if he had brought his book with him, prisoner replied that he had not. Supt James mentioned that prisoner had been travelling the racecourse for the past four or five years, bookmaking. His clerk, who was with him that day, was a man named Martin Dudley, and was an ex-convict. Prisoner's father was also a bookmaker. In 1922 Green was fined £10 for street betting – he was then only fourteen years of age. For failing to issue tickets for bets at Birmingham in 1928 he was fined £5. The Superintendent added that they had only brought three cases forward, but there were dozens of complaints at the races.

The Bench announced that they had decided to deal leniently with the prisoner, chiefly on account of his age. He would be fined £5, with £2 5s costs. "W should like to give you a warning," added the Chairman, "if it will be of any good to you. It was stated that your clerk on the racecourse was an ex-convict. You had better be very careful who you mix with or else you might find yourself in prison."

Prisoner: Will I have time to pay?

The Chairman: No, you will have to pay to-day, or else you will get a month's imprisonment.

In the meantime Green was given an opportunity by the Superintendent of wiring for money, and on giving a promise that he would send the money prisoner was allowed to leave.

Meeting Held November 28th 1930

HUNT WEEK CHANGES

A meeting of the Tenby Race Committee was held at the "Royal Gate House Hotel," Tenby, on Saturday evening. Sir David Hughes-Morgan, Bart, was voted to the chair, and others present were the *Mayor (Mr Oliver Thomas), Mr David Harrison (hon Secretary), Mr J H F Burke (Assistant Secretary), Mr A Powell, Mr J E L Mabe, Mr J H Hodges, Mr R H Farley, Mr B J Rees, Mr A Francis, Mr G Phelps (Cresselly), Mr Tudor Griffiths (The Lodge), Mr Spencer Williams (Knightston), Mr E Williams (Knightston), Mr E H Leach.

* Mayor Oliver Thomas: local bookmaker.

Mr Burke read the accounts of the last race meeting held in January 1930. It appeared that the total expenses of the meeting had been £1,033, and there was at the present time a balance of £43 in the bank. There were, however, certain unpaid accounts, including the rent of the course, and some subscriptions still to be received; when all payments had been made and monies received it appeared that there would be a debit balance of about £30.

Mr Harrison read a letter that had been received from the National Hunt stewards, forwarding a report made by the inspector of courses. The inspector suggested an alteration of the open ditch, and other improvements of the course, and the provision of better accommodation in the weighing room. Mr Harrison stated that the open ditch had been attended to.

The Chairman said that for a good many years the Hunt Week and Race Week had been held together, but next year there was to be an alteration in regard to the Hunt Week. He did not think it a wise thing to do, but the stewards of the Hunt Week had decided to have the Hunt Ball during Easter Week, when the Point-to-Point Races were to be held. Other hunt balls were to be held in the same week at Carmarthen and elsewhere, and there might be one theatrical night at Tenby. As far as Tenby was concerned the Hunt Week would disappear, and the January Week would be a Race Week and nothing else. He did not think the alteration would make any difference to the Race Meeting, as most people came in their cars and did not stay in the town. Mr Harrison stated that he had applied for and been granted the corresponding dates to those of last year, namely, Wednesday and Thursday, January 7th and 8th. Tenby would follow the Birmingham meeting, and would have a clear fixture.

On the proposition of Mr R Farley, seconded by Mr Tudor Griffiths, it was decided to hold the meeting on the dates mentioned.

A discussion followed with regard to the accounts. It was agreed that the unpaid ones should be discharged, and to enable this to be done ten of those present undertook to become guarantors in the sum of £5 each. Mr Spencer Williams, of Knightston, kindly promised to give back half the rent of the course for the coming meeting, this being equivalent to a donation of £25. Mr Harrison stated that he thought a good many people managed to get on to the course without paying, and he asked that some different arrangement should be made at the gates for the coming meeting.

The charges for admission, it was agreed, should remain the same as last year, namely 2s 6d for the course and 12s 6d for the stand (The Grandstand is now the stand). Mr Burke mentioned that it was proposed to hold a dance during Race Week. The De Valence Gardens had been booked for Monday, January 5th, but the hall would be available on the Wednesday, owing to the cancellation of the dance for the Blind Babies' Home. It was decided to hold the dance on the Monday evening, the price of admission being 2s. Mr Francis stated that Mr Harrison had kindly promised to give whist prizes to the value of £5 for the dance, and the same amount for the Farmers' and Tradesmen's dance, which is to be held later. Sir David Hughes-Morgan also kindly promised a donation of £1 1s towards each dance.

Can you now see the swift decline of Tenby Races?

* * * * * * * * * * *

This is an article of the fight for the jockey's title from The Western Mail.

BIG FIGHT FOR JOCKEYS' CHAMPIONSHIP
FROM OUR SPECIAL CORRESPONDENT
WARWICK, Tuesday.

W.Stott and W.Speck, good friends out of the saddle, are having a big fight for the National Hunt jockeys' championship. The former has ridden 32 winners since August 1, and the other 31. It is all the more interesting as they are possessed of similar styles of riding. Each is small for a steeplechase rider, but is strong and game.

Stott has been handicapped through having several nasty falls, which kept him out of the saddle for various periods, but the accidents do not appear to have damped his ardour. I do not think he knows the meaning of the word "fear" as he keeps returning as if nothing untoward had happened. The little fellow is smart over fences and hurdles. In comparison to many of the other jockeys he has not been riding long over the sticks. He did not ride much on the flat owing to increasing weight, and was taking part in private trials for a long time until Bernard Carslake advised him to try his luck under the winter code. Almost immediately he started to ride under National Hunt Rules. He met with success and he has not looked back since.

STOTT, A MODEST FELLOW

He is a modest fellow, and his many victories have not spoilt him. At the dinner he gave at Cheltenham to celebrate his winning of the championship last year, he had very little to say – in fact, he appeared to be tired of people singing his praises. Perseverance and dash are his chief assets, for no matter what class of a horse he is riding he gets all out of his mount, and believes that a race is never lost until it is over. Stott has won many a race through outriding other jockeys, and for his size he has remarkable strength.

Speck has equal courage, and is a fine finisher. His experience under Jockey Club Rules is responsible for his smooth and sound steering in a close tussle. To see Speck and Stott in opposition with not much between them on the run in is exhilarating, for the horses under them have to strain every nerve until they pass the post so powerful are the jockey's efforts. That is why owners and trainers are always anxious to secure their services. It is not often one sees either of them ride badly, and barring accidents they will hold their own for many years. Speck started to ride during the winter because he did not get sufficient mounts on the flat, although he could ride at a reasonable weight. He has told me many times he does not regret his change.

FRED REES, THE ARTIST

F. B. REES,
SIR MALCOLM McALPINE'S COLOURS

Although Speck and Stott are clever, however, for the real artistry in jockeyship one has to give credit to F B Rees. It does not matter whether he is riding over fences or hurdles he is just the same – he seems to make himself a part of the horse. One never sees him pushing his mount when it is unnecessary, but he can "drive" a horse strongly when required so to do. I have seen him ride in all classes of races, and the more I see of him the more I realise our present flat race jockeys would have to sit up and take notice if Rees's weight would allow his riding against them. He has not been well recently, and I hope he will soon recover.

Although George Duller thinks more of training than riding nowadays, Stott, Speck, F B Rees and some of the others keep the standard of jockeyship under National Hunt Rules high.

1931

The number of horses in the stables now were less than twenty, which included David Harrison's own. The time had come to have a word with O'Connor, the Irish vet, to tell him that he had spoken to Brychan Rees and they both felt that they could no longer keep him on as the second veterinary surgeon. It was very difficult for David Harrison because he was still seeing Patricia O'Connor on her regular visits from Ireland. O'Connor said that he thought the day would not be far away and that he understood, but that Harrison's worry was to be his sister Patricia, as she was in love with Harrison. He asked O'Connor to contact her to ask her to come to Tenby so that he could explain his position to her.

"I remember her being here for the last time," said Ashley Colley. "I knew that O'Connor was going, but I have no idea what happened, apart from her staying for a few months during the summer; but she was out and about a lot more than usual, because she was the kind of woman that you would notice anywhere, especially that summer. I remember it was hot and she showed more of herself in public than most women of that time would, if you know what I mean. She had a lovely figure and she showed it off. I don't remember O'Connor or her leaving at any particular time, only that he wasn't there for the next winter season. They must have sorted something out with Harrison. I know he would have had good references from Brychan Rees and Harrison. He was a very good vet and a lovely, funny man. I don't even know where he went, I don't think anybody dare ask because David Harrison was pretty keen on her, and the last thing you wanted was to get on the wrong side of him."

****

The 1931 meeting was held on January 7th and 8th.
TENBY RACES (A Western Mail Report)
TWO FINE DAYS AND SPLENDID SPORT
TOTE IN OPERATION

The opening day of the Tenby Hunt Steeplechases and Hurdle Race Meeting was held under the most favourable conditions. While the sport has been held up at a number of centres by frost and fog the Pembrokeshire fixture opened under summer-like conditions, the warm sun, combined with a slight nip in the air, being almost ideal for outdoor sport, and a splendid crowd attended.

For the First time the "Tote" was in operation here and did quite a fair amount of business.

AMONG THOSE PRESENT

Capt Hugh Allen, Major T Alexander, Mr Ivor Anthony, Captain Hugh Angell, Mr E T Allen. Capt W H Buckley, Mr E P Barthropp, Major Barclay, Mr G Baker, Mr F Brown, Mr and Mrs A Beavan. Sir Geoffrey and Lady Congreve, Mr G Cooper, Captain W Cope. Col and Mrs Delme Davies-Evans, Mr A E Dyke, Mr D Davies, Mr D S Davies, Miss D Davison, Miss L I Davison, Mr E Daniels, Mr S Evans, Mr T Edwards, Miss G V Edmonds. Mr W Fletcher, Mr and Mrs G I Fraser, Mr J Ford, Mr A Francis, Captain J Flood, Mr E Falney. Mr E George, Capt E Garland, Mr and Mrs G Gooding, Sir David Hughes-Morgan, Bart, JP and Lady Hughes-Morgan, Mrs Haddon Howard and Master J Howard, Mr and Mrs David Harrison, Mr J Hodges, Mr A E Hancock, Miss E Higgins. Mr J Jarrett, Mr Morgan Jones, Mr and Mrs D A Jackson, Mr J Jones, Mrs C Jones, Miss A C James, Lord Kylsant, Major J Kelly, Miss Knight. Col Morgan Lindsay, the Hon Anne Lewis M F H, Mr T Lewis, Miss E Lawrence, Miss G V Lawrence, Mr G Llewellyn, Miss Lyle. Sir Armine Morris, the Hon Mrs Basil Mundy, Mr N McKinnon, Mr J Morris, Mr C Mathias, Mr R C Morel, Captain G Morgan, Miss N Mackie, Mr D D Morgan, Mr and Mrs C Mason.

First Day

LAWRENNY STEEPLE CHASE
of £67 Three miles
Sir G Congreve's, Bath Chap, Owner, 1
Winner trained by F G Hunt, Hednesford
Also ran – Tetrasant (G Hardy), Dove's Pride (Speck)
Betting – evens Dove's Pride, 6 - 4 agst, Tetrasant,
7 - 1, Bath Chap
Tote: Win, 6s 3d
All three horses fell.
Bath Chap and Tetrasant were remounted, but Tetrasant refused and Bath Chap went on to win alone.

KNIGHTSTON SELLING HURDLE RACE
of £50 Two miles
Mr C Horton's, Saighton, J Hamey, 1
Mr P Sheehan's, (IRE), Buckna, Mr J Sheehan, 2
Mr D Faber's, Summer Night, G Hardy, 3
Winner trained by R Gordon, Wroughton
Also ran – Marrifirth (Speck), Jack XIII (Mr Raymond),

223

Royal Saloon (R Henton), Boneblack (Owner), Swanlake Bay
(Mr Walwyn, Copybook (Owner)
Betting – 2 - 1 agst Marrifirth, 5 - 2 Saighton, 3 - 1 Buckna, 6 - 1 Royal Saloon, 100 - 7
Summer Night and others.
Won by five lengths; three lengths divided second and third.
Tote: Win, 8s 3d

LLWYNARTHAN CHALLENGE CUP
of 50 Guineas With £50 added; hurdle race Two miles
Mrs Mundy's, Lough Mor, Speck, 1
Mr D A Jackson's, Passing Cloud, Owner, 2
Mr D D Stewart's, St Cecilia, Owner, 3
Winner trained by D Harrison, Tenby
Also ran – Perfective (O Thomas), Putney (G Hardy)
Betting – 11 - 4 on Lough Mor, 6 - 1 agst Putney,
10 - 1 Perfective, 100 - 8 Passing Cloud and
St Cecilia
Won by four lengths; six lengths divided second and third
Tote: Win, 2s 9d

GROVE OPTIONAL SELLING STEEPLE CHASE
of £70 Two miles
Lord Allendale's, Heartburn, J Hamey, 1
Mrs L Wilson's, Hackdene, D Williams, 2
Winner trained by Gordon, Wroughton
Also ran – Craignure (G Bowden), Count Vella (W Parvin)
Betting – 6 - 4 on Heartburn, 6 - 4 agst Hackdene, 100 - 6 others
Won by a neck; only two finished.
Tote: Win, 4s 9d

WROUGHTON NATIONAL HUNT FLAT RACE
of £50 Amateur riders, Two miles
Mr J H Wallace's, Georginatown, Mr L Whitfield, 1
Mrs C Jones's, Doubtful Lady, Mr R Morel, 2
Mrs Mundy's, Dove's Pride, Mr Walwyn, 3
Winner trained in Ireland
Betting – 5 - 2 on Georginatown, 11 - 4 agst Dove's Pride,
8 - 1 Doubtful Lady.
Won by six lengths; three-quarters of a length divided second and third.
Tote: Win, 2s 6d

DAILY TOTE DOUBLE
The tote double returned a dividend of 19s; double pool, £21.
There were 19 winning tickets.
TOTAL TOTE INVESTMENTS
Total Tote investments - £237 10s.

NO TOTE PLACE BETTING

DON'T FORGET

TO - NIGHT

AT THE

SUPER CINEMA, Warren Street

THE

RACE DANCE

Dancing: 9 p.m. till 3 a.m.

TICKETS, 2/-.   -   **REFRESHMENTS EXTRA**

Proceeds in aid of Tenby Races.

SECOND DAY'S EVENTS

Since the institution of the Tenby Hunt Steeplechase and Hurdle Races the meeting has achieved a reputation which is almost unique. There is an atmosphere at Tenby not experienced at any other race meeting and the sport is watched and thoroughly enjoyed in a spirit of festivity. While other cities and towns have their festivals and special occasions, the folk of Pembrokeshire make the two days' racing their gala days.

During its existence, however, Tenby has acquired one undesirable feature - that of the weather – and one good day and one bad had become almost a tradition. This trait, however, was eliminated this year, and the two days' fixture was held under wonderful conditions. With reports of snow and hail from some quarters and meetings abandoned owing to frost in others, racing at Tenby was never more doubtful on the second day. The fine day attracted an even bigger attendance than that of the opening day, and those present were rewarded with a splendid afternoon's sport.

A CAPITAL RACE

As usual a deal of local interest was evinced in the United Counties Farmers' and Tradesmen's Hurdle, for which eight of the ten entries went to the post. Mrs W H Roch's Splendid, last year's winner, was an odds-on favourite in spite of having to shoulder 13st 3lbs. The race proved a capital one, Skip On making the running for half the journey, when Splendid went to the front, followed by Phoebe III and Early Dawn. The three swung into the straight clear of the others, and though Phoebe III made desperate efforts to get on terms, Mr H S Hughes, riding a fine race on Splendid, won cleverly by a couple of lengths. The winner was accorded an ovation on returning to the paddock.

GATE HOUSE HURDLE RACE
of £50 Two Miles
Mr D Harrison's, Skrinkle Bay, Speck, 1
Mrs C Jones's, Vivacious, W Parvin, 2
Mr D A Jackson's, Passing Cloud, Owner 3
Winner trained by D Harrison, Tenby
Also ran – Betty Dhu (Mr Walwyn), Mis-direction (O Thomas), Dee-side (Owner)
Betting – 5 - 4 on Skrinkle Bay, 9 - 4 agst Vivacious, 4 - 1 Passing Cloud, 100 - 7 others.
Won by ten lengths; the same divided second and third.
Tote: Win, 4s

PARK HOUSE SELLING HANDICAP STEEPLE CHASE
of £70 Two miles
Mr R E More's, Easter Boy II, Mr R Morel, 1
Mr O A Greenslade's, Lewis Gun, G Wilson, 2
Winner trained by Roberts, Cheltenham
Also ran – Betting Tax (W Parvin)
Betting – Evens Easter Boy II, 5 - 4 agst Lewis Gun, 8 - 1 Betting Tax
Won by 20 lengths
Tote: Win, 3s
The three horses fell, but Easter Boy II and Lewis Gun were remounted and finished the course.

LICENSED VICTUALLERS' SELLING HANDICAP HURDLE RACE
of £50 Two miles
Mr J C Ainsworth's, Peccadillo, Major H Misa, 1
Mr C C Williams's, Eel Point, Speck, 2
Mrs M Evans's, Dream O'Fortune, D Williams, 3
Also ran – Jack XIII (Mr Raymond), Sonny Fitz (J H Brown)
Betting – 5 - 4 agst Eel Point, 6 - 4 Dream O'Fortune, 4 - 1 Sonny Fitz,
8 - 1 Peccadillo, 20 - 1 Jack XIII
Won by five lengths; eight lengths divided second and third.

226

Tote: Win, 19s 3d

TOWN HANDICAP STEEPLE CHASE
of £67 Three miles
Mr J H Wallace'sGeorginatown, F Maxwell, 1
Col M Lindsay'sCairbre, Mr Walwyn, 2
Winner trained in Ireland
Betting – 5 - 1 on Georginatown, 5 - 1 agst Cairbre
Won by 30 lengths
Tote: Win, 2s 9d

UNITED COUNTIES FARMERS' AND TRADESMEN'S HURDLE RACE
of £45 Two miles
Mr W Roch's, Splendid, Mr Hughes, 1
Mr J S Hodges's, Phoebe III, Owner, 2
Mr W M Lewis, Early Dawn, Mr W Lewis, 3
Winner trained privately
Also ran – Lady O (Mr V Griffiths), Erse (Mr T Griffiths),
Watchman II (Sir G Congreve), Skip On (Mr Walwyn), Possession (Mr Watkins)
Betting – 6 - 4 on Splendid, 7 - 2 agst Early Dawn,
6 - 1 Phoebe III, 100 - 8 others.
Won by three lengths; ten lengths divided second and third.
Tote: Win, 4s

TOTAL TOTE INVESTMENTS
Total Tote investments - £118 4s.

227

CHAPTER 10
THE FINAL FURLONG

1932

In 1932 the races were in a terrible state of affairs. At the meeting of the Tenby Corporation in early January, a letter was read from Mr David Harrison, the Hon Sec of the Tenby Race meeting, asking the council for a subscription. The Deputy Mayor suggested that £10 was a reasonable amount, yet Alderman Hughes suggested £5. It was then argued that it may be illegal to do so, as the money was to come from the ratepayers; so why not give the same to the Bowling Club and Football Club, which were more deserving cases anyway.

Mr Collins said that the council had no right to finance a private business. He maintained that the races, from a purely sporting point of view, were all right, but when they were fun solely for an influx of undesirable riff-raff, and for their benefit only, it was time to call a halt to it. He said that he remembered the races when he was a young lad, when it was pure sport and all the aristocracy from the Principality attended. It was said that the races were £94 in debt and the town had not given a penny to support them for many years past. He said that a raffle had been held at the Imperial Hotel in aid of the races, and a gentleman staying at the hotel won the prize of "a lamb". He immediately gave it back; it was then auctioned and given back on two further occasions by racehorse owners, and again on two occasions by jockeys, until the well known Cardiff bookmaker, Danny Davies bought the lamb and gave it to the Tenby Cottage Hospital. "Are these the people you consider riff-raff?" said the Deputy Mayor. It was voted to give £5 to the Race fund.

A Western Mail Report:

THE SAD TALE OF A RACE MEETING

TOTE TAKES £59 12S IN TWO DAYS

WASHED OUT

This is the sad story of the two-day race meeting arranged to take place at Tenby, South Wales, on Wednesday and yesterday (Thursday):

The first day was abandoned because the ground was waterlogged and racing was impossible. A decision to open the gates yesterday was deferred till about 10a.m. Owing to the doubtfulness of sport taking place the attendance was the smallest ever.

Soon after the first race rain fell with considerable violence, and continued throughout the day.

Only twenty-six horses turned out for the six races decided. Consequently there was no place betting at all on the tote. In the first race two horses fell out of four, and the winner finished alone. In the second two fell out of seven. In the third all three finished. In the fourth two out of four fell, and one ran out. The fifth event was a flat race, so there were no falls. There were four starters for the last race, and the misery of the onlookers was complete when an 100 - 8 outsider beat the even-money favourite by twenty lengths.

The tote had an awful time. Only £3 16s was taken on the first race. The total amount invested on the six races was only £359 12s. The Racecourse Betting Control Board's percentage was therefore less than £5 for all the expenses of a two-day meeting.

****

D HARRISON'S "HAT TRICK"
PROMISING YOUNG JOCKEY

Following a cold, boisterous morning, accompanied by heavy hail-storms, the weather on the first day (Wednesday) suddenly changed for the better, and when the annual Hunt Steeplechases Meeting opened the sun was shining brilliantly consequently the attendance was fairly well up to average.

Unfortunately, however, fields did not come up to the strength anticipated, and except for the first and fourth events were not representative. Still, from a backer's standpoint it was a good afternoon, for four of the five events fell to favourites, and the other winner was also well supported.

Mr David Harrison, the local trainer, took the honours of the day with three winners – White Flag and Lough Mor, owned by the Hon Mrs Basil Mundy, and Pathos, the property of Mrs N Weaver.

Local interest was also associated with the Wroughton National Hunt Flat Race, won by Slater, the property of Mr J H Whitney, the American millionaire patron of Jack Anthony's stable. Slater, who has been rather a disappointment over the jumps, was ridden by Mr H A Jones, son of Mr Herbert Jones, a well-known Carmarthen farmer and a nephew of the famous Anthony brothers of Kidwelly.

FIRST WINNING RIDE

The youthful rider – he is only sixteen years of age – has been at the riding establishment of his uncle, Mr Jack Anthony, at Wantage since October last, having gone there straight from school at Carmarthen. Jack quickly realised that the lad had ability and gave him his chance. This was young Jones's sixth ride in public and his first winning mount. His first ride was on Craftsman at Stratford-on-Avon, and, though beaten, he had demonstrated that he at least had ability as a jockey.

The only favourite to be upset was Lord Puttenden in the Knightston Selling Hurdle, with which the proceedings opened. Half a mile from home he seemed to have the race in hand, but coming into the straight G Owen sent Tuck Box to the front, and coming away from the last flights Mr H Dyke Dennis's representative won by a couple of lengths. At the subsequent auction, however, he failed to elicit a bid. The Hon Mrs Basil Mundy's White Flag had no difficulty in winning the Violet Mundy Challenge Cup, presented by Mrs Mundy herself, and which has to be won three times, while Lough Mor, also owned by Mrs Mundy, carried off the National Hunt Steeplechase, thus completing a double for W Speck. By riding Pathos to victory in the Grove Steeplechase G Owen also scored a double.

We noticed: Lord and Lady Kylsant and Lady Suffield, Sir David Hughes-Morgan, Bart, and Lady Hughes-Morgan, Major and Mrs W M Saurin, Sir Geoffrey and Lady Congreve, Mrs L Tate Mrs G Stokes, Mr Owen Anthony, Mr C C Williams, Mr J W Baillie, Mr H Dyke Dennis, Capt A Wengall, Capt Monty Williams, Mr and Mrs David Harrison, Mr R C Morel, Major Morgan Jones, Col and Mrs Seymour Allen, Mr Hugh D Allen, Capt and Mrs Hugh Allen, Miss V Allen, the Hon Anne Lewis, M F H Sir John Grey Mr R H Farley. Col Morgan Lindsay, Mr David Lindsay, Major and Mrs G R Turner, Mr David Turner, Miss M Knight Mr and Mrs A Williams, Mr and Mrs Sackvill Owen, Councillor Alfred Francis (Deputy Mayor), the Mayoress of Tenby (Mrs H J Collins), Miss Davies-Evans, Mr Williams Merriman, Mr Thomas Williams, Mr Griffith Thomas, Mr and Mrs T R Griffiths Miss Norah Pascoe, Miss T F Rees, Mr G F Rees, Mr C O Pascoe, Mr C H Williams, Mr S Berry. Major and Mrs E G Early, Mr and Mrs D O Stuart, Mr T R Mills, Mr C Thomas,
*[1] Local R. C. Priest, Father Moran, Mr Morgan Jones, Mr A Knowles, Miss Martin-John, the Hon Mrs Basil Mundy, Mrs R J Ingham, Miss Priscilla Ingham, Mr David Saunders, Mr Victor Higgon, Alderman Oliver Thomas, Major Roberts, Mr and Mrs Bailey, Mr T Williams.

The stewards were: Col Morgan Lindsay, Sir David Hughes-Morgan, Bart, Mr H Dyke Dennis, and Mr C C Williams, M F H. The following were the officials: Judge, Mr A E Hancock; clerk of the scales, Mr T H Wilton Pye; handicapper, Mr Andrew Knowles; clerk of the course, Mr O F Thomas; starter, *[2] Mr George Phelps; auctioneer, Mr J A Roch; hon secretary, Mr David Harrison; assistant hon secretary, Mr J H Fitzgerald-Burke; auditor and stakeholder, Mr Ashley E Colley; hon surgeon, Dr C Mathias; hon veterinary surgeon, Mr B J Rees.

*[1] This should ring a bell from my previous mention of a R. C. Priest.
*[2] Dick Francis's Great-uncle.

First Day

1-30 KNIGHTSTON SELLING HURDLE RACE
of £50 Two miles
Mr H Dennis's, Tuck Box, G Owen, 1
Mrs N Roberts's, Lord Puttenden, J Moloney, 2
Mr D Stewart's, St Cecilia, J Hamey, 3
Also ran – Placid (Mr D Smyly), Severn Slip (W Speck),
Leopardess (Mr D Stewart), Trainer, P Dennis. No bid for winner.

Betting – 5 - 4 on Lord Puttenden, 2 - 1 agst Tuck Box, 6 - 1 Severn Slip, 10 - 1 St Cecilia, 100 - 6 others.
Won by 2 lengths; 6, Off at 1.32.
Tote: Win, 11s

2-5 VIOLET MUNDY CHALLENGE CUP
(Handicap hurdle) value £50, presented by Mrs Basil Mundy, with £50 added. Two miles
Mrs Mundy's, White Flag, Speck, 1
Mr C Williams's, Swanlake Bay, J Hamey, 2
Mrs C Jones's, Back Isle, J Moloney, 3
Trainer, D Harrison
Betting – 3 - 1 on White Flag, 5 - 1 agst Back Isle, 8 - 1 Swanlake Bay
Won by 3 lengths; a bad third.
Off at 2.7
Tote: Win, 2s 3d

2-40 NATIONAL HUNT PLATE STEEPLE CHASE
of £100 Three miles
Mrs Mundy's, Lough Mor, Speck, 1
Also ran – Yellow Oriel (G Owen).
Trainer D Harrison
Betting – 11 - 4 on Lough Mor
Off at 2.42
Tote: Win, 2s 3d

3-15 GROVE OPTIONAL SELLING STEEPLE CHASE
of £75 Two miles
Mrs N Weaver's, Pathos, G Owen, 1
Mrs C Jones's, Salt of the Earth, E Foster, 2
Mrs I Tate's, Yes or No, J Walsh, 3
Also ran – Little Honey (G Bowden)
Trainer, D Harrison
Betting – 6 - 4 on Pathos, 5 - 2 agst Yes or No, 9 - 2 Salt of the Earth, 100 - 8 Little Honey
Won by 4 lengths
Off at 3.16
Tote: Win, 3s 3d

3-45 WROUGHTON NATIONAL HUNT FLAT RACE
of £50 Two miles
Mr J Whitney's, Slater, Mr H Jones, 1
Sir D Llewellyn's, Breconian, Mr E Williams, 2
Trainer J Anthony
Betting – 3 - 1 on Slater;

Won by 3 lengths
Off at 3.46
Tote: Win, 2s 3d

REPORT OF SECOND DAY'S RACING

Tenby Racecourse was bathed in brilliant sunshine for the concluding stage of the Tenby Hunt Steeplechases on Thursday. The attendance was larger than on the opening afternoon, and the sport much more entertaining. Heavy overnight rain had left the course a little yielding, but on the whole the going was fairly good.

From a backer's standpoint, however, it was not so satisfactory, for only one favourite was successful, namely, Sir John Grey's Winged Victory, on which odds of 5 - 2 were laid. Three other odds-on "shots" failed to materialise, and another well-backed horse, Lord Puttenden, also disappointed.

After his forward display of the previous day, the Cheltenham representative was expected to win the Licensed Victuallers' Hurdle. He did not, however, have it all his own way in the market, for there was some good money for Sprint shortly before the off. "Blower" money for Lord Puttenden, however, established him firm favourite, and when the field had covered three-parts of the journey it looked as though the confidence was justified. He raced into the straight with at least half-a-dozen lengths lead of Wait and See, but after negotiating the last hurdle he compounded rapidly, and A Smyth, riding a desperate race on Wait and See, got up to win by a neck. Subsequently offered at auction, the winner failed to raise a bid.

A WELSH SUCCESS

Mr D Stewart, the Welsh owner-rider, had the satisfaction of winning the Gate House Hurdle with Subjugate, beating a hot favourite in Perfective.

Sir Geoffrey Congreve was most anxious to win the Town Steeplechase on his gallant old horse, Bath Chap. The only opposition was provided by Mrs L Tate's Yes or No and Col Morgan Lindsay's Bellamite. It was, therefore, not surprising to find the layers asking for odds of 5 - 2 in respect of Bath Chap. Taking the lead from the outset of a tiring three miles journey, Sir Geoffrey appeared practically certain of gaining the prize, but following a mistake two fences from home Bath Chap, though still in the lead, toppled over at the final obstacle, leaving Yes or No to win comfortably from Bellamite.

There was no lack of local enthusiasm in connection with the United Counties' Farmers' and Tradesmen's Hurdle. Only six horses went to the post, but the wagering was pretty brisk. Eventually, May B III, last year's winner, became a pronounced favourite, but there was also confidence behind Gay Lad III and Bandit II. Backers were dealt their fourth bad blow when the favourite fell on the last circuit when leading, leaving Bandit II, with a lead of Gay Lad III. This was the order over the last flight. Then ensured a desperate tussle for supremacy, Mr H Hughes, on Gay Lad III, eventually overhauling his rival to win by ten lengths, with Watchman II, who earlier in the day had failed to reach his reserve, a bad third.

Second Day

1-0 GATE HOUSE HURDLE RACE
of £50 Two miles
Mr D Steward's, Subjugate, Owner, 1
Sir J Grey's, Vain Prince, J Hamey, 2
Mrs Mundy's, Perfective, W Speck, 3
Also ran – Scrambled (G Bowden), Casquet's Light (G Wilson),
Fair Measure (O Thomas)
Trainer, Owner
Betting – 2 - 1 on Perfective, 5 - 2 agst Subjugate, 10 - 1 Vain Prince
And others.
Won by 6 lengths; Off at 1.01
Tote: Win 3s 3d

1-30 PARK HOUSE HANDICAP CHASE
of £75 Two miles
Sir J Grey's, Winged Victory, J Hamey, 1
Mrs L Tate's, Mrs Shears, J Walsh, 2
Mrs Mundy's, Dove's Pride, W Speck, 3
Trainer, Barthropp
Betting – 5 - 2 on Winged Victory, 11 - 4 agst Dove's Pride,
8 - 1 Mrs Shears
Won by a length; Off at 1.31
Tote: Win, 3s 3d

2-0 LICENSED VICTUALLERS' SELLING HANDICAP HURDLE RACE
of £50 Two miles
Mr G Shakerley's, Wait and See, A Smyth, 1
Mrs N Roberts's, Lort Puttenden, J Moloney, 2
Mr A Boxhall's, Sprint, E Foster, 3
Also ran – Placid (Mr D Smyly)
Trainer F A Brown
No bid for winner
Betting – 11 - 8 agst Lord Puttenden, 6 - 4 Sprint, 4 - 1 Wait and See, 100 - 6 Placid.
Won by half a length; a bad third
Off at 2.05
Tote: Win, 9s 9d

2-30 TOWN HANDICAP STEEPLE CHASE
of £75 Three miles
Mrs L Tate's, Yes or No, J Walsh, 1
Col M Lindsay's, Bellamite, G Bowden, 2
Sir G Congreve, Bath Chap, Owner, 3
Trainer, Tate
Betting – 5 - 2 on Bath Chap, 5 - 2 agst Yes or No, 100 - 6 Bellamite
Won by 4 lengths; a bad third.
Off at 2.31
Tote: Win, 3s 6d

3-0 UNITED COUNTIES FARMERS' AND TRADESMEN'S HURDLE RACE
of £45 Two miles
Mrs Ingham's, Gay Lad II, Mr H Hughes, 1
Mr G Williams's, Bandit II, Mr E Williams, 2
Mrs C Griffiths's, Watchman II, Mr T Griffiths, 3
Also ran – May B III (Mr W Lewis), Sportsman (Mr D Smyly);
Moysland (Mr E Watkins)
Trained privately
Betting – 5 - 4 on May B III, 3 - 1 agst Gay Lad III, 4 - 1 Bandit II, 10 - 1 Watchman II,
20 - 1 others.
Won by 2 lengths; a bad third.
Off at 3.00
Tote: Win, 9s 6d

****

"ROBIN GOODFELLOW" AND TENBY RACES

In yesterday's (Thursday) issue of the "Daily Mail", "Robin Goodfellow", that journal's well-known racing expert writes:

I have never had occasion to visit Tenby while the annual jumping meeting is in progress, and it is extremely improbable that the necessity for going there at that time will ever arise in my case. For one thing, it would mean fitting in a pretty hopeless round-the-world railway journey between the meetings which come before and after it and which one must attend; while so far as the racing is concerned, Tenby has no place to fill in the general order of things connected with the N H season.

I have no quarrel with the Tenby meeting, which, from what I gather from those who have been there, is well conducted and has a social side found at very few other racing venues. It creates local employment and causes money to be spent, and for that reason one hopes it may continue. But just why it should be allowed to hold up generally the jumping season for two whole days, as it does and has done, is a thing which I do not understand.

Each year Tenby paralyses the regular racing forces nearly as effectively as fog, flood and frost. Very few, if any, starting-price bookmakers are left who will accept wagers for the meeting; the subsidiary company connected with the totalisator refuses to do any business during the two days while the tote itself operates on a scale which makes it literally "the toy" it is called at all times by its opponents.

Do the authorities who grant Tenby two clear days year after year ever stop to think of the consequences of this holding up of the daily turnover connected with racing? I do not suppose for one moment that they do. Tenby gets its two days because, as is the rule with ultra-conservative racecourse management, it had them last year - and the year before.

There was a time when racing had the monopoly of the form of sporting entertainment which it supplies. It has not that monopoly now, and yet there is very little evidence to be found that those who have the conduct of the game are cognisant of that fact. I do not think our competitors would leave their public to kick its heels aimlessly around for two days as we do.

From Thursday's Daily Mail:
5 RACES, 17 RUNNERS ON FIRST DAY
FOUR ODDS-ON NATIONAL HUNT WINNERS

The two-days National Hunt fixture at Tenby, "North" Wales, began yesterday. There were five races, and the total number of runners was 17. Four odds-on favourites won, and the price of the other winner was 2 - 1. D Harrison, the local trainer, had six runners. Three of them won. Betting was virtually confined to the course. Very few starting-price bookmakers kept their offices open.

The Tenby Observor reported:
"By the way, we are rather surprised that a great national journal like the `Daily Mail` does not know the geographical location of Tenby. Don't they keep a Gazetteer at Northcliff House?"

****

David Harrison was now in serious financial difficulty, yet it did not seem possible that after such a successful career as a trainer for more than thirty years he should have no money, especially after the coup of 1927; it should have made him a considerable sum of money, although it was a disaster for

In the County Court of PEMBROKESHIRE holden at Haverfordwest

IN BANKRUPTCY. No. 8 of 19 33 .

RE DAVID HARRISON, residing at The Grove, Tenby, in the County of Pembroke, RACE HORSE TRAINER, and carrying on business at The Stables, Frog Street, Tenby aforesaid.

NON-SUMMARY CASE

(Under Receiving Order dated the 27th day of October, 1933. Debtor's Petition.)

TAKE NOTICE that I, the undersigned Official Receiver, acting as Trustee of the property of the Bankrupt, intend to apply to the Board of Trade for my release, and further take notice that any objection you may have to the granting of my release must be notified to the Board of Trade (Bankruptcy Department), 20, Great Smith Street, London, S.W.1, within twenty-one days of the date hereof.

A Summary of my receipts and payments as Trustee is given below.

NOTE.—Section 93 of the Bankruptcy Act, 1914, enacts that " An order of the Board releasing the Trustee shall " discharge him from all liability in respect of any act done or default made by him in the administration of " the affairs of the Bankrupt, or otherwise in relation to his conduct as trustee, but such order may be revoked " on proof that it was obtained by fraud or by suppression or concealment of any material fact."

DR. *Statement showing position of Estate at date of application for release.* CR.

	Estimated to produce per Debtor's statement.			Receipts.				£	s.	d.	£	s.	d.
	£	s.	d.	£	s.	d.	By Court Fees, including Petition Stamp				5	14	6
To total receipts from date of Receiving Order, viz.							„ Board of Trade Fees, viz. :—						
Deposit on Petition.	—	—	—	10	—	—	Fees in respect of 11 Creditors and 39 Debtors, and including Stationery, Printing, Postages, Rooms for Meetings of Creditors	23	—	—			
Cash in hand......	9	17	—	11	9	10	2½% on amount of assets realized £3,585.2.11....	197	17	11			
Implements, farming stock, trade fixtures, fittings, utensils etc......	800	—	6	1,000	—	—	2½% on amount of dividend £ 2,651. 0. 2. ...	85	18	—			
Furniture.........	521	3	—	614	3	—	Ad-valorem duty on Audit, &c.	52	10	—			
Life interest under Will of T.A. Harrison......	400	—	—	1,344	4	3	Other Fees........	7	1	11	366	7	10
Book Debts.......	309	13	—	304	12	3	„ Costs of Notices in Gazette and Local Paper				3	3	6
O.R's. interest in W.C. Policy........	—	—	—	11	15	3	„ Person appointed to assist Debtor to prepare statement of affairs ...				2	2	—
Wheat supplied to Wheat Commission...	—	—	—	24	5	10	„ Auctioneer's, Surveyor's and Valuer's charges				12	19	—
Repayment of Income Tax........	—	—	—	33	14	7	Shorthand writer's charges...				1	15	6
Refund of wages overpaid..........	—	—	—	10	—	—	Law costs of petition........				18	8	2
Receipts per trading a/c.......	—	—	—	57	10	11	Travelling expenses..........				1	5	2
	£2,040	13	6	3,412	5	11	Incidental expenses..........				4	3	3
LESS:—							Total Costs and Charges......				415	18	11
Deposit returned...	10	—	—				Creditors, viz:—						
Refund of amount paid subsequent to O.R's. interest....	3	11	—				20 Preferential..............				212	4	3
Costs of execution.	72	1	7				69 Unsecured for first and final dividend of 2/10¾d. in the £ on £18,375.4.9.				2,651	—	2
Payments per Trading a/c........	45	5	10	130	18	5	N.B. The debtor's estimate of amount expected to rank for dividend was £15,892. 7. 7.						
							Balance				2	4	2
			£3,281	7	6						£3,281	7	6

Assets not yet realised, estimated to produce NIL.

OFFICIAL RECEIVER'S REMARKS:— 1. The Official Receiver carried on the debtor's business up to the date of sale, and disposed of the same as a going concern. The result of the trading is shewn in the above a/cs. 2. The debtor failed to schedule a large number of creditors in his Statement of Affairs.

Tenby Races. Whether it is true or not I cannot say but I was told some time ago that both David Harrison and George Stokes had invested a lot of money in Lord Kylsant's shipping company after the coup, without the knowledge of it being bogus. If this is the case, it could account for both the sudden death of George Stokes and the bankruptcy of David Harrison. The same person told me that a lot of prominent people in the county had also been the victims of Lord Kylsant's share deals, for which he was eventually imprisoned. I would tend to go along with this train of thought, 'as there is no smoke without fire', and if it is the case then I feel sorry for both George Stokes and David Harrison, because those two to me, whether you like them or not, were the backbone of that Tenby Race Meeting; and to be fair to David Harrison, for all his bad faults, Tenby Stable and the Race Meeting had his blood running right through its very veins right to the very end. Harrison did not pack his bags and leave, but fought the battle right to the bitter end, and you must admire the man for that. Over the last twenty or so years, I have grown to live and breathe a lot of these characters and have tended to really feel as if I was actually there; to tell them not to do certain things and guide them to do others. But this is the real world, and as it was then, they did what they did and that is that.

To me, this is the end, 'The Bankruptcy of David Harrison'. It is so sad, and I have not been looking forward to this particular part of the book, and although there are a few more years left of Tenby Races, I think somehow that my heart goes out of it here.

****

In 1933, Willy Stott, shortly after winning the Gold Cup on Golden Miller, took a bad fall on Pelorous Jack in the Grand National whilst in the lead from Kellesboro Jack at the last fence. He was forced to stop riding after medical examinations showed that he had a weak heart. Later that year he died, following a bad car crash, in which he swerved to avoid a pedestrian, thus crashing head-on into a stone wall. In an interview in the 1970's, Tim Hamey (who won the Grand National in 1932 on Forbra) who was an inseparable friend of both Stotty and Specky, said, "When I won, Stotty was more excited than I was, he was a great man and a true friend, that's the way jockeys were in those days, and when Specky was killed at Cheltenham in 1935, I was offered the mount, but he wanted it so bad that I gave it to him, it should have been me out there, not Specky. I know that a lot of people feel that riding over fences was never anything much until Lord Mildmay and others like him lifted it out of the commonplace, but it was jockeys like Stotty and Specky who won the admiration of the public, along with the Anthony brothers and the Rees brothers: they were all fearless, and in those days we jumped real fences. The years when we all rode together were the best years, and the men riding then, were the best in the game."

On the death of Specky the trainer Ben Roberts said, "He was one of the boldest riders that I ever knew, he had almost too big a heart, but racing was his life, and he was part of a breed of men, of whom we shall never see the likes again, I am afraid that this is the end of a glorious golden era for National Hunt Racing". One famous retired jockey also commented, "If the jockeys of today could see some of the tracks that we had to ride on, I don't know what they would make of them. Many of the fences were 'Island Fences' and you couldn't give an inch away; also if you were up against someone like Specky, you had no chance of getting the rails, as he hugged them like a brother, and if Stotty was coming up on your other side, it was no use shouting, you just had to fend for yourself."

Tim Hamey continued, "There were lots of characters on the race tracks in those days, real colourful characters, one of whom was Archie Hunter. He knew all the small-time crooks in the business, and he would sometimes run a book himself, which was all right if the favourite did not win the first race; he would often borrow a few quid from one of us to start a book, and if things went wrong, Archie went missing, but you always got your money back, usually in dirty ten-bob notes in a registered envelope six months later."

In 1934 Specky had won the Great Lancashire Chase for Mrs Mundy on Avenger, trained at Tenby by David Harrison. He was also involved in the great epic duel in the 1935 Gold Cup, with Golden Miller ridden by Gerry Wilson, having to be content with second place. He later spoke to Gerry saying, "Well done mate, when we are old and grey and sitting back enjoying a drink, we can at least say that we rode one great race one day in our lives." Tragically, he broke his back falling from a bad horse in a Seller at the following Cheltenham meeting and died six days later. The whole of Cheltenham turned out at his funeral, which was two miles long, and he was buried with his saddle, boots, whip and colours."

"One unforgettable moment of Specky's career was in 1932 when his saddle slipped and he won the Becher Chase literally bare-back," said Hamey.

* * * * * * * * * *

TENBY RACES
TO BE HELD IN AUGUST IN 1934

A meeting of the Tenby Race Committee was held at the "Royal Gate House Hotel" on Thursday, February 2nd for the purpose of considering a proposal to alter the date of the meeting. Mr T G Phelps was voted to the chair, and those present were Mr David Harrison (hon Secretary), Alderman O F Thomas and Mabe, Messrs R H Farley, J H Hodges, A Francis, W Johnson, Tudor Griffiths, E H Leach, Williams and Ashley Colley.

For a long period the Tenby meeting has been in January, usually in connection with the Hunt Week, which, however, was dropped this year. For some years the meeting has not been a financial success, and the attendance on the course has been small. It is only through the aid of the large sums raised by whist drives and dances that it had been possible to continue holding the meeting. The opinion was expressed that if the races could be held in August or September, when visitors are in town, the gate receipts would be very much greater. Many of the owners and trainers who are in the habit of supporting the Tenby meeting had been written to by Mr Harrison, and they were nearly all of opinion that a change was desirable, and gave their promise to support an autumn meeting.

The matter was fully discussed, and while the difficulties of making the change were appreciated, it was decided to hold an autumn meeting this year. Possible dates were discussed, and the National Hunt Stewards were asked to sanction a meeting on Friday and Saturday, August 25th and 26th, but refused and gave August 22nd and 23rd.

1934

The Hon Mrs Basil Mundy still had a number of horses in training with David Harrison. Mrs Mundy and Edith Clay had been to Ireland some years previous and bought a dark brown gelding, with a measly muzzle, by the name of Avenger, which won her the Great Lancashire Chase in 1934 ridden by W Speck, trained by D. Harrison. Her other horses were Western Flier, White Flag, the Danube, a good mare named Lochmore, which nearly always carried top weight, and a 2 year old filly named Kate Murphy. Kate Murphy won on the flat and was believed to be Mrs Mundy's only flat race success, and also a very rare occasion for the Tenby stable, winning at Chepstow in 1934.

August 22nd and 23rd 1934.
TENBY RACES RUN IN DELUGE AND SUNSHINE
TWO DAYS OF STRIKING CONTRAST IN WEATHER CONDITIONS

Big attendance and good running at Thursday's Meeting. It was, indeed, unfortunate that the weather should prove unfavourable for the opening of the Tenby Hunt Steeplechases on Wednesday. A cold wind and a deluge of rain was experienced practically throughout the afternoon, and, as a consequence, the attendance fell far below that anticipated.

In spite of the conditions the racing was exceptionally good. From a backer's standpoint, too, things worked out well, three of the races falling to favourites, while the other two winners were also well supported.

Mr P Herbert, who piloted his own aeroplane to the meeting, had the satisfaction of winning the opening event on Mr H Chaplin's Gaxonit, who beat the favourite, Sonna, by a short head after a thrilling race from the last hurdle.

ONLY LOCAL SUCCESS

Mr Herbert later rode Mrs Shears in the National Hunt Steeplechase, but though Mrs Tate's representative was installed favourite she found it a little too much to concede 2lb to Mr J Pidcock's Duneira.

The only local success was obtained in the Violet Mundy Challenge Cup, when Mr H Dyke Dennis's Tuck Up beat his three rivals after an interesting race. Vive L'Amour, owned by Lady Sybil Phipps only had Scrambled to beat in the Grove Steeplechase. I believe this was Scrambled's first race over the bigger obstacles. He fenced well, but was beaten for speed in the straight.

AMONG THOSE PRESENT

Lord and Lady Kylsant, Lady Sibell Lygon, Mr T P L Thomas, MP, Baron and Baroness de Rutzen, Miss M Molyneux, Mrs Pate, Lady Sybil Phipps, the Hon John Coventry, Col Delme Davies-Evans, Mr Ivor Anthony, Mr and Mrs E V Lea, Mr C Mathias, Mrs Aldridge, Mr Owen Anthony, Col Morgan Lindsay, Mrs Ingham, Miss P Ingham, the Hon Mrs Basil Mundy, Mr and Mrs R H Williams, Mr and Mrs David Harrison, Mr C C Williams, Mr and Mrs T G Phelps, Mr and Mrs J Rouse Mr R Corbett, Mrs Harmood-Banner. Father Moran, Mr H F Burke, Mr W Phillips, Alderman J E L Mabe, Councillor A Francis (Mayor of Tenby), Mr Ashley Colley, Mr F E Greathead, Mr O V Holmes, Mrs P Herbert, Mr R Gordon, Mr J Talbot, Mr and Mrs Meyrick Price, Alderman Oliver Thomas, Mr D D Stuart, Mrs Stuart, Miss Greenwill, Mr G Ace, Mrs Foley Phillips, Lady Meyrick, Sir Thomas Meyrick, Capt Penn, Miss Diane Allen, The Countess of Essex, Capt King Smith, Capt Phillips, Lady Joan Phillipps, Mr T R Mills, Mr Fred Williams, Mr J I Johnson, Mrs Lacey, Mr David Turner, Mr Peter Dawson, Mr E C Nicholetts, and Mr Griffith Thomas.

The 'Tote Racing Annual' of 1934 gives the following information for the race-goer.

Admission charges:
Tattersalls, 12/-
Course, 2/-
Cars, 7/6d
Carriages, 7/6d
Club Membership: There is no Race Club.

This is a very sad day for Tenby Races. To see its decline gain speed like a fast-rolling snowball makes one ask why? But the answer is now clear for all to see. With the bookies not even taking a bet on any race at Tenby, what chance have they got?

First Day

2-30 KNIGHTSTON SELLING HANDICAP HURDLE RACE
of £50 Two miles
Mr H Chaplin's, Gazonit, Mr P Herbert, 1
Mr E Dorse's, Irish Lord, Mr R Corbett
Mr J Dennistoun's, Sonna, G Hardy
Also ran – Helicon (G Bowden), Marche Militaire (E Williams)
Trainer Mr H Chaplin
No bid for winner
Betting – 6 – 4 agst Sonna 2 – 1 Gazonit, 4 – 1 Irish Lord, 6 – 1 Marche Militaire, 100 – 8 Helicon
Won by a short head; dead-heat for second
Off at 2.30
Tote: Win, 4s 9d

3-10 VIOLET MUNDY CHALLENGE CUP
£50 added (Handicap Hurdle race) Two miles
Mr Henry Dyke Dennis's, Tuck Up, G Owen, 1
Mr E Barthropp's, Hit the Deck, G Wilson, 2
Mr G Bostwick's, Uncanny II, Owner, 3
Also ran – Robinetta (Mr J Dennistoun)
Trainer D Harrison
Betting – Evens Tuck Up, 6 - 4 agst Hit the Deck, 5 - 1 Uncanny II, 8 - 1 Robinetta
Won by 15 lengths
Off at 3.20
Tote: Win, 5/-

3-40 NATIONAL HUNT PLATE, A STEEPLE CHASE
of £100 Three miles
Mr J Pidcock's, Duneira, Owner, 1
Mrs I Tate's, Mrs Shears, Mr P Herbert, 2
Also ran – Gay Lad III (Mr H Jones), Silver Plaid (Mr Ransom)
Trainer, Bissill
Betting – Evens Mrs Shears, 6 - 4 agst Duneira, 6 - 1 Gay Lad III, 10 - 1 Silver Plaid
Won by 8 lengths; others fell
Off at 3.30
Tote: Win, 4s 3d

4-10 GROVE HANDICAP STEEPLE CHASE
of £75 Two miles
Lady Phipps's, Vive L'Amour, E Williams, 1
Col M Lindsay's, Scrambled, A Price, 2
Two ran
Trainer I Anthony
Betting – 3 - 1 on Vive L'Amour
Won by half a length
Off at 4.13
Tote: Win, 2s 6d

4-40 WROUGHTON NOVICES' HURDLE RACE
of £50 Two miles
Lieut Comdr E W B Leake's, Roman General, E Wilson, 1
Lord Allendale's, High Flight, Gurney, 2
Mr H Dyke Dennis's, Witch Hazel, Owner, 3
Also ran – Eggflip (Price), Bournemouth (Mr Bowen),
Fell, Salvage (D Jones)
Trainer Barthropp
Betting – 6 - 4 on Roman General, 6 - 2 agst Witch Hazel, 5 - 1 High Flight, 8 - 1
Salvage, 10 - 1 Eggflip,
100 - 6 Bournemouth
Won by 4 lengths; 8
Off at 4.44
Tote: Win, 3s 9d

THURSDAY'S MEETING

In marked contrast to the conditions prevailing on the opening afternoon, the weather for the concluding stage of the Tenby Hunt Race Meeting on Thursday was delightfully fine. Consequently, the attendance was up to expectations. Sport, too, proved quite enjoyable. There were several falls but, luckily, riders and horses escaped injury.

The surprise of the afternoon occurred in the Park House Steeplechase. Well-backed horses in Paddy McGinty and Ross Mill came to grief, as did

Bluesand and Silver Plaid, leaving only Wroxham Bridge, the mount of G Bowden, standing. Ross Mill was remounted, but could not make up the leeway, Wroxham Bridge winning by a distance. The winner was subsequently put up for auction but failed to raise a bid. The second surprise came in the Licensed Victuallers' Hurdle, Sonna, who had run on the first day, was installed favourite, but though figuring fairly prominently in the early stages of the race, could not cope with Irish Lord and Gazonit on the flat, the former winning by a length. Once again the winner did not change hands.

A LOCAL WINNER

The local establishment, presided over by Mr David Harrison, carried off the Gatehouse Hurdle with the Hon Mrs Basil Mundy's Perfective, ridden by W Speck. The Tenby representative, on whom odds of 9 - 4 were laid, waited on his rivals until entering the straight, and then came on to win by a length and a half.

Roman General followed up his success of the previous day by winning the Town Steeplechase from his solitary opponent, Gay Lad III. The issue was never in doubt, the favourite holding his lead throughout to win by 20 lengths.

Usually all the entrants for the United Counties Farmers' and Tradesmen's Hurdle go to the post, but on this occasion the field was disappointing, only numbering three. Still, the usual sporting spirit prevailed, two of the three runners being well fancied by their connections and backed accordingly. Mrs M O Lewis's May B III was always favourite though the friends of Watchman II also anticipated success. The race, however, proved a good thing for the favourite, as Mr J Mathias, after waiting on Watchman II for three parts of the journey, took command to gain a popular victory by ten lengths.

Second Day

2-30 GATE HOUSE HURDLE RACE

of £50 Two miles

Mrs Mundy's, Perfective, W Speck, 1

Mr F Rome's, Vain Prince, G Bowden, 2

Mr E Barthropp's, Hit the Deck, G Wilson, 3

Also ran – Bournemouth (Mr E Bowen) pulled up

Trainer D Harrison

Betting – 9 - 4 on Perfective, 7 - 2 agst Hit the Deck, 5 - 1 Vain Prince, 20 - 1
Bournemouth

Won by one and a half lengths; 2

Off at 2.30

Tote: Win, 2s 6d

3-10 PARK HOUSE SELLING HANDICAP STEEPLE CHASE
of £75 Two miles
Mr F Rome's, Wroxham Bridge, G Bowden, 1
Mr J Pidcock's, Ross Mill, Owner, 2
Also ran – Paddy McGinty (Speck) fell, Silver Plaid
(Mr Bayley) fell, Bluesand (A Price) fell
Trainer W Lewis
No bid for winner
Betting – 11 - 10 agst Paddy McGinty, 5 - 2 Ross Mill, 5 - 1 Wroxham Bridge, 8 - 1
Bluesand, 20 - 1 Silver Plaid
Won by a distance
Off at 3-10
Tote: Win, 11s 3d

3-40 LICENSED VICTUALLERS' SELLING HANDICAP HURDLE RACE
of £50 Two miles
Mr E G Dorse's, Irish Lord, Mr R Corbett, 1
Mr W H Chaplin's, Gazonit, L Agar
Mr J Dennistoun's, Sonna, Owen
Also ran – Witch Hazel (G Owen), Helicon (G Bowden)
Trainer, Owen
No bid for winner
Betting – 7 - 4 agst Sonna, 3 - 1 Witch Hazel, 7 - 2 Gazonit, 4 - 1 Irish Lord, 20 - 1
Helicon
Won by a length; a.5
Off at 3.40
Tote: Win, 7/-

4-10 TOWN HANDICAP STEEPLE CHASE
of £75 Three miles
Lt Comdr E Leake's, Roman General, G Wilson, 1
Mr J O Ingham's, Gay Lad III, Mr H Jones, 2
Betting – 11 - 2 on Roman General
Won by 20 lengths
Off at 4.10
Tote: Win, 2s 3d

4-40 UNITED COUNTIES FARMERS' AND TRADESMEN'S HURDLE RACE
of £45 Two miles
Mrs M O Lewis's, May B III, Mr J Mathias, 1
Mrs C Griffiths's, Watchman II, Mr T Griffiths, 2
Mr G S Williams's, Bandit II, Mr G Williams, 3
Trained privately
Betting – 6 - 4 on May B III, 5 - 2 agst Watchman II, 8 - 1 Bandit II
Won by 10 lengths; 1
Off at 4.40
Tote: Win, 3/6

However, there was not long before there was to be an almighty argument. Mrs Mundy had been a loyal patron of the Tenby Stable for over thirty years and at the Cardiff Meeting in early 1935 all hell broke loose. Mrs Mundy and Sir John Grey were the very best of friends and were in competition in one race with Sir John Grey's Vain Prince and Mrs Mundy's Western Flyer. Sir John Grey had put £1000 to win on his horse, Vain Prince, as David Harrison had said to Mrs Mundy that Western Flyer was in no way fit and would not win. A certain person said to David Harrison, "Surely you are not going to put Specky on Western Flyer against Vain Prince in this race, are you Mr Harrison?" Harrison replied, "He's got no chance at all." Western Flyer came home ahead of Vain Prince, and Mrs Mundy was waiting in the winner's enclosure. When Specky rode in she hit him out of the saddle with her umbrella, shouting, "You'll never ride for me again," and Specky never did. He was to die at Cheltenham soon after, and on that day there was no-one more upset than Mrs Mundy. She could not stop crying, she could not forgive herself for what she had said.

Avenger ran in the 1935 Welsh Grand National at Cardiff, ridden by Fred Rimell. The competition was fierce including last year's winner, Dream Ship, owned by Mr J V Rank, who also had a favoured runner this year in Lacatoi ridden by Jack Fawcus and trained by Ivor Anthony. Other class runners were Ego and Aureate Earth. It was a fast run race with Ego making all the running, until Lacatoi took it up with a mile to go and shook off the challenge of Fred Rimell on Avenger, to go on and win by a length and a half. Said Fred Rimell later, "I remember that Jack Fawcus walked the course before the race, and found where some sheep had been grazing. This left some very good going and as the race went on he picked out this ground, and won."

August 1935

GOOD RACING AT TENBY
FINE WEATHER FAVOURS ANNUAL RACE MEETING

Tenby Hunt Steeplechase opened on Wednesday last and there was a good attendance, the weather being gloriously fine. Fields, unfortunately, were on the small side. There were three outstanding happenings. The first was the triumph of Max Barthropp, the Tern Hill trainer, who saddled four winners; secondly, the dual success of the horse, Down South, who, after winning the Violet Mundy Challenge Cup, carried off the Grove Steeplechase; and thirdly, the "hat trick" performed by J Hamey, who, after twice riding Down South to victory, went on to win on King Sable.

THE STEWARDS AND OFFICIALS

The stewards of the meeting were Sir David Hughes-Morgan, Bart, Col Morgan Lindsay, Mr H Dyke Dennis, and Mr C C Williams, with the following officials:

Handicapper, Major G Johnson; starter, Mr George Phelps; hon Judge Mr J Coventry; clerk of the scales, Mr T H Wilton Pye; hon secretary, Mr H Dyke Dennis; hon auditor and stakeholder, Mr Ashley Colley; clerk of the scales, Mr A Francis; auctioneer, Mr J Roch and hon surgeon, Dr C Mathias.

Among those present were: Lord and Lady Kylsant, Sir Thomas and Lady Meyrick, The Countess of Essex, Lady Merthyr, Baron and Baroness de Rutzen, Lady Newnes, Sir John and Lady Grey, the Hon Mrs Basil Mundy, Mr Kenneth Walker, Col Delme Davies-Evans, Mr Sackville Owen, Mrs Seymour Allen, Major Maude, Col Saurin, Mr R Gordon, Mr T R Mills (Llanelly).

David Harrison on South Sands

2.30 KNIGHTSTON SELLING HANDICAP HURDLE RACE
of £50 Two miles

Mrs Mundy's, Bob Stone, T Rimell, 1
Mr E Dorse's, Irish Lord, Mr L Dorse, 2
Mr E Barthropp's, Hit the Deck, J Hamey, 3
Also ran – Golden Coin (G Owen)
Trainer, D Harrison
No bid for winner
Beeting – 6 - 4 agst Hit the Deck, 2 - 1 Bob Stone, 3 - 1 Irish Lord, 5 - 1 Golden Coin
Won by three quarters of a length
Off at 2.30
Tote: Win, 7s 6d

3-10 VIOLET MUNDY CHALLENGE CUP (HANDICAP HURDLE)
(value £50); £50 added Two miles

Mr E Barthropp's, Down South, J Hamey, 1
Mr Henry Dyke Dennis's, Tuck Up, G Owen, 2
Trainder, Barthropp
Betting – 9 - 4 on Down South
Won by a head
Off at 3.11
Tote: Win, 3s 3d

3-40 TENBY STEEPLE CHASE
of £75 To be ridden by amateur riders Three miles

Lt Comdr E Leake's, Roman General, Mr W R Birrell, 1
Mrs L Tate's, Wrexham, Mr R Petre, 2
Trainer, Barthropp
Betting – 7 - 2 on Roman General
Won by a distance
Off at 3.41
Tote: Win, 2s 9d

4-10 GROVE HANDICAP STEEPLE CHASE
of £75 Two miles

Mr E P Barthropp's, Down South, J Hamey, 1
Mr H Dyke Dennis's, Yarmouth, Owner, 2
Also ran – Witch Hazel (D Harrison), Nimbo (King),
Treasure Island (Forwood), Scylla (Lindsay), Prince Shivaji (R Morgan), Yes or No
Won by 2 lengths: 20
Off at 4.13
Yes or No pulled up.
Tote: Win, 10s 6d

4-40 WROUGHTON NOVICES' HURDLE RACE
of £50 Two miles
Mr E P Barthropp's, King Sable, J Hamey, 1
Col M Lindsay's, Charybdis, Mr J Dennistoun, 2
Trainer, Barthropp
Betting – 6 - 4 on King Sable
Won by 10 lengths
Off at 4.41
Tote: Win, 3s 6d

Second Day

2-30 GATE HOUSE HURDLE RACE
of £50 Two miles
Mr J Whitney's, Cold Bird, J Hamey, 1
Mr Henry Dyke Dennis's, Witch Hazel, G Owen, 2
Trainer, J Anthony
Betting – 9 - 4 on Cold Bird
Won by one and a half lengths
Off at 2.30
Tote: Win, 2s 3d

3-10 PARK HOUSE SELLING HANDICAP STEEPLE CHASE
of £75 Two miles
Mr H Whitman's, Cheviotdale, Mr A B Mildmay*
Mr H Dennis's, Astridge, G Owen
Both runners refused and the race was declared void
Betting – 9 - 4 on Cheviotdale
Tote: Stake refunded

* A B Mildmay: Later to become Lord Mildmay of Flete, Lord Anthony Bingham, 2nd Baron. One of the most important and best loved figures in the history of steeplechasing, he was aptly named by "The Times" as `The Last of the Corinthians`. They wrote of him, "There was never a harder rider, better loser or a more popular winner". In 1933 he rode his first winner Good Shot, and in 1936 his father bought him Davy Jones to ride in the Grand National. The pair started at 100 – 1, set out to make the running and were still in the lead approaching the last fence. But the brand new reins parted at the buckle, and with his steering gone they ran out at the last leaving Reynoldstown to win his second successive National, the first time for 66 years since George Stevens won on The Colonel in 1869 & 1870.

Anthony Mildmay said later that he had deliberately not tied a knot in his reins because "Davy has such a tremendously long neck, I needed the full extent of rein for those drop-fences". He was Amateur Champion jockey five years in succession from 1945 – 1950. In 1948 he rode Cromwell in the Grand National for H.M. Queen Elizabeth and her daughter Princess Elizabeth. He was going like a winner when, half a mile from home, Mildmay suffered a paralysing cramp in the back of his neck, unable to assist his horse he rode on to be third to Sheila's Cottage.

As the end of the 1949 – 1950 season drew to a close he took some friends down for a weekend to his Devonshire home. As was customary he went down to the beach for a pre-breakfast swim and was never seen again.

3-40 LICENSED VICATUALLERS' SELLING HANDICAP HURDLE RACE
of £50 Two miles

Mrs Mundy's, Bob Stone, T Rimell, 1
Mr H Dennis's, Golden Coin, G Owen, 2
Mr E Barthropp's, Hit the Deck, J Hamey, 3
Also ran – Irish Lord (Mr L Dorse)
Trainer, D Harrison
Betting – 6 - 4 agst Hit the Deck, 7 - 4 Bob Stone, 5 - 2 Irish Lord, 100 - 8 Golden Coin
Won by 4 lengths
Tote: Win, 7s
There was no bid for the winner

4-10 TOWN HANDICAP STEEPLE CHASE
of £75 Three miles
Lieut-Comdr E W B Leake's, Roman General, J Hamey, 1
Mrs I Tates, Mrs Shears, G Owen, 2
Also ran – Brave Cry (T F Rimell) fell
Trainer, Barthropp
Betting – 5 - 4 on Roman General, 2 - 1 agst Mrs Shear's, 3 - 1 Brave Cry
Won by a distance
Off at 4.13
Tote: Win, 3s 9d

4-40 UNITED COUNTIES FARMERS' AND TRADESMEN'S HURDLE RACE
of £45 Two miles
Mrs M C Lewis's, Helicon, Mr J H Mathias, 1
Mr G S Williams's, Ugly, Owner, 2
Also ran – Phoebe III (Mr T Griffiths) pulled up
Trainer, Lewis
Betting – 5 - 1 on Helicon, 5 - 1 agst Phoebe III, 8 - 1 Ugly
Won by 15 lengths
Off at 4.41
Tote: Win, 2s 6d

During the 1935/36 season Mrs Mundy withdrew all her horses from David Harrison's Tenby stable and moved them to Tom Rimell at Kinnersley. Others followed Mrs Mundy and the stable was left almost destitute.

1936

This meeting was held at the Royal Gate House in January of 1936.

GUARANTORS ENABLE MEETING TO BE HELD

Another change has been made in the dates of the Tenby race meeting. For the last two years the meeting has been held in August instead of January, in the hope of retrieving the financial losses of previous years, but the position has become so serious that a meeting of guarantors was held at Tenby to consider the advisability of holding a meeting this year.

Mr Dyke Dennis, secretary of the committee, presided, and it was stated that a loss of £22 was recorded after the last meeting, and the present deficit stood at more than £300. Eight guarantors for £10 came forward, making the total amount guaranteed, including 25 other guarantors for £10 each, to £230.

As a result it was decided to continue the races, and to hold the meeting this year on October 28th and 29th, subject to the National Hunt Committee, sanctioning the dates. Application for financial assistance will be made to the National Hunt Committee in the meantime.

Mrs Mundy's horses had now been taken from the Tenby Stable to Tom Rimell at Kinnersley. Avenger was entered for the Grand National at Aintree, to be ridden by Fred Rimell. Avenger unfortunately fell in the Grand National and had to be destroyed, having broken his neck and leaving Fred Rimell in hospital with an internal

MR. T. R. RIMELL, (TRAINER).

LORD CAWLEY'S COLOURS.

G. WILSON

haemorrhage. Rimell said later, "I knew when I rode him before that he was the best horse that I had ever ridden, he was a lovely quality horse, good enough to take to Ascot". However, Mrs Mundy did not lose heart and got Tom Rimell and Victor Cartwright to go to Ireland to purchase a replacement. They bought two good horses for her, Knight of London and Custom House, both dark brown geldings, and costing a lot of money. Custom House was her most prolific winner.

1935-36 winter in the snow at Cornishdown, just before Mrs Mundy took her horses away from the stable. The second horse in the string is the grey White Flag ridden here by a young apprentice, Dick Francis. Standing is Brychan Rees, on horseback is David Harrison.

The 1936 meeting was held on October 28th and 29th.

GOOD OPENING DAY FOR TENBY RACES
MR DAVID HARRISON WINS FIRST THREE EVENTS

Tenby was bathed in glorious sunshine on Wednesday, and, therefore, it was not surprising to find quite a respectable attendance on the Knightston course for the opening of the annual Tenby Race Meeting under National Hunt Rules. Rain during the past few days had had a beneficial effect upon the track, and even though fields were not large, there was sufficient in the racing to sustain interest throughout the afternoon.

The outstanding feature was the success of the local trainer, Mr D Harrison, who carried off the first three events, two with horses owned by Mr H Dyke Dennis, the Ruabon Colliery owner, who now carries out the duties of Hon. Secretary to the meeting, and the third with Mr T Rowe's Adamant.

Odds of 11-10 were laid on Tuck Up to win the opening race, the Knightston Selling Hurdle, and the "good thing" duly materialised. Star Turn was fancied to a certain extent, and when she took a clear lead two hurdles from home it appeared as though Mr J L Hall's mare would win, but rounding the

252

bend into the straight she suddenly compounded, and could finish no nearer than fourth, the favourite winning easily by eight lengths from Bedraggled. At auction, however, Tuck Up failed to raise a bid. H Nicholson, who rode the horse, proceeded to complete his double on Witch Hazel in the Violet Mundy Challenge Cup. In this instance the odds laid on the Tenby horse were never in doubt, for though Alvarado and Tormore were in turn allowed to make the pace, the favourite only needed to be asked the question entering the straight to win comfortably by four lengths.

A MONEY-SPINNER

Decorum was expected by his connections to recover the money lost over Star Turn in the Tenby Steeplechase, but local sportsmen showed allegiance to Adamant, who is owned by Mr Tom Rowe, Maesycoed, Templeton. At the flag fall Decorum stood at evens while Adamant was at a fraction longer odds. Backers certainly showed judgement, for quite early in the race the pair had the race to themselves and fought out a rare duel. Adamant, however, proved to possess the greater stamina, for, in spite of a desperate challenge from the favourite, D L Jones got his mount home by two and a half lengths.

What a money spinner China Sea must have proved to his connections since he came under the care of Ben Roberts, the popular Cheltenham trainer, who, by the way, is a Pembrokeshire man. When flooring the odds laid on Vive L'Amour in the Town Steeplechase the horse was winning his fifth race since Roberts purchased him for Miss Carmen Cory out of a selling race at Cardiff. It has been a real Welsh triumph, for Mr Harry Llewellyn, who rode China Sea to victory, had also twice previously been successful on Miss Cory's horse.

As usual, there was plenty of interest in the United Counties' Farmers' and Tradesmen's Hurdle. Most people plumped for Ugly, who finished second in the race last year, and their confidence was not misplaced, for though Boston Cottage flattered until approaching the straight, Mr C Griffiths brought the favourite to the front to beat his brother Tudor on Boston Cottage by 15 lengths, with Busy two lengths behind.

The stewards were Mr C C Williams, M F H, Major Sir David Hughes-Morgan, Bt, Mr H Dyke Dennis, and Sir Thomas Meyrick, M F H, and the officials: Handicapper, Mr D G Sheppard; starter, Mr J D Phelps; hon judge, Mr J Coventry; clerk of the scales, Mr W Gregory; auctioneer, Major J A Roch; hon. Secretary, Mr H Dyke Dennis; hon. Surgeon, Dr C Mathias; hon. Veterinary surgeon, Mr B Rees; auditor and stakeholder, Mr Ashley Colley; clerk of the course, Mr A Francis.

Among others in the enclosure were: Mrs Victor Higgon and Miss Higgon, Mr and Mrs Sackville Owen, Mr Kenneth Walker, Capt Higgon, Mrs Seymour Allen and Miss Diana Allen, Mr F E Greathead, Mr T R Mills and Mrs G M Morse, Mr and Mrs Ernest George, Mr and Mrs Meyrick Price, Mr David Harrison, Mr and Mrs J C Clay, Col C B Wedehouse, the Misses Vaughan, Dr and Mrs Mather, Councillor and Mrs A Davies, Capt A S Mathias, Mr Graham Ace, Mr Oliver Thomas, Mr Brychan Rees, Mrs Tate, Mr Owen Anthony, Mr Morgan Jones, Capt A W Wingate, and Mr Fred Williams.

First Day

2-0 KNIGHTSTON SELLING HANDICAP HURDLE RACE
of £50 Two miles
Mr H Dennis's, Tuck Up, H Nicholson, 1
Mr W White's, Bedraggled, A Scratchley, 2
Mr B Warner's, Richard II, H Jones, 3
Also ran – Arthur (Mr L Densham), Star Turn (G Spann)
Trainer, D Harrison
Betting – 11 - 10 on Tuck Up, 9 - 4 agst Star Turn, 7 - 2 Richard II,
5 - 1 Bedraggled and Arthur
Won by 8 lengths, Tote: Win, 5s
No bid for winner

2-30 VIOLET MUNDY CHALLENGE CUP
(handicap hurdle race) £50 added Two miles
Mr Henry Dyke Dennis's, Witch Hazel, H Nicholson, 1
Sir J Grey's, Alvarado, J Bissill, 2
Mr G Bostwick's, Uncanny II, E Williams, 3
Also ran – Tormore (H Sharland), Cold Bird (H Jones)
Trainer, D Harrison
Betting – 5 - 4 on Witch Hazel, 5 - 2 agst Tormore, 3 - 1 Alvarado, 5 - 1 Uncanny II and
Cold Bird
Won by 4 lengths; a neck
Tote: Win, 3s

3-0 TENBY STEEPLE CHASE
of £75 Two miles
Mr T Rowe's, Adamant, D L Jones, 1
Mrs O Greenslade's, Decorum, G Spann, 2
Also ran – Invereshie (F Maxwell) fell, Proud Moment
(G Owen) fell
Trainer, D Harrison
Betting – Evens Decorum, 5 - 4 agst Adamant, 5 - 1 others
Won by two and a half lengths
Tote: Win, 5s 9d

3-30 TOWN HANDICAP STEEPLE CHASE
of £75 Three miles
Miss C Cory's, China Sea, Mr H Llewellyn, 1
Lady S Phipps's, Vive L'Amour, R Bunford, 2
Mr J Morant's, St Tewdric, Mr Petre, 3
Trainer, Roberts
Betting – 6 - 4 on Vive L'Amour, 6 - 4 agst China Sea, 8 - 1 St Tewdric
Won by three quarters of a length; a bad third
Tote: Win, 3s 6d

4-0 UNITED COUNTIES' FARMERS' AND TRADESMEN'S HURDLE RACE
of £45 Two miles
Mr E Williams's, Ugly, Mr V Griffiths, 1
Mr T Griffiths's, Boston Cottage, Owner, 2
Mr T Rowe's, Busy, Mr T Rogers, 3
Also ran – Grola (Mr Reed)
Winner Trained privately
Betting – 6 - 4 on Ugly, 2 - 1 agst Grola, 5 - 2 Boston Cottage 6 - 1 Busy
Won by 15 lengths
Tote: Win, 4s

Second Day

2-0 GATE HOUSE HURDLE RACE
of £50 Two miles
Mr J Hall's, Star Turn, G Spann, 1
Mr C Williams's, Irish River, E Williams, 2
Mr E Williams's, Ugly, Mr V Griffiths, 3
Also ran – Invereshie (H Nicholson), Blue Valley (Mr Rogers)
Trainer, J Hall
Betting – 6 - 4 each agst Star Turn and Irish River, 4 - 1 Invereshie, 8 - 1 Ugly and Blue
Valley
Won by 2 lengthsOff at 2.01
Tote: Win, 2s 6d

2-30 PARK HOUSE HANDICAP STEEPLE CHASE
of £75 Three miles
Mr N J Powell's, Bellamite, Owner, 1
Mrs L Tate's, Yes or No, H Jones, 2
Mr H Llewellyn's, Last of the Hapsburgs, D Jones, 3
Also ran – J P (Nicholson), Citron (Lofthouse), refused
Trainer, Price
Bellamite bought in for 85 gns

255

Betting – 5 - 4 on Yes or No, 3 - 1 agst Citron, 5 - 1 JP and Last of the Hapsburgs, 10 - 1
Bellamite
Won by 3 lengths
Off at 2.31
Tote: Win, 57 shillings

3-0 LICENSED VICTUALLERS' SELLING HURDLE RACE
of £50 Two miles
Mr Henry Dyke Dennis's, Tuck Up, H Nicholson, 1
Mr G Gregory's, Redford, G Spann, 2
Mr I Densham's, Arthur, Owner, 3
Trainer, D Harrison
Winner sold - Mr G Gregory for 85 gns
Betting – 5 - 2 on Tuck Up, 7 - 2 agst Redford, 6 - 1 Arthur
Won by 5 lengths; 1.5
Off at 3.02
Tote: Win, 2s 6d

3-30 GROVE HANDICAP STEEPLE CHASE
of £75 Two miles
Mr T Rowe's, Adamant, D Jones, 1
Lady S Phipps's, Vive L'Amour, E Williams, 2
Sir J Grey's, Alvarado, J Bissill, 3
Also ran – Martello (H Nicholson)
Trainer, D Harrison
Betting – 5 - 4 on Vive L'Amour, 3 - 1 each agst Adamant And Alvarado, 10 - 1 Martello
Won by a length
Of at 3.31
Tote: Win, 7s 9d

4-0 WROUGHTON HANDICAP HURDLE RACE
of £50 Two miles
Mr G Bostwick's, Uncanny II, R Burford, 1
Mr C Williams's, Swanlake Bay, E Williams, 2
Mr Henry Dyke Dennis's, Tuck In, H Nicholson, 3
Trainer, I Anthony
Betting – 6 - 4 on Uncanny II, 2 - 1 agst Swanlake Bay, 6 - 1 Tuck In
Won by a head; 6 lengths
Off at 4.01
Tote: Win, 5s 3d

****

Alleged 'Welching' At Tenby Races
TWO MEN ARRESTED
AT FARMHOUSE
BAIL REFUSED TO "INNOCENT MAN"

A bookmaker and his clerk who, it was alleged, had "welched" at Tenby Races on Wednesday, appeared in custody at the Narberth Police Court yesterday (Thursday).

It was stated that they had been arrested at a little farmhouse on the Tenby-Narberth Road. The two men were Jesse Colwell, 6 Richmond Street, Neath, and Martin Duddy, White Road, Sparkbrook, Birmingham.

D.C.C. Anthony Thomas, in making an application for a remand, said that on Wednesday, the first day of Tenby Races, the two men in custody were on the ground as bookmaker and clerk – Colwell was the bookmaker. In the 2.30 race there was a horse running named "Witch Hazel" and Colwell offered odds of 5-4 on. Several people put money on this horse. Witch Hazel won the race, but when the people went to collect their winnings, Colwell and his clerk were missing. The people immediately complained to P.C. Griffiths, Saundersfoot, who was close by. Later P.C. Griffiths found the men in a little farmhouse and arrested them.

REMAND ASKED FOR

"I ask for a remand in custody until to-morrow week," concluded the Deputy Chief Constable.

Evidence of arrest was given by P.C. Griffiths, who said that at 2p.m. on the 18th October he was on duty in plain clothes at the Tenby Races. He saw Jesse Colwell acting as a bookmaker and trading under the name of "Walter Roberts, Cardiff", and Duddy was acting as clerk. "At 2.40 on the same day," the constable continued, "the horse Witch Hazel won a race, and I received numerous complaints from people who had surrounded the stand of 'Walter Roberts' that they had been 'welched'. I obtained a description of the two men and went in pursuit. At 3.10 I arrested both men in a cottage on the Tenby-Narberth Road, and later brought them to Saundersfoot Police Station."

D.C.C. Thomas: On the evidence given I make application that both men be remanded in prison until to-morrow week.

Colwell then exclaimed, "This is an unfortunate chap (indicating Duddy). I am the bookmaker. I don't want this fellow here to be sent to prison for a week. He has a wife and family, and he should get a chance of bail."

"BIRDS OF A FEATHER"

The Magistrate (Alderman Palmer Morgan): Birds of a feather....

Colwell: We live miles and miles apart. I don't want him drawn into my escapades. I am sorry he got into trouble.

The Justices' Clerk (Mr W R James) to Duddy: Could you produce a surety, say up to £35.

Duddy: My parents in Birmingham would go surety.

The Justices' Clerk: They would have two days to come down here.

Duddy: They would come; my people are well to do.

"I am not speaking for myself," said Colwell, "I'm not applying for bail, but I don't want to shoulder trouble on to an innocent man. He wouldn't be in trouble if it wasn't for me." The Deputy Chief Constable said that he objected to bail in both cases. By his own statement Colwell didn't know Duddy very well.

Colwell: Sending him to prison won't do him any good. Sending an innocent man to prison turns him into a criminal.

The Justices' Clerk said that it would be possible to release Duddy from jail if surety for bail was forthcoming.

D.C.C. Thomas: I object to that.

Colwell: Well, I've done my best for the fellow.

Both men were remanded to prison until eleven o'clock on November 6th. The magistrate was Alderman Palmer Morgan.

Ashley Colley told me of an amusing incident which happened on the last day of the Tenby Races, when a certain jockey only had one mount in an early race; after the race he started drinking whisky and became slightly drunk. In a later race another jockey had been injured and could not ride his mount in the following race. Apparently, the jockey who had been drinking was the only available one to take the ride, and when he was taken to the horse, he noticed that the horse was wearing blinkers, upon which he said to the trainer, "You'd better take those off him to start with boss, one of us will have to see which way we're going".

Ashley Colley also told me of the following incident, the closing chapter in the races history: "The race committee had been running a lottery to raise funds for the races," said Ashley, "when one day two policemen came to my house to tell me that the lottery was illegal, so I told them that the races definitely would not survive without the lottery, so I phoned Mr Dyke Dennis at Park House, and he said to send the policemen up there. Mr Dyke Dennis phoned me later saying that we had to stop the lottery sweepstakes, otherwise we could face two years imprisonment.   Mr Dyke Dennis was so upset that he burnt the racecourse meetings records and minute books".

Mr Henry Dyke Dennis, with his dog Delightful Devon

259

In the autumn of 1936, Spencer Williams, who owned Knightston Farm where the races had been held since 1886, was walking his horse up St Bride's Hill from Saundersfoot, when his horse slipped and went down, throwing Spencer (who always smoked a pipe) to the ground where his pipe went straight through the roof of his mouth into his brain. "Tenby Races had claimed its last victim." Spencer was only 36.

Courtesy of The Western Mail & Echo Ltd. This was the last official notice dated July 31st 1937:

TENBY RACES ABANDONED
END OF POPULAR FIXTURE

For almost a hundred years one of Tenby's most popular "institutions" and principal attraction of the fashionable Hunt Week and Tenby Steeplechase Meeting, is to be abandoned, following a series of heavy financial losses during the past ten years. Lack of interest among members of the Committee and the ever growing financial liability resulted in a poorly attended meeting on July 31st recommending that the race meeting be abandoned.

The notice convening the meeting for Thursday last pointed out that recent meetings had been meagrely attended and only 13 members turned up at the Royal Gate House Hotel when the fateful decision was made last Thursday. With Mrs Newton Seymour Allen in the chair, there were present: Sir Thomas Meyrick, Bart, Mr H Dyke Dennis, Messrs Ashley Colley (hon. Secretary), David Harrison, Alfred Francis, R H Farley, H I James, Griffith Thomas, G Meyrick Price, E Williams, V Griffiths and E H Leach.

The following recommendations of the meeting held on July 31st were confirmed unanimously, the Chairman expressing her regret that it had been found necessary to take such a step, "That the Tenby race meeting should be abandoned; that no application for dates or for a plate should be made for January 1938; that if at any subsequent meeting of the committee it was decided to continue the races or incur any possible liability to that end, the members so deciding must be prepared to release the guarantors so wishing from all future liability by payment of their share of the liability at the date of the meeting, and that such resolution should be circulated to the whole of the guarantors."

THE CONCLUSION

Thus Endeth Tenby Races; "Here endeth the lesson." Between 1886 and 1936 Tenby had collected 50 years of racing memories; of fantastic races battled to the last; of jockeys, trainers, owners and gamblers mingling on and off the course in the beautiful West Wales setting; of dances and parties, nights out on the town and nights hidden away in adulterous passion. Tenby Races had risen from the January mud and frost to become a race meet attended by the rich and famous, and the home of the successful Stables over which Harrison so scrupulously presided. It is a sad story of corruption that in the last, it rotted the fibre of Tenby's racing community. The racecourse lost its bookmakers, without whom there was no life in the sport. The Oyster Maid scandal had obvious repercussions for the Races, evident in the historical records of declining attendance of the public and the bookies after 1927. Harrison's underhand dealings in the scandal also managed to lose him the patronage that had for so long made him one of the most respected and successful trainers in Britain. Once the rot had set in it just all feel apart at the seams. Tenby Races ended up without funds and without the lure that it once enjoyed so much. Tenby Races died, and with it the public consciousness about its importance and success in its heyday. It has also meant that the story of the Oyster Maid scandal has lain dormant for many years, the scraps of evidence that attest to it hidden from public view, and memories of it left closed until I teased them out of the woodwork. It has taken 20 years to produce this book, the full history of Tenby Races and all that I can find on Oyster Maid and her team of 'backers', but hopefully this is not the end of the matter. Tenby Races has fallen, but its memory lives on as a testament to the will and skill of the men and women that made it great. It is a much forgotten era of Welsh history, and as we have seen, it is well worth remembering.

When Tenby Races was cancelled, David Harrison and Grace moved to Badminton, as friends of the Duke of Beaufort, and resided in one of the mews flats at the rear of Badminton House. Grace died shortly after the war and David Harrison died on February 2nd 1951, aged 75. Brychan Rees died at No 2 Picton Villas, Tenby on April 8th 1947, aged 79.

THE END

APPENDIX

NATIONAL HUNT JOCKEYS CHAMPIONSHIP TABLE

Year	Name	Winners	Year	Name	Winners
1900	Mr H S Sidney	53 *[1]	1920	F B Rees	64
1901	F Mason	58	1921	F B Rees	65
1902	F Mason	67	1922	Mr J R Anthony	78
1903	P Woodland	54	1923	F B Rees	64
1904	F Mason	59	1924	F B Rees	108* *[2]
1905	F Mason	73	1925	F B Rees	76
1906	F Mason	58	1926	T Leader	61
1907	F Mason	59	1927	F B Rees	59
1908	P Cowley	65	1928	W Stott	88
1909	R Gordon	45	1929	W Stott	76
1910	E Piggott	67	1930	W Stott	77
1911	W Payne	76	1931	Stott	81
1912	Ivor Anthony	78	1932	W Stott	77
1913	E Piggott	60	1933	G Wilson	61
1914	Mr J R Anthony	60	1934	G Wilson	56
1915	E Piggott	44	1935	G Wilson	73
1916	C Hawkins	17	1936	G Wilson	57
1917	W Smith	15	1937	G Wilson	45
1918	G Duller	17	1938	G Wilson	59
1919	Mr H Brown	15	1939	T F Rimell	61

*[1] Mr Herbert Sidney owned, trained and rode his own horses, and was a regular
visitor to the Tenby Meeting.

*[2] F B Rees's record 108 wins in 1924 etc.

* F B Rees's best victories were:-

1921	Grand National – Shaun Spadah
1925	William Hill Imperial Gold Cup – Scotch Pearl
1925	Grand Sefton Chase – Silvo
1925	Grand Steeplechase de Paris – Silvo
1928	Cheltenham Gold Cup – Patron Saint
1929	Cheltenham Champion Hurdle – Royal Falcon
1929	Cheltenham Gold Cup – Easter Hero

Fred B Rees's record 108 wins in 1924 was a record until it was surpassed by Fred Winter in the 1952-53 season with 121 winners. Covering this period of 1900 – 1940.

Only four champion jockeys had not ridden at Tenby Races, and of those four each one was only champion jockey once.

****

Top- Oil painting of Delightful Devon. Below- The 1939 Waterloo Cup.

WATERLOO CUP.
FEB: 10TH 1939.
WON BY
H. DYKE DENNIS'S
"DELIGHTFUL DEVON"

ACKNOWLEDGEMENTS

Special thanks to the following for their help
The Tenby Observor (Mr Neil Dickson)
The Western Mail & Echo Ltd (Mr Mike Day)
Sheffield Sports Library (Mrs Leslie Gunter)
Messrs Weatherby's (Mr Guy Lingley)
Tenby Museum (Mr Mark Lewis)
Tenby Library (Ms Julie Sutcliffe)
Gallagher Ltd (Mr Max Krangle)
National Library of Wales (Mr Emyr Evans)
Wilson Museum, Narberth (Mrs Pauline Griffiths)
Ladbrokes (Mr Paul Pearce)
Haverfordwest Records Office (Ms Anne Palmer)
Gareth Davies Photography (Tenby)

Three books that have been most helpful in my research
"The Encyclopedia of steeplechasing" by Mrs Patricia Smyly (An outstanding book which helped me over many hurdles).
"50 years of Chepstow" by Mrs Pat Lucas
"A Murder of Crows" by Mrs Margaret Davies

My personal thanks to
My late father W. G. (Billy) Lawrence
Mrs R. C. Lawrence (My mother)
Mr Charles Birt
Mrs Maeve Reid
Mr Steve Johnson
Mr Nigel Baring
Mrs Anne Dalgety
Mr Fred Phillips
Mrs Jane Cowper
Mrs Wendy Lawrence
Mr Henry Dyke Dennis
Mrs Sue Thomas
Mr & Mrs Bill James (The Atlantic Hotel)
Mr Cedric Evans
Mr Maurice Cole (Cresswell Quay)
Mrs Ruth Evans

Mr John Pilsen
Mr Hedley Smith
Mr Mike Gough
Mr Ryan Lawrence
Mr David Nash
Mr Graham Hughes
Mr Brinley Hughes
Mrs Marion Davies
Mrs Barbara Lawrence
Mr Tom Phillips
Mrs Pat Clissold
The (late) Flo Huller
The (late) Ashley Colley
The (late) Violet Pritchard

A TRIBUTE
To my dear late cousin, John Bentley Lawrence
1940 – 1994

In 1954, John, then aged 14, went as an apprentice to Peter Cazalet in Tunbridge Wells, who trained for H. M. Queen Elizabeth the Queen Mother. The first horse he looked after was "Three Stars" owned by the Queen Mother. In 1959 he came home to Pembrokeshire and was 2nd whip to the South Pembs Hunt until in 1961 he went as a lad to Mr A Gilbert at Andoversford, Glos. In 1964 he moved to Mr J F Roberts at Cheltenham and rode as a claimer. In 1967 and 1968 he rode as a claimer to Mr W Denson, at Woodmancote, Glos. However, he could not keep his weight down and came home to Tenby for a couple of years. In 1970 he went as headlad to Mr W Maxwell at Lambourne, and then in 1973 he moved to Dorset to look after four horses for a gentleman farmer/ Estate Agent, who also bred pedigree Hereford cattle. My only memory is that his employer's christian name was Peter.

He moved back to Pembrokeshire in 1981 after his son, Julian, had to have major surgery and remained there working with horses at Haverfordwest until his untimely death in 1994 at the age of fifty-four. John died from a kidney related disease known as 'goodpasture syndrome' which is believed to have resulted from a horse-kick to the kidney area some years before, after which he spent an extended period in Chepstow Hospital receiving treatment. (Below - John on U-Din-Club age 14 in Tudor Square, Tenby, at the South Pembs Hunt Meet.)   R.I.P. Richard

LOCAL INTEREST

Shown here are trophies won by my late father, during his horse training days of the 1950's. Also shown are the details of a flapping meeting held at Cornishdown farm Tenby, in 1947, plus other items of interest.

1953 South Pembs Hunt Cup

1950 South Pembs Farmers Open

The Mildmay Memorial Steeplechase Challenge Cup

Won by U-Din-Club May 12 1953 Buckfastleigh

In May 1953 U-Din-Club won the above cup, ridden by Micky Morrissey, with the Queen Mother's horse Galena in second place ridden by Dick Francis. U-Din-Club won at 20-1. He was by Tagerdin out of The Queen of Clubs, and the sire was believed to be bred by the Agha Khan.

In the same year he won the South Pembrokeshire Hunt Cup at Lydstep. The cup was presented to my father by Major and Mrs David Harrison Allen.

In1950 , Brown Jack owned by my father won the South Pembrokeshire Farmers Open, at Lydstep also presented to my father by Major and Mrs David Harrison Allen.

My sister Jane was born when U-Din-Club won the Mildmay Cup, and special permission to my parents to christen my sister Jane Mildmay Lawrence.

My mother on Brown Jack at the South Pembs Hunt Meet at The
Stanley Arms, Landshipping in 1950.

John aged 7 on Butchers Boy at
a Tenby flapping meeting, pictured
with his father Jack on the right,
and holding Butchers Boy is the
owner Danny Rogers from St
Clears, Nr Carmarthen

Official Race Card. 1s.

TENBY RACES

(Under Welsh Horse Racing Association Rules).

THURSDAY, AUG. 14, 1947
at Cornishdown Farm

OFFICIALS:

President: His Worship the Mayor of Tenby
(Lt.-Col. P. R. HOWELLS).

Vice Presidents: T. ROWE, Esq.; Major VALDAR JONES;
I. EVANS, Esq.; H. D. HOWELLS, Esq., C.C.
T. TIPTON, Esq.

Judges: Major VALDAR JONES; Lt. A. E. WHEELER;
G. WYNDHAM COLLINS, Esq.

Official Handicapper: F. BRACE, Esq.,

Medical Officer: Dr. M. O. EVANS.

Clerk of the Course: J. H. WATKINS, Esq.

Clerk of the Scales: J. GIBBON, Esq.

Lap Scorer: B. HOOPER, Esq.

Secretary: H. V. BOWEN, Esq.

Treasurer: E. FRANCIS, Esq.

The Committee do not hold themselves responsible for any
accidents that may occur during the day. Competitors enter all
events at their own risk.

E. H. LEACH, PRINTER, TENBY

(1)—ONE MILE HANDICAP FOR PONIES 12.2 and under.

1st, £10; 2nd, £3; 3rd, £1.

		Yds.
1—WHITE FLAG II, Phillips, Tenby ...	...	Sc.
2—SILVER MIST, Squelch, Haverfordwest	... owe	25
3—JOEY, Griffiths, Clynderwen	...	3...
4—MODERN MAID, Evans, Haverfordwest	...	35
5—BLUE STAR, Johns, Gla...eid	...	40
6—LITTLE THRUSH, Evans, Dinas Cross	...	85
7—GREY DAWN, Phillips, llangynog	...	120
8—NANCE, Davies, Bronwyd. Arms	...	150
9—THE FLEA, Evans, Penally	...	170

1st .... 2nd .... 3rd ....

(2)—6 FURLONGS OPEN HANDICAP WEIGHT RACE.

1st £20; 2nd, £5; 3rd, £2.

		st.	lb.
1—SHAMROCK, Jenkins, Seven Sisters	...	10	7
2—GREY PEARL, Thomas, Neath	...	9	7
3—PRESCELLY BOY, Rees, Crymmych	...	9	5
4—SNOWFLAKE, Nicholas, Llanfalteg	...	9	0
5—SPRINGBOK, Howells, Tenby	...	8	12
6—MR. PENNY, Rogers, St. Clears	...	8	12
7—PENALLY FLASH, Evans, Penally	...	8	7
8—MONCONIA, Thomas, Neath	...	8	0
9—PROUD GILTAR, Evans, Penally	...	8	0
10—LADY GOSEN, Rees, Crymmych	...	7	12
11—GOLDEN CLOUD, Beynon, Pembroke	...	7	0
12—MONKS BRIDGE, Fox, Pembroke	...	7	0
13—PARASILK, Jenkins, Pembroke	...	7	0
14—FIRST CHANCE, Arnolds, Haverfordwest	...	7	0
15—EXPRESS, Jenkins, Pembroke	...	7	0

1st .... 2nd .... 3rd ....

272

(3)—ONE MILE HANDICAP FOR PONIES 13.2 and under.
1st £10; 2nd £3; 3rd £2.

		Yds.
1—CYMRO BACH, Rees, Crymmych		Sc.
2—BLUE MIST, Jenkins, Pembroke		Sc.
3—CUPID, Evans, St. Clears	owe	30
4—SAND GIRL, Roberts, Laugharne		40
5—THE FLEA, Evans, Penally		45
6—ZEPPA, Powell, Roch		50
7—STARDUST, Phillips, Tenby		60
8—FORTUNE, Roblin, Broadhaven		85
9—BUTCHER'S BOY, Rogers, St. Clears ...		85
10—JOCK, Griffiths, St. Clears		90

1st .... 2nd .... 3rd ....

---

(4)—1 MILE OPEN HANDICAP DISTANCE RACE
1st £25; 2nd £5; 3rd £2.

		Yds.
1—PARASILK, Jenkins, Pembroke		Sc.
2—FLEET, Davies, Goodwick		Sc.
3—GOLDEN CLOUD, Beynon, Pembroke ...		Sc.
4—MONKS BRIDGE, Fox, Pembroke ...		Sc.
5—WHITE KNIGHT, Jenkins, Pembroke ...		10
6—GREY LADY, Jones, Letterston		10
7—FIRST CHANCE, Arnold, Haverfordwest ...		25
8—CITY LADY, Rees, St. Davids		30
9—LADY GOSEN, Rees, Crymmych ...		35
10—MRS. MOPS, Lewis, Carmarthen ...		35
11—STARLIGHT, Hughes, Llandewi ...		40
12—THE GENTLEMAN, Morris, Neath ...		40
13—PROUD GILTAR, Evans, Penally ...		40
14—FLOWER GIRL, Thomas, Neath ...		50
15—SILVER BAR, Jenkins, Pembroke ...		55
16—PENALLY FLASH, Evans, Penally ...		75
17—SPRINGBOK, Howells, Tenby		75
18—MR. PENNY, Rogers, St. Clears ...		75
19—SNOWFLAKE, Nicholas, Llanfalteg ...		80
20—PRESCELLY BOY, Rees, Crymmych ...		85
21—LONG SET, Thomas, Neath		90
22—SILVER KING, Thomas, Neath ...		100

1st .... 2nd .... 3rd ....

5 pm.

(5)—1½ MILES HANDICAP FOR HORSES 14.2 and Under.

1st £15; 2nd £3; 3rd £2.

		Yds.
1—BLUE MIST, Jenkins, Pembroke	...	Sc.
2—BUTCHER'S BOY, Rogers, St. Clears	...	Sc.
3—JOCK, Griffiths, St. Clears	...	Sc.
4—VALLEY ECHO, Powell, Loch	...	20
5—MARINA, Edwards, Newport, Pem.,	...	20
6—RUBY, Rowe, Narberth	...	20
7—TRUE DESIRE, Evans, St. Clears	...	25
8—BEAUTY, Jenkins, Pembroke	...	40
9—GOLDEN CROWN, Phillips, Tenby	...	40
10—PILOT, Evans, Penally	...	60
11—LITTLE GEM, Davies, Carmarthen	...	70
12—LA QUINTA, Beynon, Pembroke Dock	...	80
13—WHITE FLAG, Lawrence, Tenby	...	90
14—PURPLE TINT, Butler, Tembrey	...	90
15—PLAIN JANE, Davies, Ammanford	...	110
16—ELIZABETH, Bradbrok, Ammanford	...	165
17—MIST, Bowyer, Oswestry	...	H.O.G.

2nd   3rd

5.30 p.m.

(6)—1½ MILES OPEN HANDICAP DISTANCE RACE.

(Minimum weight, 8st.)

1st £50; 2nd £10; 3rd £5.

1—PARASILK, Jenkins, Pembroke	...	Sc.
2—CITY LADY, Rees, St. David's	...	35
3—LADY GOSEN, Rees, Crymmych	...	40
4—MRS. MOPS, Lewis, Carmarthen	...	40
5—THE GENTLEMAN, Morris, Neath	...	50
6—PROUD GILTAR, Evans, Penally	...	50
7—STARLIGHT, Hughes, Llandewi	...	55
8—SILVER BAR, Jenkins, Pembroke	...	70
9—SPRINGBOK, Howells, Tenby	...	90
10—PENALLY FLASH, Evans, Penally	...	95
11—MR. PENNY, Rogers, St. Clears	...	95
12—PRESCELLY BOY, Rees, Crymmych	...	110
13—GREENWAY, Thomas, Neath	...	120

1st .... 2nd .... 3rd ....

274

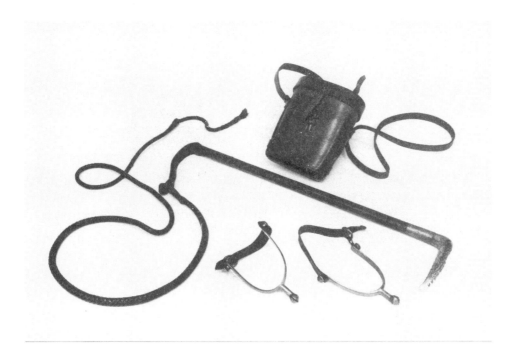

Binoculars, whip and spurs belonging to Robert Weaver Smith.

William John was born in 1883 in Frog Street, Tenby. He joined Harrison's stable as a groom in 1900, and became a local jockey. He married in 1907, aged24. He was called up in 1916 to the 2/1 Pembroke Yeomanry, and did not return from the war. His father James John was the driver of the omnibus, which was used as the transport of guests by the Cobourg Hotel.

Town Clerk's Office
Tenby, 20th May 19

G.LORT STOKES.
SOLICITOR & TOWN CLERK.

ALL PRIVATE LETTERS
TO BE MARKED "PRIVATE".

This is to certify that W. John,
2/1 Pembroke Yeomanry, was in my employ prior
to enlistment and is a capable and reliable
chauffeur.

No. **1893**
PEMBROKESHIRE COUNTY COUNCIL.   MOTOR CAR ACT, 1903.
LICENCE TO DRIVE A MOTOR CAR.
COUNTY OF PEMBROKE.

William John
of 29 Victoria Street Tenby

is hereby Licensed *to drive a Motor Car for the period of twelve months*
from the *Fourteenth* day of *June* 1915
until the *Thirteenth* day of *June* 1916
inclusive
     Signed *Robt M Wheatley*

Shire Hall,
Haverfordwest.

N.B.—Particulars of any endorsement of any Licence previously held by the person licensed must be entered on the back of this Licence.

IMPORTANT

N.B.—This Licence should always be carried, as failure by the Driver of a Motor Car to produce a Licence when demanded by a Police Constable renders him liable to a fine not exceeding £5 (Sec. 3 (4).)

In the event of the loss or defacement of this Licence a duplicate can be obtained from the Council on the payment of a fee of One Shilling.

Items found recently in the hedgerow behind the site of the Grandstand at Knightston Farm. The items were found by the present farmers, Graham and Brynley Hughes.

Prisoners in the House of Correction.

Prisoners' Names and Age.	Crime convicted of.	Date of Conviction or Committal.	Term of Imprisonment, &c.	By what Court or Magistrates Committed.
1. William Evans, 31	Sheep stealing	22nd July, 1839.	Two years to hard labour	Court of Assize.
2. Ann Evans, 28	Ditto	" " "	Three years to hard labour	Ditto ditto
3. Elizabeth Evans, 48	Ditto	" " "	Two years to hard labour	Ditto ditto
4. Sarah Dawkins, 50	Having maliciously cut down and stolen two Oak Saplings, of the value of 1s. 2d. having been previously convicted of the like offence	20th Feb. 1840.	Six calendar months to hard labour	W. B. Swann, J. T. Beynon, esqrs. Wm. Seaton, clerk.
5. George Harries, 18	Stealing Wearing Apparel	5th March, "	Eleven calendar months to hard labour; and at the expiration of that period, to be kept in solitary confinement for one month; and during such imprisonment, to be thrice whipped	Court of Quarter Sessions.
6. John Owen, 64	Sheep stealing	9th " "	Six calendar months to hard labour	Court of Assize.
7. Joseph Roos, 37	Forging a Promissory Note	" " "	Two years to hard labour	Ditto ditto
8. Wm. Archibald Barns, 19	Stealing a Diamond for cutting glass	10th April, "	Twelve calendar months to hard labour: the first and last fortnight of the said term, to be kept in solitary confinement	Court of Quarter Sessions.
9. Thomas Davies, 30				
10. James Griffiths, 28	Being rogues and vagabonds	21st May, "	Ten weeks to hard labour	H. Phelps, W. Thomas, esqrs.
11. Esau Williamston, 23				
12. Thomas Cozcus, 60	Stealing Timber	30th June, "	One calendar month	Court of Quarter Sessions.
13. Cara Davies, 60	Stealing Money from the Person	" " "	Twelve calendar months to hard labour; during the last fortnight of the said term, to be kept in solitary confinement	Ditto ditto
14. Mary Gunter, 24	Stealing a Brass Pan	" " "	Two calendar months to hard labour; and during the last fortnight of the said term, to be kept in solitary confinement	Ditto ditto
15. Isaac Hughes, 28	Trespass	" " "	Two calendar months, or pay £3 18s. 6d.	T. S. Biddulph, clerk, H. Mannix, esquire.
16. Ann Llewhellin, 20	Misdemeanor in the Narberth Workhouse	2nd July, "	Two calendar months	C. C. Wells, H. Mannix, esqrs.
17. Thomas Davies, 17	Stealing Hay	3rd " "	Three calendar months to hard labour	Court of Quarter Sessions.
18. William Jenkins, 16	Misdemeanor in the Pembroke Workhouse	4th " "	One calendar month	John Adams, G. Dunn, esqrs.
19. Martha Williams, 18	Stealing a Portable Desk	25th " "	Six calendar months to hard labour; and during the first and last fortnight of the said term, to be kept in solitary confinement	Court of Quarter Sessions.
20. David Williams, 22	Fraudulently Embezzling Money	" " "	Six calendar months to hard labour	Ditto ditto

THOMAS JONES, GOVERNOR.

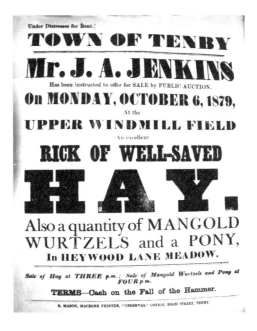

Shown courtesy of Charles Burt.

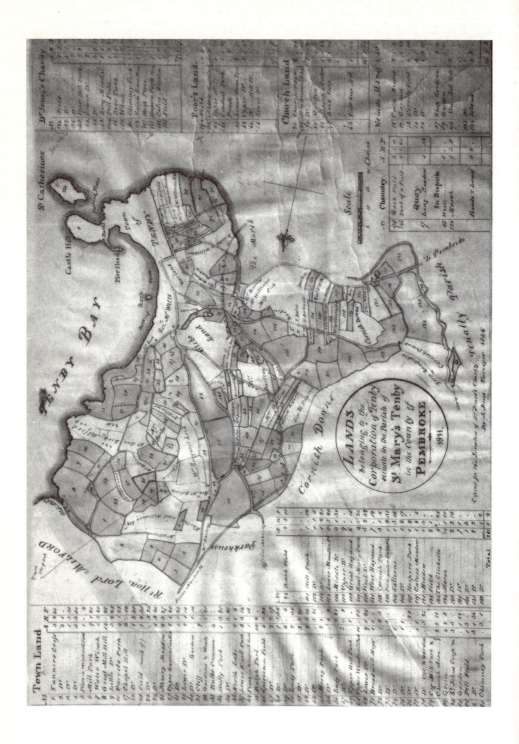

278